THE ENVOY

Mastering the Art of Diplomacy with Trump and the World

GORDON SONDLAND

BOMBARDIER
BOOKS

Published by Bombardier Books
An Imprint of Post Hill Press
ISBN: 978-1-63758-528-3
ISBN (eBook): 978-1-63758-529-0

The Envoy:
Mastering the Art of Diplomacy with Trump and the World
© 2022 GDS Literary LLC
All Rights Reserved

Cover Design by Tiffani Shea

This is a work of nonfiction. All people, locations, events, and situation are portrayed to the best of the author's memory.

Post Hill Press
New York • Nashville
posthillpress.com

Published in the United States of America
1 2 3 4 5 6 7 8 9 10

To Max and Lucy

TABLE OF CONTENTS

PROLOGUE

The Treaty Room is a large and ornately decorated meeting space located on the second floor of the White House, on the right side of the semi-circular columns that give the building its neoclassical look. The room has always been used as the president's private study, but since President Andrew Johnson it has also served as a place where Cabinet members meet. In 1898, it was the space where President William McKinley signed the US peace treaty with Spain—hence its name.

On a hot and muggy day in August of 2019, I am making my way to this very room with the forty-fifth president of the United States, Donald J. Trump. The president stops suddenly and pulls out a card from his suit pocket. It's a cheat sheet that includes a few key meeting details. He asks me, "Wait, how do you pronounce this guy's name? EYE-o-hannis?"

"No, no," I say. "Yo-HA-nis." There's a bit of exasperation in my voice because I've already pronounced the name several times. I repeat a little louder, "YO-HA-NIS."

"When did I meet him?"

"A couple of years ago."

"What does Romania want?"

I fill him in on a few quick tidbits about the president of Romania and how we're friends with them because we're both opposed to a natural gas pipeline that Vladimir Putin wants to build from Russia to Eastern Europe. Trump nods.

I was supposed to give Trump a full briefing earlier that morning with the US ambassador to Romania and a phalanx of State Department officials, but instead, at the appointed time, I find myself wandering the West Wing looking for him. Fortunately for me, I had been especially nice earlier that morning to the receptionist who has the power to issue blue or green White House passes. The blue pass is like a VIP backstage pass that grants roaming access to all parts of the Old Executive Office Building—now known as the Eisenhower Executive Office Building (EEOB)—and the White House. The green pass restricts you to the EEOB and limited parts of the White House.

With my blue pass dangling from my neck, I make my way down the halls. When I get to the Oval Office, the door is open, country music blasting from inside. Trump, sitting at the Resolute Desk, catches a glimpse of me outside the door and beckons, "Get in here and tell me which song you like."

An aide is standing in the office with him, her face like a deer in headlights. "He's choosing which song to use for his walk-on," she manages to yell over the noise. He's vetting the theme music for his next rally. Really. Trump does focus on some details, and this is an important one. Never mind the fact that the Oval Office sounds like a country western bar, and we are supposed to be prepping for a visit with a foreign leader. He skips forward through a couple of tracks.

"Mr. President, Iohannis is showing up any minute. Don't you want to be brought up to speed?" I yell, scanning my briefing paper. At this moment, a group of officials and dignitaries are gathered in the Cabinet Room for an advance discussion, waiting for us. DJ Trump gives me little further response, so I walk down the hall to meet the others. I enter the room and see the empty chair where I should have been sitting: at the end of the table with my mouth shut.

Everyone stands when the president enters a few minutes later. We then walk together down the colonnade and into the main building of the WH with a swarm of aides in tow. As we wait in the Treaty Room for the foreign leader's motorcade to arrive, Trump reaches into his pocket and pulls out a box of Tic Tacs. He shakes a few into his hand and scarfs them down. He looks over at me, since I've held out my hand in his direction.

"What the fuck, aren't you going to share?" I ask him.

Slightly sheepish, Trump pulls out the white mints and shakes some into my hand. When you call him out on not acting like a normal person, it catches him off guard—and then he kind of likes it. People do it too infrequently.

A few moments later, Iohannis enters the room. Trump greets the Romanian president as if they are long-time golf buddies. This is Trump in his element, when he gets to gab with other powerful men. He and I share a background as hoteliers, and that line of work requires schmooze skills: we know how to make small talk with just about anyone. This kind of country club chatter is a way of life for Trump. It plays to his strengths and feeds his ego.

Then Iohannis turns to me with a big smile. "Gordon!"

"Hi Mr. President, welcome!"

Trump watches bemused as Iohannis and I exchange pleasantries. Trump will find a way to make sure we all know who's in charge, just give him a second. "So, I see you know our ambassador to the EU?" Trump asks. Iohannis answers with an embarrassingly effusive comment about me, making matters worse.

"Did you know Ambassador Sondland is also a hotel guy? His doesn't have as many hotels as me, and they aren't as nice, but he does OK." Yup. There it is. Iohannis laughs politely.

I didn't mind this sort of thing because in a job like mine, you had to take the good with the bad, and that meant putting up with Trump's insecurity. Over time, though, I realized that working with Trump was like staying at an all-inclusive resort. You're thrilled when you first arrive, but things start to go downhill fast. Quality issues start to show. The people who work the place can be rude and not so bright. Attrition is a huge problem. And eventually, you begin to wonder why you agreed to the deal in the first place.

That sums up my experience as ambassador to the European Union under Trump. I'm not embarrassed to say I was able to get the President's attention with a $1 million donation. How I learned to deal with Trump—to manage his unorthodox management style—and the lessons I learned about how real politics and diplomacy work are the reasons I'm writing this book. But the reason *you* should read it is that I'll share a new view on the Trump presidency while also pointing out some legitimate issues of the US as an economic and political power.

This book offers the same frank assessment of both Trump and his enemies that I gave in my impeachment testimony, which got people across the political spectrum thanking me for my frankness. It's the same with everything I do. What you see is what you get. I don't have an axe to grind; I don't canonize the man or claim he's the second coming of Hitler, though I will never forgive him for what happened on January 6. He's an extremely sharp, decisive, and divisive figure who happens to have attention and ego issues that get in the way of his mostly sound policy positions.

He represented the antithesis of what I learned about lifelong politicians in Washington. Their main purpose for existing is to continue to exist. And the same goes for the lifetime bureaucrats like John Bolton or Alex Vindman who hide behind their love of country and belief in Democracy and Truth. Their "we'll be here when you're gone" mentality pervades everything they do. I'll show how, on the other hand, Trump brought with him an outsider's clarity to the problems that have plagued the government for many administrations, from foreign diplomacy to trade issues to how things get done inside Washington.

I certainly think Trump treated me differently because I was also a successful hotelier, but it's not just my place in business that won his respect. It's an attitude that you have to have with him in order to survive. None of the politicians in office, from Ted Cruz to Josh Hawley to Taylor Greene to Tom Cotton, know how to adopt this approach. They're sycophants who built careers on dissembling and playing roles that aren't authentic. That's not the way to get things done when it comes to a guy like Trump. To deal with a bully, you have to stand up to him. To deal with an egomaniac, you have to feed that ego. To deal with a decision maker who sees black and white and not shades of gray in every decision, you have to give him two options and paint one of them—the one you want—as obviously far more attractive.

Most Trump supporters aren't as extreme as the Capitol rioters, but they do believe in Trump as a symbol of something that's missing in this country—something he restored for them. But he is also a man with a fragile ego who wants more than anything to feed that ego the way an addict would feed a habit. This need must be met at all costs, but as long as you know how he works and what motivates him, you can deal with him accordingly. And no matter whether you love him or loathe him, Trump is not going away.

That's why I'm writing this book. That and the fact that people still stop me in line at the grocery store or in the airport and give me high fives—a mix of Republicans and Democrats. Business associates, random strangers, and close friends all still ask me, "How did you *do* that?" How did I survive Trump? How did I survive being shredded by the intelligence committee? How did I stay out of jail? How did I come out intact? These are just a few of the questions perhaps you too want the answers to.

Yes, I'm the quid pro quo guy, but you know what? Everything in life is some kind of a quid pro quo. The fact is that when you give someone something—time, affection, devotion, money, loyalty—you expect something in return. It's how diplomacy works. It's how life works. This give and take is how we intuit where we stand in relation to each other. It's how we conduct business, form relationships, and come to believe in and understand another person. The problem is not that quid pro quos exist—they're never going away. It's being too myopic to stop negotiating or to stop attempting to beat the other person at their own game. I've seen many smart people make this mistake with Trump. I've seen them do it elsewhere in life. I myself have not been immune.

Some of my success in landing on my feet is purely dumb luck. But some is not. For starters, I am a college dropout and the son of immigrant Holocaust survivors. My drive to make something of myself—and above all, to be successful—was the fuel that powered me all the way into the White House and into the EU ambassador role in Brussels. I ended up in both of those places and the hotseat at a congressional hearing in no small part due to my relentless nature, my sometimes unhealthy drive and ambition, and a big serving of both candor and humor. It's been a special formula of luck, pluck, and fucking up that's helped me achieve great success. It's also created huge problems for me and those close to me. After being the only official to honor the subpoena to appear in front of the House Intelligence Committee and tell the truth on the stand, Trump fired me, Democrats lauded my honesty, and Republicans couldn't quite figure out what I really wanted—or what the hell just happened.

So here is my slice-of-history story, which is also a behind-the-scenes view of how diplomacy is conducted at the highest levels at a time when the US-EU relationship was at a critical crossroads. Many of the foreign policy initiatives advanced during

Trump's tenure were thoughtful and effective—go ahead and balk; I'll explain. Unfortunately, because of Trump's narcissistic and self-promoting personality, the soundness of his policy initiatives didn't matter so much. In fact, many of his policies were initially accepted and then rejected by foreign leaders because of Trump's inability to shut up after he made the sale. Trump and other senior leaders love making great plays and then fumbling the ball at the end. It's like they don't know how to take "yes" for an answer. I would know; I've done it too.

For better or worse, I've also never been afraid to speak my mind and do what I feel is the right thing, like honoring a congressional subpoena when others didn't—even though I knew it could be career suicide, suing the former secretary of state because he lied to me, or pissing off the president and many others with my insouciance. Life goes on, and so will I.

INTRODUCTION

GREETINGS FROM BRUSSELS

Air Force One touches down at the Brussels Airport on the hazy afternoon of July 10, 2018, a few minutes behind schedule. I watch the venerable 747 taxi to a remote part of the field. The giant aircraft with the baby blue nose rolls to a stop within an inch of its designated mark. Presidential movements carry an expectation of flawless precision, as if the American president would be somehow diminished in the eyes of the world if the wheel of his plane did not stop exactly on the painted line. The careful choreography carries through to the line of waiting vehicles, including "the Beast" (aka the presidential limousine), a spare Beast, and at least twenty-five black Suburbans containing hordes of secret service agents with weapons at the ready.

POTUS has come to town for the 2018 NATO summit. I stand waiting as one of a handful of delegates to personally welcome him to Belgium—not bad for my third day on the job. Those of us in the welcoming committee have been wrangled into place by a nervous staffer, like cattle being ushered toward the slaughterhouse. Toward the end of the receiving line stands Kay Bailey Hutchison, former US senator and US ambassador to NATO, and Ron Gidwitz, my Foreign Service Institute "Ambassador School" class colleague and now ambassador to Belgium. At the very end of the line is yours truly, the freshly minted US ambassador to the European Union.

We stand at attention and watch the president and Melania deplane, she impeccably dressed in a camel-colored Burberry trench coat and stilettos, and he with his perfectly arranged coif glistening in the Belgian sun. (I later witnessed that curiosity being built from scratch in the small bathroom just off the Oval Office. While I was talking about the latest happenings in the European Parliament, the president used his tools, including a flat brush and copious amounts of Aqua Net, to construct a masterpiece of hirsute engineering from his wispy locks.)

The president and his hair make their way down the airstairs toward the lengthy receiving line. I watch and listen. With each handshake and platitude, I see him growing more bored and annoyed. None of his buddies are here to greet him, and NATO is definitely not his favorite club. He'd already been threatening to pull the US from NATO entirely, pout-tweeting lines like, "NATO countries must pay MORE, the United States must pay LESS. Very Unfair!" It's true that the US puts far more money into the alliance than any European country—close to 70 percent of the total—and we need to do something about that. But more on that later.

The assembled dignitaries offer their pro forma greetings: "Welcome to Brussels, Mr. President," or "We're honored to have you here." As the president approaches me at the end of the line, I remember the repeated admonishments from a curt White House advance staffer the day before. The warnings weren't about hot-button topics to avoid. Instead, they consisted of a lot of unwelcome instructions: Do not to get in the president's car. Do not ask to join him. Under any circumstances. This gave me a whiff of a phenomenon I'd grow to be very familiar with in my time as ambassador: the staff's primary goal often seems to be to hinder, delay, and prevent access to the Boss. Yes, good staffers must act as gatekeepers. But they also need to have good judgment about who to let in when there's something larger at stake.

So, my instructions were as follows: greet the president with a short welcome, turn around, and return to your own car. You will rejoin the president upon arrival at the first reception. *Do not*, repeat, *do not* get into the president's car. Problem was, I'd already realized within hours of arriving at my post in Brussels that access was the coin of the realm. If I had the right access, I could accomplish a great deal. If I had no access, I would get little to nothing done.

From everything I'd seen of him in the media, our limited interactions in person, and from all I'd heard from those who knew him well, the president seemed easy to read. He likes irreverence, success, attitude. Another off-the-shelf greeting would get me nowhere with Donald Trump.

I need a hook, something to grab his attention. A bunch of hawkish staff and secret service are eyeing me warily. The president steps in front of me and shakes my hand. "So, you're the new EU ambassador. How's it going?" he asks. His eyes wander over to the waiting motorcade. "To tell you honestly, sir, my balls are sore." He stops scanning, zeroes in on me with undivided attention. He takes up the line. "Why are your balls sore?" he asks, a hint of a smirk around his mouth. "Because the Europeans have been kicking the shit out of them since I got here three days ago," I reply. His eyes are lively now. "Get in the car. I wanna talk to you." Mission accomplished. I feel the staff burning holes in my suit with their eyeballs as I walk over and duck into the Beast with POTUS and FLOTUS (first lady of the United States). A few small steps for a man, a giant leap for an ambassador. I have just accomplished the first objective that would help me get my job done: access.

When someone mentions small change, what comes to mind? A few coins, not enough to count for much. A minor adjustment in direction or behavior or something not worth your time and attention. Why bother with the small stuff when there are far more important or lucrative issues that demand attention? Conventional business wisdom loves to warn people of perils of the cliché, losing sight of the forest for the trees.

The thing is, seemingly insignificant events or minor adjustments—in approach, in attitude, in priorities—can have profound effects. A casual remark creates an unexpected connection, which evolves into an important relationship—a relationship that changes the course of your career or your future. Small change can ruin lives or make history. As a pilot, a small change of a degree or two in flight coordinates can mean the difference between arriving safely at your destination or veering hundreds of miles off course—and maybe into the side of a mountain.

If you know who I am, it's because of one of two things: the fact that I served as the US ambassador to the EU—more specifically, as a political appointee nominated by President Trump—or that I appeared as a key witness, perhaps *the* key witness, in President Trump's impeachment trial. I ended up in both places thanks to a series of seemingly small moments, choices, and happenings that led to a chain reaction of events. The cumulative effects upended my life and made a small but indelible mark on a peculiar moment in history.

One storyline about me says I'm a rich guy without any relevant experience who got the ambassador job by writing a big check. There are some elements of truth to that. But most of it is a fiction—both the part about me and the larger narrative about political appointees. Political appointees with business skills are often mocked or disdained in the media or among career diplomats, but in reality, they are critical to how we conduct some of the most important diplomacy and foreign policy.

There are also two wildly divergent and equally false storylines about the role that I played in Trump's impeachment trial. At one point, the Democrats were absolutely sure that I was a shill for the president—that I would blatantly lie to protect Trump's interests, say whatever I needed to in order to stay in his good graces. After my public testimony, the story changed: that I was a traitor to my party and that I'd sided with those who wanted nothing more than to see the president impeached. The far more mundane reality was that my only agenda was simply to tell the truth, get the hell out of the courtroom, and get back to work. Too bad the committee was less interested in facts and more interested in dumping the president. It was clear from the enthusiastic testimony of other witnesses that they were on board with this objective. It wasn't mine. Had I received any legal cover that precluded me from testifying—for instance, a letter from the Department of State saying, "We refuse to produce Ambassador Sondland absent a court order," I would have gladly avoided the whole charade. I didn't—so off I went. I was the only political appointee to honor the subpoena, unlike others who dodged their duty to appear in court.

Despite what you might take away from the disparaging stories and spoofs about me, my ego isn't so big that it obstructs my vision. I know that I was being "used" by both sides as a tool to complete a task. And once the job is done, you're no longer useful.

I've made my peace with that. After all, although it didn't play out anything like I imagined, doing my duty in the impeachment trial ties into the reasons I wanted to become an ambassador in the first place: to uphold the values of this country that I truly believe is the best place in the world where you can enjoy the freedoms to fully achieve your potential and to pursue whatever happiness means to you. And I do have a story to tell, my story, which is more surprising and amusing than even the ones that *Saturday Night*

Live or the *New York Times* dreamt up. So as it turns out, I'm not quite finished.

Though I credit my confirmation as ambassador to the EU in no small part to luck, it also required intent, opportunity, and capability. More specifically, it was the intent to serve, the opportunity to use my long-standing commitment to Republican candidates to put myself in position for the job, and the capability from almost forty years in business, dealmaking and negotiating to get things done. Serving as an ambassador was something I'd seen colleagues and competitors do, and every last one of them described it as the most rewarding experience of their lives. I wanted to have a chance.

That said, I was an unlikely candidate for the job, even for a political appointee. Many of my peers and friends who became ambassadors had distinguished business careers as well as advanced degrees from venerable institutions. I, on the other hand, was a college dropout, son of immigrants, and a bit of a "rough around the edges" character. The tension of growing up modestly in a wealthy community coupled with a personality where envy and jealousy were primary motivators make me a cut-to-the-chase kind of guy. As a young businessperson, this made me ruthless. As an ambassador, it made me impatient and incisive: I knew I had a limited time at my post in which to make an impact. At every opportunity, I dispensed with pointless meetings or insignificant busywork to drill down quickly to what mattered. You don't need to check all the "right boxes" to succeed at a high-level job for which you might be overlooked—more than anything else, you need to show you can be effective.

That's not to say the job itself was always easy; it wasn't, but it was full of memorable moments. History itself is often made by accident or circumstance. As even career diplomat William Burns admits, it's not the lofty long term that often matters. "It's the short game — coping with stuff that happens unexpectedly — that preoccupies policymakers and often shapes their legacies."[1] I'm here to tell you, and I'll surely show you, most political appointees are adept at playing the short game in a way that many of their career counterparts are not. They know the clock is always ticking—if you're not closing a deal, you're wasting time and taxpayer money.

In my work as ambassador, I did what I could to move beyond the small stuff, like ceremonial photo-op events or following needless rules of protocol. My mandate was to advance the understanding between the US and the EU in a way that would benefit our mutual interests. And even though I myself no longer hold the job, I think it's more important than ever.

We're now facing a moment of unprecedented global peril, when we need to rededicate ourselves to acting as true partners. We owe it to ourselves, and to future generations, to do whatever it takes to come together. While the United States and the European Union sometimes disagree about tactics, we always share the same goal: security and prosperity. We need to stop our small squabbles and stand together on the big issues that really imperil us all. I'll share some ideas later about how we can be more aligned in pursuit of our larger goals.

Some of the anecdotes you'll read here may seem self-aggrandizing or silly to scholars. But this is my view of how the work of diplomacy really gets done: what's all too often portrayed as mysterious and doctorate-level complicated—it's really not. No matter what level of engagement we're talking about or how high the stakes, it still involves dialogue and interaction between human beings. Same as the decisions made at the highest levels of business and commerce: it's still just a bunch of people, negotiating, and dealmaking—another simple truth. Almost everything in life is a

---

1   David Ignatius, "A cautious diplomat who couldn't stop U.S. mistakes," *The Washington Post*, March 14, 2019, https://www.washingtonpost.com/outlook/a-cautious-diplomat-who-couldnt-stop-us-mistakes/2019/03/14/d69fd026-4297-11e9-922c-64d6b7840b82_story.html.

quid pro quo. There's nothing inherently wrong with that, nothing nefarious about it. If I give you something, in most cases I expect to get something in return. That's what an exchange is all about. That doesn't mean there's never room for altruism or empathy, but those circumstances are the exception, not the norm. Though transactions are what make businesses and countries run, they are not the only thing.

I've certainly made mistakes in my own interactions with others (many of which I'll share here), and if I could go back in time, I'd do some things differently. But I'm grateful for everything that I've had the opportunity to experience, thankful for the sacrifices my family made for my success, and proud to be a citizen of the unique country I still regard as having no equal in the world.

CHAPTER ONE

FATEFUL MISTAKES

February 7, 2020, Washington, DC. I step out of the dim cocoon of the hotel lobby into the oddly humid morning. The air is unsettled, unseasonably warm. I set out in the direction of Constitution Avenue just as it starts to rain. No umbrella, so I pull my jacket close around me like a security blanket. One of the only pleasant side effects of all the recent stress—I'd lost a few pounds. Also, I had a growing immunity to bullshit that used to drive me crazy. Tepid coffee at breakfast? Who cares. Bad traffic? No big deal. Small change.

I had survived the worst three months of my life. Somehow. In those weeks, I was served with a congressional subpoena, testified under oath for ten hours in front of a House committee in closed chambers, and appeared as a key witness in a public hearing to impeach the president of the United States. On the sidelines, I'd been falsely accused of retaliation, and my home life was in shambles, a deeply painful situation for my family. For a few days, my face was plastered on the front page of every newspaper in the country. On one especially surreal morning at Dulles Airport while waiting for a flight back to Brussels, my image appeared on CNN over and over on the screen of every airport TV I walked by.

People stared and gawked, looking back and forth from the TV to the real me as I strolled down the carpeted hallway.

Still, I emerged—battered but intact. I'd kept my job as ambassador to the EU. For the time being, I'd kept my family together. My hotel business, which I hadn't been involved in since I'd taken post, was being managed skillfully by my very capable, if very pissed off, wife. I'd mend fences. I'd move on. It was all going to be OK. That morning as I walked down Constitution Avenue in the direction of the State Department as I had many times before, I figured the worst was behind me.

After all, I had asked for the meeting, not the State Department. Ulrich Brechbuhl, counselor of the Department of State, was essentially the fixer, Dr. No, and wingman for Secretary of State Mike Pompeo rolled into one. He was the one who got things done when the work was too sticky or mundane for the Secretary (S, as he's referred to in diplomatic circles) to want to handle. He was also a college buddy of Pompeo's at West Point, and since S liked me, Ulrich did too (whether genuinely or out of deference to S, I wasn't sure and didn't really care). I'd usually meet with Brechbuhl whenever I was in town, and I figured this time was no different. I'd survived the impeachment trial. I made it through Christmas and survived a testy New Year's with my family. I'd been back at post in Brussels the past few weeks. All the media attention had turned from scrutiny to adulation, only giving me more clout as a diplomat and greater access to whomever I wanted to meet with in Europe. In the States, I got kudos on both sides of the aisle for my balanced testimony in the impeachment trial. In reality, all I did was focus on and recount what I knew personally, and I thought the publicity about me and my testimony was overblown. The left-wing media seemed to feel like I was a crusader for justice, the right wing didn't seem to have an opinion anymore, and all of that was fine with me. I decided to shut up and get back to work. That's all I intended to do.

So on that Tuesday morning, I have no inkling that anything was amiss. I arrive at the State Department and walk down the long hallway of Mahogany Row, so called for the line of wood-paneled offices of the top brass. I enter Brechbuhl's office and shake his hand, ready for a congenial meeting. He shifts his eyes away from mine a moment too soon. Then he fires me.

It was a hell of a job, and I've had many. The attraction is obvious—and I wasn't impervious—as an ambassador, you're a big deal. People treat you with deference. You have bodyguards, a phalanx of staff, and a motorcade with sirens wailing and blue lights flashing that deposits you daily at an impressive office. In many cases, you feel as close to royalty as you can get. In a sense by becoming ambassador, you cease being yourself—instead, you are a stand-in for the United States of America, writ large. Everyone in the executive branch stationed at your post works for you, regardless of which department they are assigned: the treasury person, commerce person, the in-country staff, people who are detached from various cabinet agencies like justice, agriculture, defense—all of these people are tasked to your mission and, more specifically, to you.

The US mission to the EU has a particularly high number of people from various cabinet agencies given the fact that it's a multilateral post of significant importance. In some ways, it's like a miniature White House, and you're the president's representative. But what makes the job so interesting and desirable is even bigger: when the novelty of pomp and privilege fades, you can accomplish very consequential things for your country and your fellow citizens if you have a mind to. You have the tools, you have the access, you have the stature, and now it's incumbent on you to advance the interests of America as articulated by the president of the United States.

On the other hand, you are still you. Whatever skills and experience you bring to the job you will use. Whatever personality traits or character flaws you possess, those will emerge too. Any expertise or family history you have in a particular area can also make a big difference.

My interest in Europe is personal and long-standing, and my interest in serving the United States certainly has its roots in my family's story. I was the first of my family to be born in the United States, to immigrants who came here under duress, fleeing the persecution of the Nazi regime.

My mother, Frieda, was born in Berlin in 1921. Her father was born in Russia and was conscripted into the army during World War I. He ended up a prisoner of war in Berlin and stayed in Germany when he was released, opening a clothing retail and wholesale business. They weren't wealthy, but my mother had a comfortable childhood.

My father, Gunther, was born in 1915 in Lippink, Poland. In the ashes of WWI, his father moved the family to Berlin, where they became a fixture of the local Jewish community. Then Hitler came to power in 1933. By the time my father graduated from high school, his dream of going to college was fading from view.

My parents were married on January 16, 1938. Thousands of Jews were vying for coveted visas that would allow them to move abroad. My mother's family, who had retained Russian citizenship through my grandfather, got lucky. My father and his family did not. My parents made the excruciating decision to separate.

My pregnant mother and her family set sail on the diesel-powered *Alcantara* for Montevideo, Uruguay, which they knew nothing about but turned out to be a beautiful, inviting city. At seventeen, my mother Frieda found herself supporting her family as a pregnant refugee who couldn't speak the language, working in a clothing factory. A few months later, my sister Lucia was born.

My father Gunther, after evading the Gestapo, joined the French Legion, which, contrary to its glamorous image, turned out to be a rag-tag group of criminals, deserters, and vagrants. He was sent to Berguent, Morocco where he worked for two years on the Trans-Saharan Railway project and was then sent with the British army to fight the Japanese in what is now Myanmar. When Japan surrendered, my father found himself with no country, no home, no possessions, and no money. He had a wife he barely knew and a daughter he'd never seen, and they were living on a continent where he'd never set foot.

On the other side of the ocean, my mother was doing her best to secure a visa for him. Day after day, she went to the immigration office. One afternoon, after another futile attempt, she sat down on a bench outside the office and burst into tears. An elderly janitor saw her and summoned the minister of the interior, who promised he would grant a visa for my father the very next day. He kept his word.

On May 2, 1947, my father was finally on his way to Montevideo. My parents had not seen each other for eight and a half years.

Their reunion was happy but not easy. My father's frightening anger and bad moods, very likely undiagnosed PTSD, strained everyone. My mother was industrious and hardworking at her job as the chief dressmaker for a department store, but money was tight. My sister was a good student and an obedient child (at least they had one who behaved). But my father wanted them to join his family in the United States, in Seattle. It took years to wade through the red tape to get US visas. My parents and sister arrived in 1951. My sister had never traveled more than an hour's radius outside Montevideo, and she found America huge, varied, and strange—as if she'd landed on the moon. Soon enough, though, my sister was eating pizza with her teenage friends, going on dates, and joining the cheerleading squad. My parents bought their first car, which my mother never actually learned to drive, and their first house. A few months after my sister's high school graduation in 1956, my mother had some shocking news to share. She was pregnant.

My mother had a second surprise chance at parenthood. She adored me, and my sister doted on me—after all, at her age, *she* could have been my mother. My father, though, who had never been around an infant, had a hard time with my sudden appearance. His home had been invaded by a squalling, needy little creature. My parents bought a dry-cleaning business and poured their energy and efforts into making it a success. I quickly became an independent and self-driven child. I had no siblings my age to roughhouse with, play with, or commiserate with.

It didn't take long before I realized my parents were weird—they spoke German, they were older, and they didn't have the same hobbies or interests as many of my friends' parents. I was a bit of an oddball myself.

My sister was married by this point, and she and her husband moved to Mercer Island with their infant son. A lot of Jewish families were relocating there, and my parents soon followed. One of the most important things about my six-by-three-mile-wide world on Mercer Island was that one side of the island was home to the well-to-do, and the other end was working-class. We lived on the latter, but my parents arranged for me to attend middle school on the former. That seemingly small act, determined by an arbitrary and invisible line down the middle of the island, changed my life. Suddenly, I found myself thrown in with kids who vacationed in Hawaii, whose parents dropped them off in luxury cars, and who lived in large homes with manicured lawns and hired help. I wanted what they had. Badly. In class, I saw they were no smarter, more capable, or more talented than I was. And they certainly weren't as driven.

I remember going skiing with my parents at a slope just outside Seattle. We'd pile in with our German neighbors; the adults would chatter away while the kids squashed uncomfortably in the back of the station wagon. I hated skiing at first. I remember standing out in my flimsy coat and secondhand ski pants freezing my ass off. But the worst of it was that I would run into my schoolmates. We didn't have the money for chairlift tickets, so I was stuck riding the Poma or T-bar lift. I'll never forget seeing the smirks of my middle school classmates looking down on me, literally, from up on high.

Though many years later I became infamous thanks to the Latin phrase "quid pro quo," it's actually the "status quo" that defined my early life. I was not at all satisfied with the status quo I found myself in. My parents were happy with their modest lives, given what they had survived: the Holocaust, my father practically starving in an African labor camp, and being separated for eight years while my mom had to take care of her family on her own. They thought they were doing well in their new American lives. I saw things differently. I decided I'd work as hard as I could and do whatever I needed to do to make it, to be as successful as my friends' families. No, that wouldn't be enough. I wanted even more. One of these days, I told myself, I'm going to buy up a whole day's worth of chairlift tickets and ride the damn thing as many times as I want. Alone. I wanted what the people around me had, and no one was going to stop me from getting it.

I realize now that my restless ambition was part of the reason I had an uneasy relationship with my father. I think it made him feel inadequate. I grew to see I couldn't escape the jealousy that followed me home from school every day. But I could channel it. I was determined to provide for my parents what they couldn't provide for me. The only new car my dad ever owned was a tan Buick that I bought him in cash when I was in my early twenties, after my first big real estate deal. I'd never seen him smile the way he did when we drove it off the lot together. For weeks he refused to peel off the window sticker.

My mother was the one who organized every social activity and every encounter. She was a dynamic, lively woman—a real presence. When I went to social engagements with my parents, their friends were often older like them and didn't have kids my age. I didn't mind so much. I always preferred the conversation of adults. Sometimes they'd forget I was in the room, and that was when the really interesting stuff came out, like the gossip about who drank too much or who was sleeping with whom. The bad part was that I had a hard time relating to my peers. Adults were impressed by me in a way that kids my own age were not. Kids were not impressed by me at all. But soon enough I discovered something that mattered to me more than any of that.

When people nowadays hear that I love to fly, they too roll their eyes, another weekend warrior with money to burn. They also figure I must be a dilettante; I must take a casual, passing interest in flying, the way they said I approached diplomacy. Again, nothing could be further from the truth. Flying was not a casual hobby for me then or now. It's a passion that's endured through all kinds of career ups and downs, heartbreaks, successes, and life changes. When I want to escape myself or silence my thoughts, the best place for me to do that is in the cockpit of a plane, up in the clouds.

My first taste of flying came when I went with a friend of my mom's to Fancher Flyways in Renton, Washington, a little suburb of Seattle. For $10 you could take an intro flight that is probably $200 or $300 now. That's how they got their hooks into people like me: all it took was one high.

The instructor walked you around the plane to show you how to do a preflight check. Then you'd climb into a small two-seat Cessna, a 150 or 152, and they'd put you in the pilot seat. The instructor would sit next to you, taxi the airplane, and take off. I remember putting my hands on the wheel for the first time. In reality, the plane has dual controls. You were only being given the impression of being in charge—but it was a powerful illusion.

I came down fast when I learned how expensive it was to learn to fly. The hourly rate for instruction was three or four times what that introductory flight cost. But I'd had a taste, and all I wanted to do was to get back up there. I decided that I wanted to be a pilot, and nothing could stop me. I went home to my parents, and I told them my plans, begging for lessons. I got a janitorial job at a department store, a union job where I earned $2.50 an hour, so I could save money. Every dime I earned I put towards flying. My mom and dad got so tired of my constant begging that they called in my sister and brother-in-law. Herb and Lucia sat me down and generously agreed to contribute to my wages so that I would have enough to pay for regular, scheduled lessons.

I remember soloing for the first time on a brilliant blue-sky afternoon. You do the same lessons over and over and over again, probably close to a hundred times. And then one day after you land the plane as usual and taxi back, your instructor says, "Go for it." You can't be tentative. You have to trust yourself and take off.

I experienced this thrill again vicariously when I became a flight instructor myself a few years later. I enjoyed getting the same reaction out of my own students, that initial disbelief and nervousness followed by elation.

It's an awesome responsibility to send someone off alone into the sky for the first time. You have to feel totally confident in their abilities. Then you hold your breath, hope for the best, and watch them take flight. But the hard part is still to come. Everyone loves the exhilaration of takeoff, but what really counts is being able to bring the plane down safely out of the sky. You can only stay up in the clouds for so long—it can't last forever.

I've thought about what produces that feeling of euphoria when I'm in the cockpit. Part of it is the sense of power and control. Then there's the pure sensation. Once you're up there cruising, it can be very soothing, like being suspended in water. But in the same way that we aren't naturally equipped to survive hundreds of feet below the surface, we are also not meant to reach altitudes of forty thousand plus feet. It can be simultaneously thrilling and terrifying.

Flying also requires intense and complete focus. In my regular life, I jump from task to task; I can be restless. Flying focuses me; I have no choice but to be attentive and disciplined.

As a novice, you are hypervigilant about everything. And then you start to get cocky, around two hundred or three hundred hours. At this point, most pilots go through an inevitable rite of passage, a serious scare. If you survive this episode and get over your fear enough to keep flying, by the time you get to five hundred hours, you have enough muscle memory, judgment, and humility that you'll probably be fine for the rest of your life.

I was in that cocky period when I had my close call in the early spring of 1978.

On this day, a group of four or five want me to fly them to an airport in a mountainous area of Eastern Washington. I immediately accept because I want the hours. We take off from the Renton airport with no incident, and we're about ten minutes in, thirty or forty miles east of the airport. I look out the window and see oil streaming down the side of the engine. I feel my stomach drop and every part of me tense. I know that I have to get us down, fast. Moments later, one of the passengers notices the oil too, and then all hell breaks loose in the cabin.

I circle back toward the airport and make my first mistake. I shut down the engine that I thought had a leak. Now I only have one operational engine, which is hugely dangerous. If anything goes wrong with the second engine while one is already disabled, you're going to fall out of the sky. Flying on one engine also makes the plane much harder to maneuver. I call the control tower and declare an emergency, tell them I am flying on one engine, and they tell me there is a storm approaching from the east. Soon, it is going to start getting windy.

After the longest seven or eight minutes of my life, I manage a gradual descent and get us back on the ground. Then I have to taxi back in with only one engine while the wind is pushing us. Once I get rid of the irate passengers, I walk over to the right side of the plane and climb up to see if I can tell what is wrong. I open up the hatch and see that I'd left the oil cap off. That is it. There is absolutely nothing else wrong.

Within half an hour, my humiliation turns to relief. It turns out that leaving that cap off probably saved my life and the life of those other four people too. Had I not made that small mistake, and had that oil not been streaming down the side of the engine, I would have continued the flight to a mountainous part of Eastern Oregon I was not familiar with and attempted to make an instrument approach into an airport I was not familiar with, in the middle of what turned out to be a huge storm. I learned my lesson. Not only am I overly, even irritatingly thorough and complete with every single preflight check I do, I never fail to remember on takeoff that the more days you live, the fewer you have left. The experience was also a lesson in the dangers of hubris, one that certainly translates to diplomacy.

The second you think you know enough not to go the extra mile, check your facts or seek the counsel of others with more experience; that's when an official can get him or herself, and by extension, their country, into real trouble. Flying, like anything in life, is the same but different each time you do it. The analogy to diplomacy is prepare as best you can for an important summit or meeting. Follow certain steps to get to a point of negotiation and control for all of the variables you can because the unknown lies in the other person. You can't control them or the way they react, just as you can't control windspeed. You can modify, course correct, and adjust as necessary. Sometimes that means aborting the whole flight or conversation to try again at another time. Land safely while you can, and another opportunity will present itself. Crash and burn, and not so much.

This view of mine has matured from an earlier mindset that used to dominate my way of thinking. I used to think of every interaction as a zero sum game. If I win, you lose. If you win, I lose. That's one of Trump's problems as well: he struggles to see that it's possible for both sides to win, and that has come with a cost in negotiations with our European allies. Getting caught up in the small stuff during a negotiation can derail a much bigger deal from being done. Think about closing on a multi-million dollar house, but the seller and buyer end up squabbling over who keeps a particular light fixture or piece of furniture that has minimal value. Or a bureaucrat gets caught up on one small detail and imperils an entire trade agreement or treaty. Real-life business experience in negotiating and closing teaches you that when two people walk away from a deal and they both feel they got screwed, it's probably a good deal. They've reached their maximum tension point. One walks away thinking, I am unwilling to pay one dollar more; the other person walks away thinking, there's no way in hell I'm going to sell for one dollar less.

Whether it's in a relationship, a monetary transaction, or a diplomatic disagreement, that feeling means both sides have reached an agreement without compromising on their ultimate goal. The negotiation has resulted in forward movement for everyone without a clear-cut win or loss. That's the mindset I've learned to get past, though not without plenty of bumps and bruises, close calls, and bad weather along the way.

When something captures my interest and I come to care deeply about it, whether it's learning to fly or serving as head of the US Mission to the EU, I give it my all. But I only know how to do it as myself—in most instances, when I get myself into a bind, my own ambition, my own dogged determination to push through, to achieve, can prove to be my undoing. If I keep going, I'll eventually get there, I tell myself. But sometimes getting to the destination requires a pause, a recalibration, or a recharting of the course. I certainly was reminded of this several times while I was ambassador.

I came to my post in Brussels determined to effect real change, to advance America's interests on issues like trade, security, and energy—and to really take Europe to task in terms of living up to their reputation as our most valued and long-standing partner. When I got involved in issues in Ukraine, I did so because the country is of key geographic and strategic importance, and its relationship with the US and EU is therefore important. A strong understanding between the three of us was in everyone's best interest. But with the way things played out, that goal was suddenly tossed aside in a storm the likes of which no one saw coming.

CHAPTER TWO

SO YOU WANNA BE AN AMBASSADOR...

June 28, 2018. I pace in front of the TV in a room at the Four Seasons in Georgetown. C-SPAN flickers on the screen. I feel like an animal at DC's National Zoo a few miles north up Connecticut Avenue, walking a deep path back and forth behind the glass. (OK, I did have a much nicer cage.)

Today is the day they are finally going to approve my ambassadorial confirmation, according to a voice vote of the Senate. Supposedly. I am number 927 of some 2,100 numbers. When they call out the approvals, they do it by number, but not in order. I'd turned C-SPAN on as soon as I'd woke up hours before and haven't left eyeshot of it since.

Progress through the roll call on the Senate floor is not swift. They first have several treaties to ratify, things like the Treaty with the Republic of Kiribati on the Delimitation of Maritime Boundaries, as well as many, many appointments besides mine to approve, including those of three other ambassadors.

Although most ambassadorial nominees are easily confirmed by the Senate, each year a handful are blocked and then subjected to investigations and public hearings. Most of these are still approved, but they stir up dust and controversy and slow down the process considerably. Some of these nominations are then axed. Or worse, the White House might lose hope in your nomination and reevaluate. For me, the risk felt real. Plus there was a real urgency. The NATO summit was only two weeks away. It would be a huge, missed opportunity to not be at post in Brussels before then. But first, I needed to actually get the job. They needed to call my damn number.

I've seen a lot of side conversations happening on the Senate floor in my hours of C-SPAN watching. Now one in particular catches my eye, and I don't like the look of it. It is between the two senators who are responsible for advancing my confirmation. One's a Republican and one's a Democrat; they are friendly, but they don't really have much in common other than knowing me, so I deduce I am the likely topic of conversation. Then I see Minority Leader Senator Chuck Schumer walk by, one of "my" senators grabs him by the arm, and the three men hustle off-screen. I stopped my pacing abruptly. Uh oh.

I'd made it this far: forty years of fundraising and grunt work in umpteen campaigns; countless phone calls, dinner parties, and handshakes; and far too much time and money to tally. Now I am finally going to be confirmed as ambassador to the European Union. Right?

A week earlier, the Senate Foreign Relations Committee had held my confirmation hearing, along with those of three other ambassadors. Republican Senator Thom Tillis of North Carolina and Democratic Senator Ron Wyden, both friends of mine, introduced my candidacy and spoke on my behalf, which I much appreciated. It's great to have a bipartisan introduction to the committee since there's a natural suspicion about any candidate from the opposite side. After they introduced me, I had to make comments about my background and qualifications. I also answered some tough questions about my priorities for the ambassadorship and how I would handle issues like Russia rejoining the G7, Trump's disdain for the EU, and our trade imbalance. Ron Gidwitz was a part of the same hearing for his candidacy as ambassador to Belgium. During the vetting process, Senator Tillis had introduced me to Gidwitz. We had stayed in touch, texting and calling each other to commiserate and compare notes as the process lumbered on. The whole thing had been a classic case of hurry up and wait. Now our day had come, when it would all be official. Except for the fact that "my" two senators had vanished from the floor with the Senate minority leader.

I call Tillis, then Wyden. Voicemail. Mitch McConnell is droning on laconically on C-SPAN. Schumer reappears on screen, but there's no sign of Tillis or Wyden. No one is returning my calls. An interminable half hour later, Wyden calls back and says that my name had been on the calendar for a unanimous consent vote, but he had caught wind that a Democratic senator was trying to derail as many of Trump's ambassadorial nominees as possible, and it seemed this jerk had somehow removed my number from the roll call. Tillis and Wyden had pulled Schumer aside to tell him. Wyden tells me they watched Schumer physically rewrite my number and Gidwitz's back onto the list. But would they stay there? Who's to say the same thing wouldn't happen again? I'd gotten this far, and now some idiot's kindergarten antics were going to derail one of the most important days of my life.

I can't stand it anymore. As soon as there is a break on the Senate floor, I immediately leave the hotel and get a car to Capitol Hill. I call Tillis on the way, and he tells his staff to let me into his office. I arrive in time to see the session start up again on C-SPAN. I sit with Tillis's chief of staff Ted Lehman and Ron Gidwitz, glued to the TV. Finally, I hear it: number 927. A few moments later we hear Ron's number, 929. I breathe a huge sigh of relief. It is really happening. We are going to Brussels.

There was another course-changing event much earlier in my life that didn't end with me getting what I wanted. I don't believe that we have a fate in life that we're destined to live out. But I do believe that things happen for a reason.

After my sister and brother-in-law, Lucia and Herb Pruzan, generously funded my flying education, I went all in. I decided that I was going to be an airline pilot. Nothing else mattered to me as much as pursuing that goal. I spent as much time as I could flying and progressed from one rating to the next—I quickly went from my private rating to my instrument rating to my airline transport rating. I got my instructor's license at age eighteen and did menial work around the airpark, washing and helping with maintenance and upkeep on planes like small Cessnas, Pipers, and Beechcrafts so that I could earn money to fly more. When I was old enough, I also started teaching flying lessons.

In 1975, I graduated from Mercer Island High School, where the perennial bumper sticker read "MI-HI?" I enrolled at the University of Washington the following fall, but my head was actually in the clouds—not marijuana ones either. When I enrolled at UW, a charity called the National Council of Jewish Women gave out scholarships to Jewish kids in Seattle, and I got one. My tuition came to $180 a quarter. Flying, making money, and trying to meet girls were my only real preoccupations. At nineteen, I go to an interview with a chief pilot at Western Airlines and know right away that I had passed. Sure enough, within days, there is a telegram from Western Airlines inviting me to the flight simulation stage. They fly me out first class to Los Angeles for the test, and who should be sitting next to me on the plane but the newspaper columnist Abigail Van Buren of the column Dear Abby. We get to talking, and I tell her about my plans to be a pilot. I'll never forget what she tells me. She says, "You're putting a lot of stock in this one job. Don't do that. Because even if you get it, which isn't guaranteed, you're sure to be disappointed at some point." Out of thousands and thousands of people who would write to her heartfelt letters and ask her for advice, here I am, just by chance, sitting next to her on Western Airlines. And you know what, her advice haunted me, even if it also helped.

I bombed the flight test. It was the worst thing that ever happened to me—and the best thing that ever happened to me. Had I become an airline pilot, I would have likely been miserable. Everything I loved about flying—the feeling of freedom, the thrill of traveling through the sky, the navigating and record keeping— all of it would have come to feel like a forced march instead of a release.

My biggest motivation in going to college was the fact that airlines required a four-year degree. They had a program where you could take the test midway through college to secure a job for when you graduated. Now my desire to go to class vanished. I hated spending my time in huge lecture halls and auditoriums while a professor I could barely see pontificated about esoteric stuff that had nothing to do with the real world or the skills I'd need to survive in it. After my sophomore year ended in 1977, I was sick and tired of it—not that I had much of a clue as to what I wanted to do next.

I knew I couldn't make a reasonable living by just continuing to teach flying lessons. I talked to my brother-in-law, Herb, who I always trusted and looked to for advice. He asked if I'd ever thought about commercial real estate. It too was an "eat what you kill" business, at least back then. I figured I'd give it a try.

I started out at a regional place run by a guy called Meyers. He always wore a gold chain and a shirt unbuttoned a few buttons too many. He had a keen eye for the ladies and a great toupee. Basically, he was the prototypical old-school real estate guy. You earned your keep by making commissions; you'd keep half and give half to the company. If you weren't producing earnings after a short time, there were other people in line ready and waiting for your job. They'd kick you out and bring someone else in to sit at the desk.

I remember being new to the job, sitting at "my" desk. I have a list of people in front of me, owners of commercial properties in Seattle. I'm supposed to cold call them, out of the blue, to ask if they want to sell their property. I'm not prepared to have these conversations—no one has trained me, there's no script, and there's no reason to think any of them would have a reason to sell. So as I'm sitting there looking at the list of phone numbers, I'm stalling, stalling, avoiding, and stalling. Meyers is making his regular rounds through the office. I'm trying my best to avoid eye contact with him because I know what's coming, but I feel his gaze land on me. It's like a magnet was drawing him over directly to my desk. "New guy. What the hell are you doing? What are you waiting for?" Meyers reaches over, turns the phone around, looks at the paper, dials the first number, and hands me the receiver.

I start to mumble who I am and why I'm calling. I manage to ask the person on the other end what amount they might be willing to sell their property for. At least they don't laugh or hang up right away. Meyers is mouthing to me "Too high! Too high!" even though he has no clue what's been said. So I tell the person, "Look, the price is too high." (I didn't know the first thing about what the range should be. But the automatic thing you tell anyone selling anything is that the price is too high.) They hang up on me. I totally screw up that call and the next few, but after the fourth or fifth one, I start to get on my game. I don't know anything about real estate, but I do know how to talk to people and to convince them of things.

I have a tendency to cut to the chase. It likely began because I dropped out of school, immediately realizing I'd have to make my way in life using the CliffsNotes. I couldn't rely on deep academic knowledge of any particular topic to help me. Instead, I used my quick-wittedness and my willingness to learn on my feet through trial and error, many times over a long period, to help me succeed. Doing that over and over has given me the confidence to know what I know, what I don't, and how to get to the answer I seek with the shortest line of inquiry possible. I don't get hung up on credentials or formalities. Instead, I focus on results. I watch and learn from others who focus single-mindedly on their chosen objective and are wildly successful.

Later, when it came to diplomacy, I would listen to erudite diplomats expound on heavily researched white papers. And often I would get grumbles or dirty looks when I'd interrupt with one question: What's the point? What are we trying to accomplish in this meeting? Are we trying to get the EU to do something or not to do something? Try to convince someone of a particular course of action? In business, this is the focus—the final objective. Getting to that objective is helped by an understanding of the nuances of interpersonal interaction. When sitting at an EU roundtable with a bunch of experts, I was rarely the most well-read on the subject being discussed. But after many years as a hotelier, I do know how to read people. I can figure out who can be pushed, cajoled, or convinced and who would be totally turned off by any kind of pressure. I can assess what people want and what I can give them in return. This is a big part of why businesspeople excel as political appointees. More often than not, they implicitly understand these fundamental but unspoken parts of human interaction.

So when I was first learning the ropes in real estate, I soon learned it boiled down to "make the call now." Don't procrastinate. You feel shy, awkward, embarrassed—so what? Just do it. The more phone calls you make, the better you get at it. I still look at my schedule and determine the three toughest conversations I need to have that day, and I make those calls first.

Learning life lessons is all fine and good, but I'm still not making money. I'm still living at home so I don't have huge expenses, but my bank balance is slowly dwindling. About ten months in and I haven't made many sales at all. I'm starting to get desperate. The last of my money from my flight instruction days has all but vanished. Meyers is barking at me on a daily basis, and I know the end is near if I don't sell something, quick. Then a surprise prospect comes along, a full city block for sale.

I look at the property, and I don't know anything about how to underwrite it. It has a parking garage, office buildings, and retail space. I'm puzzling over it, trying to figure it out. Then I get a phone call from a broker in San Francisco. He says he represents a Canadian development company interested in building a high-rise office building in Seattle. I think about the block property. Theoretically, this Canadian company could buy it, tear all the buildings down, and build their high-rise there. I call the broker back and tell him my idea, which he likes. He flies to Seattle to meet me. When he sees that I'm just a kid, barely in my twenties, that almost kills the deal right then and there. But for some reason we click, and he decides to take a chance and move forward on it with me.

We work on the deal for two or three months, and in the meantime, I go totally broke. But I'm not letting go. I stay determined and relentless. Other potential buyers try to intervene, and I really have to elbow my way in and convince the seller's lawyer to work with us. Finally, my persistence pays off. The deal closes. For $15 million. In 1979.

Making a good living back then would have been $40–60,000 a year. And here's this $15 million deal; my share of the commission is about a quarter of a million dollars. I take that check to the bank and grin as I hand it to the teller. She is a cute girl, and she always scoffed at me and my efforts to flirt with her; I'm sure she's noting my dwindling account balance. Now I see the look on her face as I hand her my check, and it dawns on me what has really just happened.

I found that real estate suited me in a lot of ways I couldn't have anticipated. It rewarded ambition, imagination, and hard work, all the things I'd needed an outlet for in my life without really knowing it. Later, my ambassadorship satisfied these same ambitions and instincts: the pursuit of the shiny object, though this time that object was some kind of policy achievement, not closing on a big deal. Diplomacy allowed me to transpose my private sector skill set into a public sector job. The end goal was still getting to a "yes"… and then getting congratulated for the "yes," too. Back to real estate. After a few years, I decided I didn't want to just sell. I should try out partial ownership in some of these income-generating properties. Instead of taking commission when doing a deal, I asked if I could invest the commission I would have earned into the property. In that way, I wound up owning a small piece of a lot of different properties. I also started getting involved in hotels.

I hooked up with a business partner in Seattle named Bob Dunn. I was trying to buy a hotel called the Kennedy Hotel, which was run by a cantankerous guy named Jack Baird, who was a real character. He set the same rate for his hotel year round. He'd also put a slip of paper under the mattress that said, "Yes, we clean here, too," for any curious guest snooping around. When I looked into buying the Kennedy, Jack Baird told me I should talk to his associate Bob Dunn, who turned out to be the real decision maker anyway. We hit it off. We bought the Kennedy together and sold it a few years later to the national hotel chain Kimpton, who turned it into the Hotel Vintage Seattle as it remains today.

Bob Dunn was a tall, good-looking, tan, perfectly coiffed guy. He was a lawyer by trade but became a real estate investor. He gave me this funny phrase: "We need to put this property on a 'checky' basis." "What the heck is that?" I asked him. "It's when you go to the mailbox every month and there's a 'checky' in it." He wanted his properties to actively produce income. I was in my mid-twenties and he was in his sixties when we started a small group together called Dunson Equities. He introduced me to a phrase that became one of my favorites, one that I still use frequently: "I'll do it, or see that it's done." Bob was a member of the King County council, and a true middle-of-the-road Republican. He was in favor of fiscal conservatism, a strong military, and compassion towards fellow citizens but with the understanding that it did not mean free handouts forever. He opened a lot of doors and introduced me to people who mattered in Seattle. He also helped me figure out that I felt like a Republican too.

It's funny how people formulate their political beliefs. Some people are raised with a very strong point of view that's handed down from one or both parents, and they stick to that—or become the antithesis of it. In vetting me for the ambassador job, the committee saw my long-standing contributions to Republican campaigns. But they also saw my sister's even longer history of giving to Democrats (being eighteen years older, as well as wealthier, she got a good jump on me). Looking back, I can see that my parents were Democrats, but not partisan ones. My sister is the kind of Democrat who would never even consider voting for the "other side." It's too bad, because I truly believe that Republicans and Democrats used to have more common ground. That common ground came from the simple fact that both sides loved our country and both were proud to be Americans. I also believe that it's an underlying, unifying truth that we've made mistakes and will make more, in all areas of our conduct. In other words, our country is not perfect. But it is exceptional. That comes from our strong political structure and the fact that history has shown that we give anyone, regardless of race or religion or wealth or class, the ability to go as far as they want to go. Our default setting as Americans has been to help others because we believe we all thrive in a better world. I don't think "Ds" and "Rs" fundamentally disagree on that. The nuances are in how we best believe we can achieve this better world: Should we task the government to do it, the private sector, or could we both work together? We also don't have an expansionist foreign policy. Yes, we want to have a sphere of influence. But we don't want to take over the world (I'm looking at you, China and Russia).

Though I didn't exactly figure out my political identity until my early twenties, I did have some warning signs of early-onset Republicanism. For instance, I was exposed to unions at a few of my earliest jobs. One of them was working at the local Seattle TV station, KOMO, doing odd jobs helping around the studio with the hopes of getting into broadcasting. I got the idea through my high school radio station, through a class called DECA. It was a "distributive education" class intended to teach real-world skills. The teacher, Mr. Gribble, had a knack for getting students to think for themselves and to solve their own problems. He was a retired successful executive who taught the class purely because he liked to. He had a lot of associates from the business world who would come in as guest speakers. I remember he used to tell us, "Business approach, business acceptance. Casual approach, casual acceptance." I can't tell you how many times I've thought about that: You need to take yourself seriously if you ever hope to have anyone else do so.

One of my DECA classmates was a girl named Linda who was extremely shy. Mr. Gribble insisted she be the lead cashier at the student store, which our class staffed. He wanted her to have maximum contact with customers to help her get over her nerves. At first, she was mortified, but over time, her confidence grew. One day, I am hanging out at the store with a few friends, and one of the biggest jocks in school walks in. He knows Linda is painfully shy. She is also quite cute. "I need a jockstrap," the football player announces loudly, hands on his hips. Look up "cocky" in the dictionary, and you'd see this guy's picture. Poor Linda goes three shades of scarlet. She turns around and starts to look through some things on the shelf. I wonder if she's about to burst into tears when she whips around back to him. Without hesitation she says, "Sorry, but we don't have any that will fit you. We don't stock anything that small." We all stand in silence for a moment, completely dumbfounded. Clearly Mr. Gribble and DECA had changed Linda, just as it had changed me—we both experienced the magic that happens when you meet a teacher or a mentor at a particular time that teaches you something that lasts forever, not necessarily in the classroom, either. I learned from Mr. Gribble to lean into what you're least comfortable doing because that's where you have the most opportunity for growth.

In my DECA days, I was working as a gopher at KOMO while in school. Everyone who was officially employed by the studio was a union member, but I was an unpaid summer intern, so my employment was more informal. One day, a tour group comes in to take a look around the studio. In those days, the TV cameras were massive; they were mounted on huge contraptions with cables snaking out every which way across the floor. As the tour group comes through, I notice them tripping on the wires, one after another. I go over to the enormous camera and push it to the wall so that the cables would not be in the way. Almost immediately, I am pulled aside by a senior staff member and sternly reprimanded. As a non-union member, I am not, under any circumstances, to touch the equipment. If I did so again, he threatened to file a grievance. Instead of being thanked for my concern, I was reprimanded.

Featherbedding took precedence over safety—only a union member was allowed to touch the equipment, as if my fixing the dangerous cables was somehow impinging on the right of a union worker to do his or her job. Thus began my distaste for the way unions work: there is no such thing as a meritocracy. It's like being in a cattle line—it doesn't matter who is better or more effective at the job, only who got there first.

Going into business with Bob Dunn was a great move for me. We had some big business successes. He also introduced me to the political scene in Seattle, which helped me realize that I had no interest in running for office myself. The grunt work of campaigning, raising money, and chasing donors and votes never appealed to me. Besides, I never thought I was electable—I was too rough around the edges, I didn't have a degree, and I didn't want to wait in line. What I wanted was a seat at the table. I instinctively knew that the people who called the shots weren't the ones with the lofty titles. It was the people with the money who really had a vote. If I wanted to have some say in who was running the local government or the national one, the most direct way to do that was to keep making money. That sounded just fine to me.

I realized that what I was really after was access, and getting it meant not always going after the headliner. The people who have the title, the office, or the accoutrements of power often don't make the decisions. You'll always hear people say there's a board, there's a committee, or there's a team. That's a practical smokescreen. Generally speaking, there's always one decision maker at the heart of the matter. I don't mean the figurehead. I mean the one person who has real influence over others when it comes to a cause or a campaign.

I always try to figure out who really "holds the pen" and how I can get to them. There are usually cadres of people in the way, and if you try to go through them to get to the decision maker, your message is garbled by the time it reaches that person. Every single staff member your message travels through acts as a filter. It's not entirely their fault; the essence of their job is to protect the decision maker. They are there to insulate that person from demands and noise. But they also take the opportunity to add their two cents to your message. It's like a tumbleweed: as it rolls along, it picks up more dead grass and dirt, until when it reaches the final destination, it's grown to ten times its original size and contains all kinds of stuff you never intended.

In my business, personal, and political life, I want to make a beeline for the decision maker. It's a character trait in line with my "cut to the chase" attitude. I want to get an answer and move on—whether it's the answer I want or if it means I have to take a different path to achieve my objective. It's a more practical concern than an ego-driven one. I don't want to expend time and energy in endless loops of conversation with intermediaries. The decision maker will give you credible guidance about what can and can't be done in a way that others on the sidelines can't. Once I have that direct line to the principal, the staff in the middle also have a different attitude. Once they know you have the ear and the interest of their boss, they know they can't bullshit you.

There are things that require time, like making wine or building trust. There are no shortcuts. All the same, I've always been hounded by a sense of urgency. Time is the only commodity you have that's not replaceable. A businessperson always has expenses running, no matter what else he or she might be doing. If you're an ambassador, a president, or any kind of elected official, you have a ticking clock. You only feel it if the expiration or the cost directly affects you. It's central to why career bureaucrats don't have the same attitude about getting things done as political appointees: the career person wants to sustain his or her job. The appointee wants to get as much done as possible in a limited amount of time.

I've always been in positions where the end feels imminent, where entrepreneurship matters, and where you only eat what you kill.

So, how does one go about gaining access to decision makers or to people who will help you reach your ultimate goal? If your objective is to get close to the next would-be governor, for instance, a bunch of small donations might get you a generic thank you note via email. If instead, you collect those donations into one sum, you'll find for $2,000 you can attend a luncheon, sit at a table with the candidate, make a personal introduction, and make it clear you're the one who wrote the check. It's a far more effective way to spend the same amount of money. In 1985 or 1986, I go to a charity auction, and one of the items is lunch with the governor of Washington, Booth Gardner. I buy it and then invite five people along. Then I have access to him along with the goodwill of the people I invited, who also get to know one another.

With these thoughts in mind, I show up at the Republican National Convention (RNC) in 1988. But my attendance at the convention isn't the result of a well-plotted, meticulous plan. It was my drive for access, sure, but it also required a chain reaction of random events: meeting people who introduced me to others, and then to someone else, and on and on. It was like trying to cross a river by jumping from one rock to the next. Only when I got to one spot could I see where I wanted to head next and how to get there. Each forward move made possible the next one. I find myself standing alongside some of the Bush family while George H. W. Bush delivers his points of light speech, which was written by Peggy Noonan and was one of the most moving and inspiring pieces of political rhetoric I'd ever heard. It was another random occurring event that was far less lofty but just as memorable.

I'm waiting in the lobby of the convention center just after parting from Jim Munn. Jim was a lawyer in Seattle whom I'd done business with on a hotel deal and the one who had invited me to come along to the convention. I'm alone, waiting for the elevator to arrive, and I look over my shoulder at the guy standing just behind me. I recognize him instantly. I clear my throat, work up my nerve, and turn around. I say something like, "So, Mr. Trump, Gordon Sondland. I heard you just bought a property from Westin. I did too, and it seems we're both getting screwed." His feud with Westin is very public; I'd been reading about it in the papers. My quibbles with Westin are far smaller in scale but just as annoying. Trump gives me a dismissive look and turns away. In essence, he totally ignores me.

That evening, I'm having drinks at the hotel bar with Munn and his buddy John Sununu, who went on to be White House chief of staff for President George H. W. Bush. Trump sees the three of us together and comes up to introduce himself. He is very friendly, almost effusive—acting as if he'd never seen me before in his life. What a jerk, I think. Later, in 2016, I remind him of this episode when I was invited by Steve Mnuchin to a meeting at Trump Tower to discuss coming on board to help the Trump campaign. I said to Trump, "You know, you were kind of a dick to me when we first met. It was in New Orleans in 1988, do you remember that?" He demurred. I continued. "And then later that day, we ran into each other again, but this time I was with Jim Munn and John Sununu, and you were very friendly. What the hell was that about?" He smiled. "Well, of course I was nice to you then, you were with someone important!" My "small change," a seemingly unimportant run-in thirty years prior, afforded me a chance to establish a connection that really mattered in the end.

Another chance event that changed my life happened not long after the 1988 convention. An offer comes in on an old historic office building in Portland, a property that could have been purchased, renovated, and made into a hotel. A friend and mentor of mine, Howard Wright, whose company built high-profile projects like the Seattle Space Needle and some other iconic buildings in the US, flies down to Portland with me as a favor. The broker takes us through the place, which is totally unimpressive. When we finish the tour, Wright takes me aside and says, "Gordon, this building is a disaster. You're going to have nothing but problems and cost overruns trying to renovate it. Instead of this building, why don't you focus on that broker over there? She's pretty cute." Never one to turn down good advice, I try to figure out how to approach this broker by the name of Katy Durant. For a while, I keep our correspondence going under the guise of being interested in the building until I work up the nerve to ask her out properly. She is smart, funny, driven, and beautiful. We start dating and marry a few years later, in September of 1993.

We made a great team in business and life. Katy inspired me to help others. We worked together to give people in our community greater opportunities, the life opportunities everyone in the United States should have: to go to school, to get good medical care, and to make a good living. Katy has always been a far more private person than I. She takes no enjoyment from being in the spotlight. Her generosity was never motivated by a need for public recognition, and though we decided to part ways recently, I would feel remiss in not mentioning here what an extraordinary role she's had in my life and in my success. We have two wonderful children, Max and Lucy, now in their early twenties. Watching them grow up and thrive makes life worth living.

Katy and I made a great team. It seemed like there was nothing we couldn't do. Though we had our own spheres of interest and separate circles of friends, we also developed into something of a local power couple in Portland. We were the big fish in a small northwest pond. In the early '90s, the city was a dynamic and exciting place, if always a bit far-left for my tastes, though nowhere near as extreme as it is today. That didn't bother me so much because it didn't stand in my way. And as I discovered, I actually liked a Democrat or two (other than my wife).

My ability to find middle ground with most reasonable people allowed me to do things like serve on the board of the Portland Museum of Art for over a decade. It was excellent preparation for being an ambassador, even if I didn't know it at the time. Being on the board, especially during my time as chairman, meant dealing with big personalities and even bigger egos while finding a way to manage them and still making people feel special. I took on various tasks with great relish and worked with the director and senior staff to grow the museum and its profile. I also had a chance to network with other illustrious museums around the world.

My interests in art went beyond my role at the museum. I'd started collecting in my mid-twenties, and over the years, Katy and I built up quite a collection, which we hung in various homes and loaned to museums. When George W. Bush decided to run for president in 2000, I hosted a fundraiser for future Vice President Dick Cheney at our house. Pulitzer Prize–winning photographer David Kennerly had graciously made the introduction with the Cheneys. At that time, Cheney wasn't the polarizing figure he'd later become; in fact, many referred to him as "the adult in the room" and lauded Bush for picking someone with foreign policy experience when Bush himself was sometimes perceived (inaccurately) as passive or uninterested. I had volunteered to have the event for Cheney at our house, because again, access. I'd started to think about getting myself in position for an ambassadorship and figured I still had a way to go.

The ambassador job offered many elements that I found appealing: being involved in international engagement at a high level, working with big ideas, creating change on a large scale, and plenty of opportunity for personal interaction. Plus, as we've already established, I like attention and shiny objects. An ambassadorship affords access at the highest level, by virtue of the title and station. My ambassadorship in particular was a great opportunity, as opposed to many other postings; since the EU position was ill-defined, historically that meant I would have the chance to shape the job to my liking and to pursue the objectives I thought most important. I also found that I could directly transfer some of my real estate skills to diplomacy. There's a saying in real estate that for every deal, there's a finder, grinder, binder, and a minder. The finder discovers the potential deal in the making, the grinder negotiates hard, the binder seals the deal, and the minder follows up on the terms and makes sure things run smoothly. Engaging in diplomacy shared the same elements—and I excelled at most of them. I admit I wasn't so enamored with the minding part and all its minutiae, but luckily, plenty of other smart and capable people at the State Department are.

So I set my sights on becoming an ambassador, but I knew I still had several intermediary steps to complete to put myself in position. I meet with the head Republican fundraiser for the West Coast and tell her, if you ever need us to host an event for the right candidate, we'll be glad to consider it. She comes and pays us a visit at the house and feels it would be a great space for a future event. Then a few months later she calls and says, "Cheney is in fact coming to town, would you like to host?" I tell her we will be happy to. Doing so will give me proximity to the potential vice president of the United States. Volunteer, show up, follow through. I tell myself: do this over and over, and it's inevitable that these small steps will move you forward in business, in life, and in whatever you do. The more opportunities that you create, the better access you have, and the more likely you will have success in executing on whatever your life plan may be. The only way you create your own resources is to be out there interacting with people, gaining greater access. As seasoned diplomat and former undersecretary of state George Ball was fond of saying, "Nothing propinks like propinquity"—a line used by Ian Fleming in his James Bond novel *Diamonds are Forever*. Power is directly proportionate to proximity to the president, regardless of title.

There are two main reasons you want access. One is basic and venal: people like to be with others who they consider important. But access also has a benefit, as I have mentioned above, in that it allows you to accomplish much more in a shorter amount of time. At one point, I believed in access as an end to itself, but now I see it as a tool to accomplish a task. Nowadays, I care less about what people think of me (notice I said less; I didn't claim not at all) and more about what I am able to accomplish with purpose.

At the event, I stand off to the side chatting with Lynne Cheney when she points out a painting on the wall in our foyer, a portrait of two infant girls, remarking how much she likes it. I tell her I had bought it at a charity auction and that it had once been owned by Nelson Rockefeller. It had once hung in the Naval Observatory, the designated home of the vice president in Washington DC, when Rockefeller held the position. "When you all win the election, I'd be honored to loan it to you," I say.

After Bush and Cheney indeed win, I want to make good on my promise. Through Kennerly, I get in touch with the Second Lady's staff, and she asks me to send her a slide of the painting to take a look (and refresh her memory). It is almost a month later that I hear back. But the call comes from the White House. Mrs. Cheney had shown a photo of the painting to Laura Bush. Mrs. Bush loves it too. Then she learns that the painting is called the *Houston Twins*. Rank has its privileges, so Mrs. Cheney graciously offers my loan to Mrs. Bush.

Katy and I fly out with our painting to loan it to the Bushes. They put on a private lunch for the two of us in the residence and lead us on a tour. The Bushes are kind, open, and welcoming. President Bush asks me one question about Butch Swindells, a banker I knew from Portland. I tell Bush that Swindells had worked his ass off on the presidential campaign on Bush's behalf, which is absolutely true. About a month later, Butch learns he is being nominated for ambassador to New Zealand. I had more and more of these kinds of conversations—hoping and knowing that others were likely having them about me too.

While Bush was in office, we loaned them a second painting by renowned Black artist Jacob Lawrence. Thus began a twenty-year friendship with the Bush family that continues to this day. And while I never aspired to move into the White House myself, I was fine with a few of our paintings taking up temporary residence there.

Back on the West Coast, one of the Democratic Portlanders I discovered I liked was Ted Kulongoski. I first met him when I was supporting his opponent in the 2002 race for governor. Despite being on the other team, I was immediately taken by Ted. His father had died when he was four, and he grew up without a family in an orphanage in St. Louis. After high school, he joined the marines. He went to college on the G.I. Bill and became a lawyer. He ran for and served in the Oregon House and Senate, then became Oregon insurance commissioner, then attorney general, then an Oregon Supreme Court justice, and eventually became governor. I greatly admired his up-from-nothing ambition.

My decision to support Ted was as pragmatic as emotional: he was way ahead in the polls, and it became clear he would beat the Republican candidate. I decided I wanted to have a seat at the table of a Democratic governor's administration, who was also a sensible centrist. He had his liberal leanings, but he was also ready to tell the unions when they were overreaching, which he had the credibility to do so from years as a labor lawyer. The emotional part was that

I liked him a lot as an individual. He's a gentle person, plainspoken, and smart as hell.

During his campaign, I bring up an observation from working in the hotel business about how much income movies brought to town when they were filming in Portland. If we can get more of the movie biz to come to our state, it will be a boon for our economy and for local jobs. I tell him we don't do enough to encourage film productions to come to Oregon. After he wins the election, he calls me and says, "Why don't you come run the film commission and see if you can come help us attract more movie business to the state. And before you get to that, how about you come help me on my transition team?"

Working on Ted's transition team was great experience for me. It was a big team, thirty or so people. We had meetings around a massive rectangular table in a hotel ballroom where we would discuss appointments, policy, and what Ted would keep and discard from his predecessor. Many of us then broke off and had smaller meetings. I met regularly with Ted and his economic development lead and chief of staff. I told him that to be a success on the film board, I would need access to him along with his willing participation to meet with production heads and senior executives at movie companies. We are competing with other states that have generous film grant programs—other countries too, like Canada, Romania, and Australia. Oregon had some advantages and some disadvantages as a location: We weren't necessarily the most financially compelling option for these studios, but we had other appeal. I was able to greatly increase the number of movies being filmed in the state with Ted's willingness to show up and participate in making a direct pitch to movie companies. I was reappointed to the film commission twice. I also got to hang out with a few movie stars now and again, some of whom would stay in my hotels.

Katy also developed a strong rapport with Ted and his team. One night, Katy and I go to dinner with Ted and his wife, and Katy and Ted get into a heated discussion. On the way home, I say something like, "That's not a great way to make a first impression with the governor and his wife." Katy replies, "I was just telling the truth, and he didn't like it." The next day, the governor calls me and asks for my wife's number. He calls her moments later. When she gets off the phone, she gives me a little smile. He had appointed her to the Oregon Investment Council. She did such a good job that the two succeeding governors also reappointed her. She eventually became the chair, and she grew investments tremendously over the years she served, from $40 billion to about $100 billion.

In the meantime, I had become more and more involved in the hotel business and started my management company, Provenance, in 2000. I quickly realized that I was biting off a great deal more than just operating a real estate portfolio. Hotels are living, breathing beings. If you own or manage a warehouse or an office building, you collect a check from a tenant, worry about maintenance and upkeep, and move on to the next task. When you own or run a hotel, it's a whole different thing. You not only house and feed a guest. You also act as their home away from home, their gateway to a city. You provide a refuge and an escape. You keep secrets. You provide neutral territory during family events. You are present for momentous occasions. You are Switzerland with a heart.

On the business end, you really have to understand the financial metrics and be able to make good predictions. You start the day empty, and unlike other forms of real estate with long-term tenants, you have to refill your space each and every day. The people who come to you do so from around the world. They speak multiple languages, and no two want exactly the same thing.

The hotel business is the perfect laboratory in which to employ nearly every skill necessary to be a successful businessperson, diplomat, or even a decent human being. It requires an eye for detail without losing the big picture. Graciousness, tact, hospitality, and prescience go with the territory. You also learn some unexpected lessons, like the fact that the guest that pays the least steals the most, or the higher the price of the room, the fewer amenities are expected. Why do you need a coffee maker when you're sure to order room service or an ironing board when you're sure to have your clothes washed and pressed professionally? You learn to deal with and accommodate all kinds of people and requests. And you can't be in the hotel business without hospitality being in your DNA: You're doing more than offering someone a service. You're inviting them into your "home," and they are your guest. That's part of why so many political ambassadors at high-profile posts end up spending a lot of their own money when entertaining. A State Department budget is not sufficient for entertaining a high-level diplomat, unless your idea of fine hors d'oeuvres is a plate of Pringles and can of Cheez Whiz. I can't think of a better knowledge platform to prepare for a diplomatic role.

From time to time, my hotelier skills directly translated to my next act as a diplomat. One such situation arose in 2006. Al Gore was in town to give a speech at a world affairs event. He booked an in-room massage. We have a list of approved therapists, male and female, who are legitimate and licensed. He got back from his speech; the masseuse was waiting. She was in the room for a couple hours. It was past midnight when she came back down to the desk. She seemed perfectly at ease, according to the clerk who recounted the story to me and later to the court. She thanked the clerk for the booking and went on her way. The next day, she called the general manager. She said that she realized she had undercharged, and she asked us to revise the bill and charge Gore another $100–200. We said no. The service was rendered, you got paid, so you can't come back and re-bill. She was a little miffed but again, no big blow up.

And then, about thirty days later, she accused Al Gore of assaulting her. (This was right when he had announced separation from Tipper, so there may have been some hope of a monetary benefit in her accusation.) From all that we heard in the hotel, the encounter had been amicable. When she came down to the desk, she wasn't rattled or offended. Her claim developed after the fact, after she'd asked for more money and had been denied. We cooperated fully with the authorities, and the rest lives on in history (or infamy). There was a lot made of the story in the media. I'm a partisan Republican and not necessarily a fan of Gore's politics, but that doesn't matter in this situation or when it comes to right and wrong. Partisanship should stop when truth or fairness is involved—in business and in life at large. The truth is the truth whether you're a "D" or an "R." While it would have been a good political move for me, perhaps, to help destroy his reputation, I wasn't going to do that. And in the end, because she "failed a polygraph test, thanked the hotel management two days after the alleged incident for sending business her way," and "ha[d] not provided as repeatedly requested medical records she claim[ed] [were] related to the case,"[1] the whole thing was eventually dropped.

Back to Ted. As our work together continued, I decided to try and make some efforts to bring him over. Gradual incrementalism, as it were. When I was working on the John McCain campaign for the 2012 presidential election, I saw my chance. I liked that McCain was gruff and irascible, but I also saw that those qualities belied a total genuineness, something I knew Ted would respond to.

I became the finance chair for the McCain campaign's northwest region. I knew that to win at my long game, to become ambassador, I needed to have direct visibility to the candidate. Being success-

---

1   Ned Potter, "Al Gore Cleared in Sexual Assault Case by Portland District Attorney," *ABC News*, July 30, 2010, https://abcnews.go.com/Blotter/gore-affair-district-attorney-case-criminal-prosecution/story?id=11292348.

ful in fundraising is one way to achieve that. There are essentially two pathways into a campaign: the policy route or the fundraising. If you don't have knowledge and expertise that can be useful to the person running, then you have come up through fundraising ranks. You become attractive to them because of your contacts and your ability to attract and secure donations. And everyone knows, if you don't have money, you don't have a campaign. The problem for a bundler comes if the candidate has tons of their own money, for instance, with someone like Mike Bloomberg—then you have less utility. For McCain, I spent a lot of time on the phone calling people and asking them to turn up at an event, to contribute, and to tell others to contribute. Bundling is like multilevel marketing: at the top is a sales manager figure, and they have a team that goes out to pound the pavement, and when the money comes in, both parties get recognized. After working on multiple campaigns, you become known as a perennial bundler. Some people do it just to help their candidates and their parties. Some want a position in the administration, for instance, an ambassadorship. This is the way it works, in every city, on both sides of the aisle.

I decided to work on Ted because I knew he was a huge Hillary Clinton supporter in 2008 and found Barack Obama perhaps a bit arrogant and was not entirely aligned with him on policy issues. In other words, he gave off some vibes that he was willing to have an open mind about McCain. I helped McCain with the first event in his campaign for which he worked with the Secret Service. We helped arrange it at the Sheraton Hotel near the airport in Portland, so he could get in and out with minimal hassle. Then I went to work setting up a meeting between Ted and McCain. Ted was a marine, and John was in the navy; they both were self-made guys, salt-of-the-earth types. "I see you guys really bonding," I told each of them.

To have Ted meet McCain in public would have been polit-ical suicide, so we snuck Ted into the Sheraton very carefully, where McCain was already holed up in a hotel suite. They sat down together and immediately found a point of commonality: both were huge baseball fans. They went from baseball into many other subjects—it was a warm, friendly meeting. Afterward, Ted said he was honored and flattered to meet McCain, who echoed that sentiment. The following days fanned the spark and kept that relationship going. It looked like there was a possibility that, with assurance from McCain on certain policy issues, Ted was ready to endorse him. A sitting Democratic governor endorsing the Republican candidate...it could have opened the floodgates. Then McCain dropped a bomb. He announced Sarah Palin as his vice presidential pick. As soon as the news came out, my phone rang. It was Ted. "Gordon, tell John not to call me again." That was that. Ted felt Palin had no capacity to be president of the USA, and hav-ing her one heartbeat away from that job was not acceptable. I had to say that I felt similarly on the issue.

Ted is still a friend of mine. He wrote me the most incredible letter I've ever received from a sitting official. As he completed his last term as governor, he wrote me to say that many people don't recognize "the importance of outside advisors—from both par-ties—who offer fresh ideas, pose counter-arguments, make intro-ductions, and bring private sector expertise. For the last eight years you have been exactly that kind of outside advisor—very much to my benefit and the benefit of all Oregonians."[2] Politicians tend to take credit for things that they haven't done rather than give credit to those who have helped get things done. Not Ted. He is and has always been forthcoming, gracious, and completely egoless.

As for me, two out of three of those isn't bad, right? By 2012, I was getting somewhere. I don't doubt that my ego-driven energy

---

2   Ted Kulongoski, personal communication, January 4, 2011.

was largely to thank. While showing up, hosting events, volunteering, lunching with the governor, and seeing a presidential nominee give a history-making speech, you eventually you start to run into the same people time and again. You get into a group of the same few people doing the same things you want to, the people who will work together to get something done. I wanted to be with other people like me, who, instead of expending energy worrying about grievances, focus on repairing and solving the problems at hand.

That meant a move to the Mitt Romney / Paul Ryan campaign, where I got more deeply involved than ever by doing more events, giving more money, and meeting more people. I remember being at a dinner for the big bundlers—if you imagine concentric circles, I was in the innermost circle called the Victory Council.

There were fewer than one hundred of us nationally. Each was made known to Romney by his finance committee. One way or another, every single one of us would have had a position or a continuing relationship with the administration had Romney been elected. I was approached by Spencer Zwick, the extremely capable chairman of Romney's finance committee, and asked to be on the Romney Readiness Project, his transition team, which was a huge honor. It was the summer of 2011, and they had a smart, strategic, and cohesive plan for what was going to happen on day one after the elections if Romney won. The group had already assembled "landing teams," who would go into the cabinet agencies with detailed plans of who stayed and who went from the last administration. An interesting thing about transition teams is that once the nomination is secured, your campaign has the official status equivalent to those already in government. You have a headquarters building not far from the White House. You have access to government resources for staffing and materials. It's like a carbon copy of the sitting government, which of course continues on until the new president is inaugurated. There are huge benefits to having a strong transition team and a plan in place to allow you to hit the ground running when elected. If you wait to figure it out when you get there, you will have wasted a year of your presidency.

Case in point, Trump. A classic business guy who thinks that everyone overstates everything; that every issue is really far less complicated than experts or old hands will tell you. Trump's whole shtick was, I don't need a transition team. I don't wanna jinx myself by setting all that up before the votes come in. I'll figure it out when I get there. He was totally wrong on this point, and when it comes down to it, he was just being superstitious. In a sense, it was typical businessman wariness—just because the deal closed doesn't mean the check will clear. But in this case, you have to make some victory predictions. After all, the bureaucracy will keep the engine running while you figure things out but not necessarily in the direction you want it to. If you don't have the proper transition preparation, you waste an entire year just getting your act together, and you can't accomplish nearly as much with your precious time in office. What's more, your campaign doesn't pay for the transition team's work—the government does. Creating a transition team means you have a whole network in place of volunteers who are willing to serve, just for the off chance to have a job in the administration. Heads, you win, and you have a structure in place to help you hit the ground running and implement your policies right away. Tails, you lose the election, and people like me have done work that they are honored to have been asked to do regardless. The experience gives everyone a better chance of success the next time around. I have no doubt if Trump had been way ahead in the polls and it was predicted he would win, he would have taken his transition team way more seriously—and the country would have been better off for it.

Romney had an incredible group of people led by Governor Mike Leavitt and Jamie Burke, who literally wrote the book on transition teams. Once they lost, they created a guide on how to put together a thoughtful and well-designed team to serve a future candidate. Levitt is extremely thoughtful and capable. He would have made a great chief of staff if Romney had become president. Being on the transition team positioned me to be noticed by those conducting the ambassadorial nomination process. I made it clear to them that I was committed, thoughtful, dedicated—and interested in the ambassadorship. Even though I didn't end up reaching my ultimate goal quite yet, the experience was very worthwhile. I met brilliant people in government and business.

That's not to say that the loss wasn't a huge downer, because it was. I take my fifteen-year-old son Max with me to watch the returns at Romney's campaign headquarters in Boston. There is a dinner for the top donors and bundlers, and then a certain subgroup of us (including Zwick, Ryan, and Sununu) are invited up to the green room, which is decorated with all kinds of campaign paraphernalia. We sit and have cocktails, hors d'oeuvres, and watch the returns come in on the big-screen TVs set up all around the room. Zwick approaches me and says, "We really appreciate everything you did for the campaign, and hopefully we'll have good news tonight. I'm sure you'll be very happy if you want to serve in the administration."

As the night goes on, we try to keep morale up, but it is looking more and more clear that Romney is going to lose. As it so happened, Trump is there, sitting with his wife Melania directly across from me and Max. Max is more starstruck by Trump than by Romney. Later, from the very early days of Trump's campaign, Max said that he was going to win the presidency. Max never wavered in his prediction, through all the scandals and highs and lows. But that night, Trump is not a candidate, just a guy there grumbling about how Romney is a loser and a waste of time.

I disagree. As president, I believe Romney would have had developed good policies and executed them well. People would have taken him seriously, and he would have guided us with a firm and steady hand through the shitshow of 2020.

CHAPTER THREE

WRITE A BIG CHECK; BE A PAIN IN THE ASS

Once Romney lost in 2011, I wondered whether I should shelve my ambassadorial aspirations permanently. I wanted to be an ambassador for George W. Bush. I wanted to be an ambassador for John McCain, Mitt Romney, and Jeb Bush. Had I been given an ambassadorship under any of those administrations, it would have likely turned out very different for me than what had happened with Trump, given who those men are, the types of presidents they were or would have been, and how I would have worked with them.

I was not a supporter of Trump initially. In the 2016 election, my first love was Jeb Bush, initially due to my relationship with George W. and Laura. I worked with Jeb and traveled with him. We raised money together very early, even before his exploratory committee. (I'm also an investor with him in private equity deals now.) I thought he had the right human qualities and political experience and was raised in the right ecosystem to be a great president. People say he comes across as quiet or even laconic, but in reality, he's very tough and has lots of energy. He just doesn't display it by tweeting at 3 a.m. or being voluble. He could do a lot of campaigning without needing to be briefed, had great experience from being governor of Florida, was brother and son of two former presidents, and spoke fluent Spanish—just to name a few skills and qualities. I was a huge supporter and also became a friend.

Despite there being eleven candidates still at that point, Trump just acted as if he were already the nominee. He'd start tweeting and immediately the press would ask the other candidates to respond to what he'd said. The agenda that Trump had set for that week was how Americans should speak English. He was railing about it every time he got a chance, and it irked my friend Jay Leno, whom I'd worked with on a fundraiser for wounded veterans and who was not a Trump fan. Leno said, "I've got a line for Jeb. He should interrupt Trump and say, 'I'd rather say something thoughtful in Spanish than something stupid in English.'" I passed the line along, but Jeb couldn't bring himself to say it because he's too much of a gentleman. He did come out with one good self-deprecating quip that night. He said if elected, he'd want his Secret Service code name to be "Eveready: it's very high energy, Donald."[1]

I was very disappointed when Jeb Bush suspended his campaign. Many people close to me had spent a lot of time and money on the campaign. We also had high hopes that he would be a thoughtful and highly competent leader for our country. There was no candidate left in the race that really spoke to me. I was getting a lot of calls from other finance campaigns, but I decided to hang back. Whoever the "Rs" were going to put forward, I was going to support. I just wasn't sure how emphatically or at what level. What I did know was that I didn't like where the country had been led regarding tax policy or foreign policy after eight years of Obama. Case in point: my company had taken over management of a union hotel in San Francisco. There was a dispute, and we took the issue

1   Nick Gass, "Jeb and Trump have a bromance moment," *Politico*, September 16, 2015, https://www.politico.com/blogs/debate/2015/09/gop-debate-jeb-bush-donald-trump-humor-bromance-213756.

to the National Labor Relations Board, a group of Obama appointees. They had no interest in the substance of our claim. They are supposed to be a judicial tribunal, but they simply reached a decision by invoking the maxim: "It doesn't matter what you're arguing, we always vote with the union."

I also had no stomach for Obama and John Kerry's style of diplomacy: basically, their sentiment was that no one in the world liked us after what happened under George W. Bush's tenure, so we had to go around apologizing, kissing ass, and making friends. And just know, this is not a party issue. I didn't take umbrage at Bill Clinton's style of foreign policy, which included appropriate, discrete apologies for missteps. But you don't go around groveling, apologizing for your existence.

Obama came into office focused on his "pivot to Asia" and only worked with European allies as a means to an end. The irony is that all of the recipients of his apologies then act like petulant children: they want our military protection, our financial investment, and our products delivered to their markets on their terms. A cynical person would look at our relationships abroad, especially with Europe, and see this: we want you to buy from us, protect us, and shut the hell up. Trump's instincts, while not well explained or executed, were accurate more often than not when it came to identifying the problems between the US and the EU, for instance, the imbalances in our trade relationship.

We need to reset the whole "You offended us, now come apologize" paradigm by both the US and EU. We have to stop saying, "We're family," which is the rhetoric both sides employ when one of us, usually Europe, wants something. After WWII, we gave them everything they needed for recovery and more. We helped them rebuild; we even gave them an edge in trade with us, an advantage they could use to repair their economy. Now they don't really need us. They are bigger than we are in population at 448 million people (after the UK withdrawal) versus our 328 million (pre-2020 census). They are closing in on us in nominal GDP. Out of the top fifty economies in the world, fifteen of them are EU members—yet they don't give us credit for putting them in that position. They don't say, "The US is a special friend, our long-term ally, so we'll make an exception for them." Nope.

Looking back at history, in the aftermath of WWII, if we had said, "We're going to rebuild you or help you, but there are strings attached: we get a special deal with you on trade later when you're on your feet," they would have readily signed. Instead, we came up with the Marshall Plan, "directed not against any country or doctrine but against hunger, poverty, desperation and chaos. Its purpose should be the revival of a working economy in the world so as to permit the emergence of political and social conditions in which free institutions can exist."[2] Between 1948 and 1951, the United States provided $13.3 billion ($150 billion in 2017 dollars) to sixteen European countries. In 2020, that's like every single person in America giving Europe $864.36.[3] And as a result, European economies recovered quickly and soon were thriving: "by 1951 European industrial output was 43 percent greater than before the war."[4] They've never looked back, nor given us much thanks—at least not in any tangible, economic sense.

Despite Trump's narcissism and inability to clearly explain some of his policies (even when well grounded) he's essentially right about many things, including how out of whack our relationship with Europe has become. Were he just to go the extra mile to

2   John Glenn, "'Your Eighty Dollars': The Marshall Plan 70 Years Later," U.S. Global Leadership Coalition, June 9, 2017, https://www.usglc.org/blog/your-eighty-dollars-the-marshall-plan-70-years-later/.

3   "Value of $80 from 1950 to 2022," CPI Inflation Calculator, accessed March 24, 2022, https://www.in2013dollars.com/us/inflation/1950?amount=80#:~:text=In%20other%20words%2C%20%2480%20in,)%20is%20now%201.18%25%201.

4   "The United States to the rescue," Encyclopædia Britannica, accessed March 24, 2022, https://www.britannica.com/topic/history-of-Europe/The-United-States-to-the-rescue.

THE ENVOY

bring people along with some explanation of what he is doing and why, he would have been far more effective at prosecuting those policies. I think it's impatience, not inability—he's undeniably successful at communicating to the American people at rallies. Why can't he shift that to addressing the nation as a whole, not just his partisan followers? I believe his transactionalism gets in the way of his communication. Nancy Pelosi and others have struggled and failed to understand this key point and work around it.

I wait until Trump became the presumptive nominee and then I get in touch with Steve Mnuchin, his finance committee chairman, later his secretary of the treasury. Mnuchin did a great job, but I don't think he or anyone working on the campaign had any notion they were going to win. Trump likely figured, hey, getting to be the presidential nominee is pretty sweet for my brand, for my visibility; I'll get millions or even billions of dollars' worth of free airtime over the course of six months…not a bad perk. There wasn't a huge downside for him in losing.

There were plenty of others like me who had supported other candidates until very close to the nomination. But Mnuchin was there from the beginning, and that wasn't lost on Trump when he later offered him a cabinet position. Mnuchin is an evenhanded, thoughtful guy (who was once a Democrat). This has allowed him to have solid relationships with people like Speaker Pelosi, even as they have their ups and downs. They both see that the other is reasonable and has the best interests of the country at heart. Mnuchin helped dampen Trump's worst instincts and talked him off many a ledge. As I weighed my options in 2016, the more I learned about Mnuchin, the better I felt about him. Over time, as Mnuchin did his work courting other major fundraisers and bundlers, most of the Jeb team eventually migrated to Trump.

I ask Mnuchin to arrange some time for me to sit down with Trump. "Come to NYC," Mnuchin tells me, "We'll get together, the two of us, and then I'll introduce you." I fly to New York in December of 2015, and it's freezing cold. Mnuchin meets me for dinner at the Polo Bar. It was an easygoing conversation. I can tell I like this guy. One thing catches my attention: Mnuchin's description of how he had worked with Trump on a very profitable deal. He said that Trump was very logical and sane; he asked all the right questions and gave great advice, none of these wild antics I'd heard about. Mnuchin's experience in having done business with Trump made the candidate seem a lot more credible in my eyes.

The next day, I go to *TRUMP TOWER*, emblazoned on the building in enormous gold letters. The street is thronged with security. I'm waiting outside Trump's office, and I see Jeff Sessions leaving. Trump ushers me in, and we start talking. I bring up the fact that we've actually met before at the convention in New Orleans in 1988. I tell him what a dick he was to me; that helps break through the formality and awkwardness. Then we get down to the matter at hand: why I should give him my money. He has a good pitch for me: The past eight years have been a disaster. We can't let this go on. We can do so much better. The other side doesn't understand money. They are not dealmakers. They don't know how to close. Now finally someone is speaking my language. It is time to get down to work in getting this guy elected.

July 14, 2016. I am at a fundraiser for Trump in LA. I work hard to help plan and herd people there. Everyone who attends writes a check for at least $100,000. One donor alone gives close to $2 million. The location itself isn't much to look at: the property is an old house Trump had bought right across the street from the Beverly Hills Hotel. He was trying to get zoning approvals to tear it down and build a commercial property there. For now, for our purposes, it will suffice. Trump has very few staff with him, and it is immediately clear he handles a lot of things on his own. Once the event is in full swing, I stand in the back against the wall. I want the guests to be the ones sitting down with Trump. He is the presumptive nominee but is still a few weeks away from being officially named as the Republican candidate.

Trump goes around the room and asks each person seated, one after the other, who we think he should pick as vice president. When it is my turn, I say, "I think you should pick Mike Pence." My impression of Pence was that he wouldn't try to usurp Trump politically or optically, and he'd be grateful for being given the position as opposed to feeling entitled to it or owed it. As a result, it would fit in well with Trump's style—there's only one boss. Other candidates mentioned including Chris Christie, Newt Gingrich, Jeff Sessions, Mike Flynn, and Bob Corker. They all had too much ego and personality that wouldn't have made for a good long-term relationship. I'm not saying I'm clairvoyant. There were a few other people there who raised Pence's name as well. And lo and behold, in the days soon thereafter, he announced that he had chosen Pence as his running mate.

I was struck by the fact that he took the time to ask each of us our opinion, and whether he actually cared or not what we said, he did a good job of pretending to. But the thing that really struck me about Trump that afternoon, the thing that made me sure that this man would be president, was when Bill O'Reilly interrupted the evening. This was hours after a horrific incident in Nice, France where eighty-six people were killed and hundreds injured when a truck drove into a crowd. A call comes in from Bill O'Reilly. Would Trump make a statement about it? Live? In five minutes? Trump says he is going to step away for a few minutes and goes upstairs to call O'Reilly. "Turn on the TV," he says, "and you all can listen to me from down here if you want." Without any kind of pause or preparation, he goes on the show and immediately comes out and calls the incident an act of terrorism—not violence, not tragedy. He doesn't need to be prepped, briefed, and have a statement carefully reviewed. He simply says what he thinks; he is unafraid to call it an act of war, with no equivocating. We all look around at each other. I could tell we are all thinking the same thing: this man can win. (Of course, Hillary got on the show a bit later, presumably after a significant briefing and no doubt demanding her people help her play catch up.)

The positive impression that he made on everyone present was that there were no limits on what questions he was willing to respond to. He was open to a real, free-flowing conversation with no briefing papers, no script, and taking all questions as they came. And he answered with his characteristic candor and aplomb. He could perform on the fly; he could multitask and wasn't so heavily packaged that he was afraid he'd break his plastic case by responding off the cuff. Those elements of a true leader appealed to me, and they were on display that day.

My involvement with the Trump campaign was controversial in uber-liberal Portland. Senior staff of mine were telling me that by coming out in support of Trump, there was an enormous backlash building against my company, Provenance Hotels. The two local newspapers in Portland absolutely hated Trump. They downright loathed him. So yes, some local activists made a big deal about it in Portland, and that was not pleasant. Having people picket outside your office and your places of business is not pleasant. Losing money because of bad press is not pleasant. Being chased down the hallway in the airport is not pleasant. Seeing your family followed by reporters is downright terrible. But now that I've experienced what global media scrutiny is like, that level of backlash was like someone giving you a little push on the playground versus being hurled down a flight of stairs and kicked in the face when you land.

Still, it was a lot of strain and stress, and the polls weren't leading me to believe it was worth the damage to my business or to my family's reputation in our far-left city. One of the core group of people helping to run my company at the time was Muslim. He told me that he was personally troubled by Trump's actions, especially when Trump attacked the parents of Khizr Khan, the father of a Muslim-American soldier killed in Iraq. It seemed like if I wanted to keep my core businesspeople or my good standing in Portland, I would have to drop out of supporting Trump. So I did.

In retrospect, I consider this a huge mistake. When my colleague came to me and said we need to get out of this campaign, I should have said, "You are welcome to withdraw your own support. But I'm going to continue supporting Trump because I'm a lifelong Republican, and this is the nominee of my party, so I'm supporting him. Whether I agree with everything he does or even think he's the best Republican for the job is now beside the point— he is the nominee, so he is now my choice for president."

I should have kept on keeping on. That's what belonging to a party is all about. I still would've gotten some flak in the local media, but I would not have gotten stuck with the label of hypocrite, which is next to impossible to remove. It certainly came back to haunt me in the Trump impeachment debacle.

The response to the harsh criticism I received for supporting Trump was very visceral, and it hurt from a business and public relations standpoint but also personally. Back then, I wasn't accustomed to that level of scrutiny and malintent. The minute I was criticized in such a public way, I tried to fix it by stepping away, hoping to blunt the criticism. Little did I know what was to come.

On election night 2016, I am at home in Portland. I figure Trump is going to lose. Watching the demeanor and tone of the news media change over the course of the night is something to behold. I had known before that CNN was not a neutral news organization, but on that night it is as if they held a funeral on TV. It is nothing like what a venerable newsman like Walter Cronkite or Mike Wallace would have done.

Great, I think. I've done this lead up four times with four different campaigns: Bush, McCain, Jeb, Romney. If I want to make a play for an ambassadorship, Trump could be my last shot, and I may have already blown it. Will there be another Republican nominee before I'm too old to care? Will I want to be working my ass off and raising money when the next campaign comes around? When you're up at bat, do you swing or let the ball go by? Do I make my big play now, or do I sit around for the next however many years and hope that someone with higher standards and better management skills not only makes it into the White House but also picks me to serve as ambassador?

I decide to ask for input from friends and colleagues that I trusted the most. There are a few who really hate Trump. They don't dislike him. They detest him. And yet the unanimous response is "Go for it. You've wanted this chance for decades and you might not get another opportunity. You should also do it for the good of the country. You're not doing it for Trump. You're doing it for the United States." That said, the day I took the job there were a few people in my circle who made it known they would not speak to me again.

The shiny side of the coin that was Trump's lack of hierarchy and adherence to procedure created opportunities for me that I could have never had in a more structured administration and allowed me a seat at the table on many more issues. I could make the ambassador job my own. I was free to shape and direct things far more than I would have been able to under a more tightly controlled administration. For instance, under the Romney campaign or administration, there would have been instructions, guidance, and recommendations for everything. Trump gave me broad discretion and very broad direction. That made the job far more enjoyable. It also made me more prone to encountering unseen landmines....

OK, let's do this, I decided. To get myself in good stead with the president-elect once again would be a challenge. The campaign was over, so I'd have to do something to support the inauguration—something big and splashy. I looked into the tickets available for the inauguration, and there were multiple tiers—as the price goes up, benefits go up. The highest level was the million dollar ticket, which entitled you to attend any inaugural event with VIP seating. Even the half a million dollar ticket had a dramatic drop off in access. So I went big. I later learned about fifty to fifty-five people or companies bought the million dollar ticket. And by the way, only two or three of those got an ambassadorship, so that clearly wasn't the only thing that got me the job.

There is a long-standing tradition of giving big donors ambassadorships, but times have changed since Richard Nixon. When the Nixon administration asked a wealthy donor for a contribution in exchange for the ambassadorship to Costa Rica, the donor quipped, "Isn't $250,000 an awful lot of money for Costa Rica?" The Foreign Service Act of 1980 helped to limit this sort of thing by codifying that the president nominates ambassadors who are then vetted and approved by the Senate. The Senate, through its Committee on Foreign Relations, then holds a public hearing to review the character, knowledge, and policy views of the nominee. This is an opportunity for the nominee to put forward a statement of their interest in the position, outline qualifications, and provide details relevant to their candidacy.

Within the Department of State, there are 266 PAS positions (presidential appointments with Senate confirmation). The Trump administration left big gaps at the senior levels of the State Department for a long stretch of time, which was especially annoying and confounding to people like me who were eagerly awaiting an appointment. Of the twenty-two assistant secretary positions, seven remained unfilled a year into Trump's tenure, including many key strategic allies of the United States like Egypt, Georgia, Saudi Arabia, South Korea, Turkey, and the United Arab Emirates. Even as of July 31, 2020, at least ten ambassador-level positions remained vacant as they had been all throughout the Trump administration, and thirty-eight positions were pending Senate confirmation or had been returned to the White House.[5] It wasn't all Trump dragging his heels though. The Senate has the power to reject a candidate, which hasn't been exercised in over a century, but it will refuse to vote, stonewalling until the White House ultimately recalls the nomination.[6] The White House blames Congress for the situation and vice versa. Often empty roles are then occupied by people in an "acting" capacity. Many acting heads of mission are amply qualified, and placing them as acting chief of mission, rather than full ambassador, gets them off the hook of needing official Senate approval.[7]

I had a long way to go before I needed to worry about any of that. First, I had to get back in the good graces of Trump's inner circle. On December 7, 2016, there is a big breakfast being held for donors at Cipriani in Manhattan. The president is there to speak to the group of lobbyists and businesspeople, many of whom had dropped out of the campaign and were now there trying to get back in line. Once inside, I find my name card at a well-placed table towards the front. The president-elect gives some remarks. "They said 'Never Trump,' now they're 'Only Trump,'" he quips. He makes a few other snide remarks about fair-weather friends that makes me wonder if my idea is going to work.

---

5 "Appointments - Donald J. Trump," American Foreign Service Association, accessed August 1, 2020, https://www.afsa.org/appointments-donald-j-trump.

6 Dennis Jett. "How Rich People like Gordon Sondland Buy Their Way to Being US Ambassadors – 5 Questions Answered," *The World from PRX*, November 18, 2019, https://www.pri.org/stories/2019-11-18/how-rich-people-gordon-sondland-buy-their-way-being-us-ambassadors-5-questions.

7 Cory Gill, "US Department of State Personnel: Background and Selected Issues for Congress," Congressional Research Service, accessed August 1, 2020, https://fas.org/sgp/crs/row/R45203.pdf.

I find Mnuchin. He greets me kindly, tells me that the team is disappointed I had dropped out but is glad to welcome me back into the tent. Then I pull out the envelope I'd brought with me. "I'm sorry that business circumstances made me drop out, but I'm glad to be here to support the president, which I plan to continue doing," I say. Mnuchin opens the envelope. A big grin spreads across his face. "I need to show this to Trump. Let's go find him." He takes me backstage. I repeat my mea culpa to Trump and then Mnuchin pulls out the check to show him. The president-elect claps me on the back. "Welcome back."

Then I had to wait. A long time. There were plenty of people who had stayed on through thick and thin, through the pussy tapes, tax return stuff, and all the other blips along the way. Those were the people who got first crack at ambassadorships. When the campaign was in its darkest days, Mnuchin, Sessions, Jared Kushner, and other loyalists, including big bundlers, came to NYC for a phone-a-thon. They had to sit there all day long calling business acquaintances and friends, asking for money when it looked like the campaign was going to fold. All of these people ended up on the committee charged with nominating ambassadorships. That is how it works with every candidate, though, with minor variations. It's all the same thing, though the media is far more critical of Republican donors who serve as ambassadors as opposed to Democratic donors. "He bought his way in," they say, not "this is how he got to know the candidate." For Republican nominees, the attacks are visceral and venal, while Democratic political appointees are noted as having gone to the best colleges and universities. Except it's a farce—they are all bundlers and donors on both sides.

A narrative developed that because I wrote the checks for my million dollar contribution in the name of several companies I own, I was trying to disguise my contribution. I was said to be too wussy to admit that I was still a Trump supporter. In truth, I had been advised that some portion of my contribution might be tax deductible if given through my companies. I was told later that advice was erroneous, and I paid taxes on all of that money with after-tax dollars. But the thing is all of those companies are legitimate, and more than that, my whole point in making the gift was that I wanted the large amount to be noticed. At the inauguration itself, people who made big donations were acknowledged on a board in full view of the public. Once I felt like I could reengage, I proudly gave the money. In the end, I raised nearly $4 million for Trump—and that was before I dropped out. It wasn't my million dollar donation to the inauguration that got me the ambassadorship. It was thirty years of grunt work fundraising for Republicans that put me in a position where those on the committee making decisions knew who I was and what my decades-long contributions had been.

Katy, our kids Max and Lucy, and I flew out to Washington. On the night of January 17, 2016, we went to the chairman's dinner. Pence and Trump were both there. Ambassadors from all over the world were in the audience, and I got to rub elbows with a lot of them. The inauguration itself was cold, wet, and miserable. It was absolutely worth the hypothermia though. Had I done anything less, I don't think that it would have paid off with the same result. The optics of having been one of the only people to write a check like that set me apart.

It's widely known that political nominees for ambassadorships generally come from a pool of fundraisers that have significantly aided a presidential campaign. The exceptions are when the person has another tie to the president, for instance, a close friend from private life, a former business partner, or someone to whom the president owes a political favor. Some diplomatic posts are more suitable or desirable for career people. But other ambassadorships are like a plum gift you give to a supporter or friend: positions you've promised them along the way for something they've done to help you get elected (quid pro quo...). The plums are places like Paris, London, Rome, Berlin, and Sydney.

Being at the inauguration reinforced that I was putting myself in position for consideration. I supported the president and was clearly not a never-Trumper, as some were alleging, including Elliott Broidy. I'd worked with him on several campaigns for McCain, Romney, and Trump. Broidy was a senior bundler and the vice chair of the finance committee for Trump, in charge of the western US. He was an effective fundraiser, good at calling and asking for money and great at hosting parties. His other alleged skills, according to more than one news outlet, included impregnating prostitutes and illegal lobbying on behalf of the Chinese.[8] [9] When I start making it known to the Trump team that I am interested in an ambassadorship, they are skeptical at first. "We appreciated your gift to the inauguration, but others have raised far more than you have," I hear. "What about the other $4 million I raised before I dropped out?" "Huh?" they respond. "What are you talking about?" I go back through my emails and forward a message to Mnuchin that I had originally sent to Broidy, tallying my work and detailing from whom I had gotten donations. Broidy had sent back a response, telling me, "Great job. Thanks for your hard work." When I show it to Mnuchin, he is stone-faced, but I can tell he is pissed. I later learn Broidy had been taking my numbers and quietly adding them to his own ledger of money raised.

Unless there's been a commitment to someone—for instance, I'm now president, and I promised you, back when you hosted a big fundraiser for me at your home, or based on our friendship dating

8   Gideon Resnick, "Elliott Broidy's Mistress: I Was Pregnant When My Lawyer Keith Davidson 'Recruited' Michael Cohen to 'Solve' Problem," *Daily Beast*, March 4, 2019, https://www.thedailybeast.com/elliott-broidys-mistress-i-was-pregnant-when-my-lawyer-recruited-michael-cohen-to-solve-problem.

9   Kenneth P. Vogel, "Elliott Broidy Pleads Guilty in Foreign Lobbying Case," *The New York Times*, October 20, 2020, https://www.nytimes.com/2020/10/20/us/politics/elliott-broidy-foreign-lobbying.html.

back from college, that you get to be ambassador to Ireland—then the president usually has a more passive role in doling out the rest of the ambassadorial positions. He relies on a committee, which includes people like the head fundraising team for the campaign, the national finance chair, and people who they themselves get their own pick of positions. Then the committee sits down with a list of the names of people in the running, the desires of each of those people, and a list of all the open spots. What happens next is something like the ninth circle of seating chart hell: who goes where, who deserves what, and who did more to help the campaign than whom. But it's not like someone completely unknown walks in off the street, drops a big check, and boom—gets a plum assignment.

About a month after the inauguration, I follow up with Mnuchin reminding him how much I wanted to serve. Reince Priebus was an old friend from when he ran the RNC, and he was now the incoming chief of staff, so he was invaluable to helping me follow up. I kept in touch with everyone I knew who mattered, including Mnuchin, Johnny DiStefano, the director of personnel, Senator Gardner, Senator Tillis, etc. This is how the nomination process works in its most organic form. You have to answer repeatedly: what have you done for the candidate and the party? It required being pushy but not too pushy, and I was just one of many people making the same phone calls to many of the same people. Mnuchin advocated heavily for me because he liked that I came back in and came back strong in my support of Trump, and I really worked hard for the campaign in the short time I was involved. He says, "Yes, yes, we know what a help you've been. The loyalists get first dibs on the plum assignments, but we also know you've toiled for thirty years. I know. Reince Priebus knows. I can make no guarantees, but we'll do our best for you."

I watch England, France, and Italy all go to donors in the first wave as the weeks and months ticked by. I stay in touch with Mnuchin and also call around on the Hill to other people I know would help me out, including Senators Tillis and Wyden. Once I know that I am seriously in the mix, then I pull out all the stops. I don't mind spending my political capital to ask people to weigh in for me. I learn I almost didn't make it into the second wave, either; it was widely known that I was a Bush guy, and some wondered if I'd be loyal to President Trump. I'm pretty certain Mnuchin is the one who stood up for me and said, "Gordon worked hard on the campaign. He will be loyal and get real things done over in Europe." I think that's one of the reasons he's pissed at me now—because I think he viewed my testimony during the impeachment trial as disloyal. He thinks I had a choice about how I testified, even though I didn't. He didn't understand my particular and peculiar legal situation, which I'll get into more later. I have nothing but respect for Steven. Without his advocacy, I would have never had this opportunity. He did a great job of managing a lot of the president's worst instincts and will clearly be one of the most successful alums of the Trump administration.

So I work the phones and bide my time. It is late spring of 2017 when Mnuchin calls and says, "I might have an opportunity for you. Luxembourg. Are you interested?" I say, "Absolutely. I'd be honored to serve wherever the president wants me." Then...nothing. Weeks go by. I know that the committee has many people weighing in on decisions, and each of them has scads of people like me calling them day after day. There are a lot of people involved in the process, and the same objections kept coming up: Are you really a loyalist? Are you really going to support the president and his policies? It was a balancing act, staying in people's viewfinder without being a pest. Finally, in the fall of 2017, I get another call. What about either Belgium or the EU? Word is that the president had said he knows I am a no-bullshit kind of guy, so he thinks I might be good at the EU gig. It was said to be hard work. Belgium would be a far cushier position: beautiful house in Brussels, more low-key, and far fewer demands. I ask for a day to think about it.

My first call is to President Bush. I ask, "Should I even serve in this administration? I know you and Trump aren't the best of friends. I respect your opinion. Do you think I should do this job?" He says, "Yes. You absolutely have to say yes. One—I think you'd be good at it and two—you have to serve your country when you're asked." Then he tells me, "Gordon, being ambassador to the EU is a substantive and important job. In Belgium, you'll be kissing babies and cutting ribbons. That's not you." He puts me in touch with Rockwell Schnabel, who had been his appointee to the EU. I have lunch with Schnabel, and he tells me about the key role that the EU ambassador can play in the transatlantic relationship, if that person has a mind to. I hear from him that if I am going to be successful, I need strong access to the president. He tells me he had been offered Rome by Bush (one of the most coveted posts: London, Paris, and Rome are the big three) but was then offered the EU, and he jumped at the chance. "Sold," I say. I call Mnuchin back and say, "Yes."

I wished my mom were still alive to see me make that call. It's a proud moment, when you're the son of immigrants fleeing war and genocide and a college dropout, to be selected by the president to represent the country on the international stage. I thought about my mother as a pregnant sixteen-year-old banished from her home-land, separated from her husband, and headed on a boat to a South American country she'd never seen, where she didn't speak the lan-guage. Fast-forward and now her son was going to be confirmed as America's ambassador to the EU. I knew she would be proud.

The job wasn't entirely mine yet. Nomination is only the first step in a laborious process to get to the post. In fact, it took almost a whole year from the time I got my verbal assurance to the day that my flight took off for Brussels in June of 2018. That gave me plenty of time to learn more about the EU and the job I was heading there to do and to think about what I wanted to achieve. My biggest goal would be to bring the US and EU together to act as an unstoppable Western Bloc to counter malign forces and authoritarianism around the world. I started to consider what sort of "small changes" we could undertake that would move us towards to achieving this in an incremental way.

After I accepted the nomination, I had to get my security clearance. This involved a lot of paperwork and a lot of people close to me being interviewed about my qualities, habits, and character traits. I had to do a bunch of financial disclosures, which were really complicated. After I was finished being vetted, it was time to go to the Foreign Service Institute in the Washington suburbs for ambassador training, aka "charm school," for three to four weeks in April and May of 2018. Charm school doesn't run unless there are enough appointees ready and waiting to take the course. The students are a mix of both political appointees and career ambassadors, and it was fascinating to see the stark differences in conduct and personality between the two groups. The career people look like frightened puppies. This is the biggest job and the culminating opportunity they have been working toward for their entire career. Most political appointees have already held high-level positions before, so they have a different attitude and outlook. Charm school ran the gamut in terms of our coursework, from protocol to political theory to assessing threats.

I brushed up on my European history, too.

The European Union formally came into existence in 1993 with the Maastricht Treaty. The EU was an unprecedented transfer of political power, from nation-states to a supranational organization with three domains in its purview: political and security, judicial cooperation and home affairs, and economic integration of members. The Maastricht Treaty also introduced the European Economic and Monetary Union, which would later introduce the common European currency, the euro, on January 1, 1999. (The euro is not a requirement to be a member of the EU, with countries including Denmark and Sweden opting out.)

In 2004, the EU added many country members from eastern and central Europe: Cyprus, the Czech Republic, Estonia, Hungary, Latvia, Lithuania, Malta, Poland, Slovakia, and Slovenia. The final few members included Bulgaria and Romania in 2007 and Croatia in 2013. The rapid intake of so many countries, all with different economies and populations, led to a stall in adding more members that has held to this day (with only one country left, the United Kingdom in 2020). There will surely be new countries added in the future, most likely geographically proximate. These countries, as of now, still have work to do to ensure their governments and economies are stable enough, they have the financial and fiscal responsibility, and they have a level of democratic governance to reach EU standards. Switzerland and Norway are exceptions—countries that were invited to join but chose not to and who gloat every time something regarding the EU goes awry. They have strong links to the EU though, obviously; they behave more like social members of a club rather than full members.

Today the EU has twenty-seven member states, the second largest economy in nominal GDP after the United States, at $15.6 trillion, and a total population of more than 448 million. It has a unique sovereign status and oversees many trade, border, digital, and agricultural issues through three primary institutions[10]: first, the European Parliament, which represents the EU's citizens and whose 705 members are elected directly by them. The European Parliament shares legislative and budgetary power with the

---

10   "Institutions and bodies profiles," European Union, accessed March 24, 2022, https://europa.eu/european-union/about-eu/institutions-bodies_en.

Council of the European Union (somewhat analogous to the US Congress). Second, the Council of the European Union represents the governments of the individual member countries. It is made up of the heads of state or government from each of the EU member states. The presidency of the Council is shared by the member states on a rotating basis and is comprised of representatives from each member country. Third, the European Commission (EC) represents the interests of the EU as a whole and is made up of a cabinet of twenty-seven commissioners, one from each EU country. The president of the EC, currently Ursula von der Leyen, and before her, Jean-Claude Juncker, holds a powerful and important role that they are elected to by the European Parliament.

The EU emerged from World War II as a means of rebuilding and uniting Europe, but by the end of the twentieth century, it had become an increasingly important force in global politics. Former Secretary of State Henry Kissinger was said to have asked the question, "Who do I call if I want to call Europe?" For a long time, no one really knew. Enter the US ambassador to the EU.

There are now three US diplomatic missions in Brussels: the US Mission to the European Union, the US Mission to NATO, and the bilateral US Embassy to the Kingdom of Belgium. Brussels is one of only a handful of cities to host multiple missions, which makes for a unique embassy environment.

The United States ambassador to the EU engages on issues at a different level than country-specific bilateral ambassadors: issues of trade, competition, negotiation of some international agreements, monetary policy, energy, and military engagement that are also vital to US political, economic, and national security interests.

As the official statement of the US mission to the European Union states,

A strong, united, and integrated Europe as envisioned by the EU's founders benefits Europeans and Americans alike. Europe's security and success are inextricably linked to our own. Our economies, cultures, and peoples are intertwined, and a Europe whole, free, and at peace helps to uphold the norms and rules that maintain stability and promote prosperity around the world.[11]

In the past ten to twenty years, the European Union has become a stronger, more political body, requiring more day-to-day attention and engagement. It increasingly flexes its economic and regulatory muscles, for instance, by pursuing major US firms such as Apple, Amazon, and Google for alleged anticompetitive behavior and privacy concerns. As a result, the US ambassador to the EU position has taken on more significance in recent times. It's now a far more important job than it was a decade ago.

To be effective, any ambassador must be a leader, a manager, a shrewd negotiator, and a public figure capable of articulating complex policy.[12] The chief of mission (COM), aka ambassador, has "full responsibility for the direction, coordination, and supervision of all Government executive branch employees in that country"[13] and serves as the president's representative to the host government, local businesses, and civil society.

Functionally, the ambassador is the COM and oversees all departments at an embassy with the assistance of a deputy chief of mission (DCM). Each COM is under general supervision of the US secretary of state and often works closely with the assistant secre-

---

11   "Why The EU Matters," US Mission to the European Union, accessed May 24, 2022, https://useu.usmission.gov/about-the-mission/.

12   "What are the roles of a diplomat?" National Museum of American Diplomacy, accessed March 24, 2022, https://diplomacy.state.gov/diplomacy/what-are-the-roles-of-a-diplomat/.

13   "Foreign Service Act of 1980 (P.L. 96-465)," United States Department of State, Section 207, accessed July 31, 2020, https://www.usaid.gov/sites/default/files/documents/1868/fsa.pdf.

tary of state for their region. Although the dynamic varies from mission to mission, the COM tends to focus on implementing policy and on being a public figure for the United States (creating the schedule and mapping the routes), and the DCM focuses on the internal management of the mission (making sure the trains run on time). Missions can range from dozens to hundreds of employees, including US citizens and locally employed staff (LES). This includes representatives from potentially dozens of government agencies who might need to station a representative in the embassy. At the US mission to the EU, besides the US Department of State, there were staff from the Foreign Agricultural Service, Office of the US Trade Representative, the Foreign Commercial Service, the Department of Homeland Security, the Department of Justice, the Department of Defense, the US Agency for International Development, and many more.[14] Lots of personalities and duties to manage.

I was ready to step up to the task. As I prepared to head to post in mid-2018, one of my biggest concerns was not my job, but my boss. Besides or perhaps because of his penchant for invective, I noted Trump's inability to attract and keep people who were willing to push back on him. I also noted his lack of curiosity about his appointees, including me for that matter. He didn't interview me for a very critical job. The job itself was highly unstructured and had been adrift and vacant for almost two years—the mission was in bad shape, the residence needed repairs, and the staff were largely left to their own devices. In the absence of an ambassador, Adam Shub, deputy chief of mission, had been left in charge. Before him, the job had been in the hands of a political appointee and former private equity manager, Anthony Gardner, who hadn't moved any policy anywhere. I reached out to him, and he had little interest

14   "Sections and Offices," US Mission to the European Union, accessed July 31, 2020, https://useu.usmission.gov/sections-and-offices/.

in talking to me even though I asked for his advice and counsel as I took on the job. We were introduced by mutual acquaintances prior to my being confirmed, but when I extended a hand to him to try and establish a rapport or at least a line of communication, he was not having it. Instead of coming to meet me, giving me his best thinking, he chose to make snarky remarks in the media instead of paying it forward. A textbook example of the deeply entrenched problems of partisanship. He could have been a great resource for me and helped transfer information and institutional knowledge, but instead, he intentionally refused to be of service. He stuck with the "do nothing and get nowhere" approach he'd followed during his own time as ambassador.

Gardner had spent the vast majority of his time working on the ill-fated Transatlantic Trade and Investment Partnership (TTIP), a wide-reaching trade deal between the United States and EU. TTIP failed for a multitude of reasons: widespread opposition within the European public, secrecy of negotiation sessions, potential erosion of labor standards and the European welfare state, and minimal support from the public in the United States. Basically, it was a huge waste of time. Gardner had limited access to anyone who counted—no fault of his, more of the labyrinthine workings of the State Department system, but he did little to challenge it. I also watched Trump's interactions with EU leadership and wished he would stop the catty name-calling and bullying. It didn't help advance America's economic or security objectives. I felt that I was heading to post and assuming leadership there at a critically important time from an economic and security perspective.

Still, I didn't doubt that I could do what the job required, and I felt I understood Trump's style and motivations better than most. After vetting, nomination, training, and confirmation by the Senate, finally it was time to head to post. I would have the title and all the trappings of the office but no box to be trapped inside other than the loose confines of what Trump wanted to achieve, most of which I agreed with. It appeared I was off to build a bespoke job for myself. I liked that idea.

> Less often recognized, is the fact that despite all the organization, automation and modem communications systems which characterize and contribute to the interdependent nature of the international system, human beings are still the critical components of interstate relations. Somewhere, at some time, individuals have to sit down and work out all the details of how their respective countries will interact and respond to the many issues arising from international relationships. The traditional institution for communication, representation and negotiation on behalf of the United States in world affairs is the President's personal representative: the Ambassador.[15]

---

15   "Ambassador in US Foreign Policy: Changing Patterns in Roles, Selection, and Designations," Congressional Research Service, July 1, 1981, accessed July 31, 2020, https://www.worldcat.org/title/ambassador-in-us-foreign-poli-cy-changing-patterns-in-roles-selection-and-designations/oclc/7996841.

CHAPTER FOUR

HOW TO MAKE FRIENDS AND PISS OFF STAFFERS

After greeting President Trump on the tarmac and getting in the Beast with him when he arrived in Brussels for the NATO summit, I wanted to make the most of the moment. Once you set expectations, you best deliver. Once you have the ear of the president, you better have something to say. I had already thought of a topic of mutual disgust: bloat.

The building that housed both the EU and Belgian missions in Brussels was overdue for renovations—both due to wear and needed security updates. The Obama administration had previously decided they were going to build a new, elaborate embassy compound in a suburb thirty minutes outside of the city rather than fix up the existing one. I knew Trump was still stewing about another Obama embassy project. The new London embassy, which opened in 2017 after a drawn-out process, resulted in an ugly and expensive behemoth that was located in an inconvenient suburb. Trump had recently been mouthing off in the press about how awful it was and the "bad deal" Obama made. (In reality, the plans to move the embassy were set before Obama's tenure.)[1] As we sit across from each other in the back of the Beast, I nudge Trump and say, "So I hear you're going to see Woody [Johnson] in his brand new embassy next. If you like that one, you'll never guess what they've come up with here in Brussels."

I tell him about the plans for the new US embassy compound. He says, "I want you to kill it." I tell him that the plans were already well along. Contractors had already been hired and that there will be a lot of pushback from the OBO, the Bureau of Overseas Building Operations. Or maybe it stands for "oblivious bureaucrats overspending." The OBO states that its mission is "to provide safe, secure, functional, and resilient facilities that represent the US government to the host nation and support the Department's achievement of US foreign policy objectives abroad."[2] But I found their objective was to be as opaque as possible about process, spend as much money as they could, and argue that every single expenditure was somehow related to safety and security.

Gidwitz and I, given our background as real estate developers, had already been asking OBO a ton of questions about this project, and they didn't like it. How much would it cost? Between $300–700 million. OK, pretty big range there. They always argue security and safety in order to spend more money. The minute you utter those words, it's like a kid yelling "Safe!" during a game of tag. Suddenly, you can't touch them. Money is no object. If you push harder, they throw shade by asking you, "So, what's the life of a diplomat worth?" Okay, fine. But again, everything has to be balanced against something else. Trump's point on London was, even though the previous building didn't meet all modern standards, it

1   Caroline Davies, "Trump hits out at 'lousy location' of US embassy in London," *The Guardian*, April 29, 2018, https://www.theguardian.com/us-news/2018/apr/29/trump-hits-out-at-lousy-location-of-us-embassy-in-london.

2   "Bureau of Overseas Building Operations," U.S. Department of State, accessed March 24, 2022, https://www.state.gov/bureaus-offices/bureau-of-overseas-buildings-operations/.

was an incredible and irreplaceable location; the move would have improved security but drastically reduced effectiveness. What dignitary wanted to shlep out to the boonies in bad traffic to come to a meeting? And here we were about to do the same thing in Brussels? It would be a huge headache and quite frankly, an impediment to diplomacy.

"I don't care what you have to do," President Trump tells me. "I want you to put a stop to it." "Do I have your authority to kill it?" I ask him. "We may need to settle with contractors that have already been hired, there might be other costs we need to absorb…" "Tell those idiots to stop," he says. OK. I had my first mission from the Boss.

We arrive at the Belgian embassy, and the second Trump gets inside he goes around, opens all the curtains in the living room (which are closed for security, not for looks), and says, "Look at this location! Beautiful! No way are we going to move out of this place!"

On my next visit to DC, I go to the OBO, in charge of all buildings owned and run by the State Department worldwide. These are the folks who end up hearing about it when an ambassador wants new $200,000 wallpaper in their kitchen. About a dozen people are in the meeting about the Brussels project, including the head of OBO. I say, "I have to break the news to you that this project for the new embassy in Brussels is not happening." A lot of pissed off looks and protestations. "Look," I say, "I'm just the messenger. If you want to call the president and talk to him about it, you'll hear in no uncertain terms he wants this thing axed." Gidwitz takes up the cause after the meeting, and the plans are officially shelved. Case in point of how Trump often makes instant decisions, and his instincts are usually right. Does he execute them with finesse? No.

I encountered this issue of bloat again and again in my time as ambassador, in many manifestations. In any other enterprise outside of government, you have finite resources—there's a budget, and it runs out at some point. Once the funds are extinguished, if you haven't achieved the goal or completed the project, you are out of luck unless you can go back and scrounge up more money. Inside the government, there's always funding to be found somewhere. There's infinite time to work towards a goal. In this situation, how is performance measured? Not by how well or efficiently you do the job, but how well you can keep yourself *in* a job.

Much about the global diplomatic system is anachronistic. It's a game with its own customs, traditions, and rules. There are individuals holding various offices and positions who desperately want to stay just where they are. It is built to survive. The consummate insiders who are career public servants have a great deal to protect in terms of lifestyle, prestige, abundant free travel, and, for those in the upper ranks, a sense of power. Those insiders insist that the rules be followed. Communications between persons of equivalent rank must be protected, lest someone of a lower rank should dare to reach out to a more senior person—and have a better idea.

This system creates abundant employment (although the career bureaucrats always insist that they are shorthanded). Everyone has an assistant or a deputy or both. If you play the game, you move up. If not, you move out. It is designed to accomplish very little tangible benefit when measured by the amount of personnel and the amount of money being spent on its endeavors. For careerists, it's all about the journey and the process, not the results. In other words, it's another day to enjoy the perks.

In looking at the ambassador role more specifically, there is a constant debate surrounding political appointees versus career foreign service officers (FSOs) that frequently revolves around competency. There are two types of ambassadors: (1) career FSOs that work their way up the ladder by spending their entire career in the diplomatic corps until they reach the level of ambassador and (2) political appointees who are nominated directly by the president and are usually strong supporters of a president's campaign or have a personal connection to the president. Traditionally, about 70 percent of ambassadors are career FSOs and 30 percent are political appointees. Under the Trump administration, closer to 40–45 percent of ambassadors are political appointees, which reflects his mentality as a businessperson.

Here's my take: many who disdain political appointees say that a career-groomed Georgetown foreign service graduate is more qualified to hold the position of chief of mission than the head of a hedge fund who knows relatively little about foreign policy but knows how to manage people and make and close deals. The former has subject matter expertise, but the latter understands business, knows how to negotiate, knows how to get things done, and has access to the commander-in-chief. Who do you want running the embassy?

There are always going to be exceptions to the rule, people who perform poorly on both sides, like the career person with charisma and the political appointee who is a dud. But in general, careerists often lack that extra dose of emotional intelligence and people skills because they are so steeped in their expertise and in academic study. For this reason, the businessperson or layperson political appointee has a big edge over the career person: they know how to negotiate, and often, they know how to charm. As a political appointee, you certainly need subject matter experts on your team, no matter how well-versed you think you are in foreign policy. But you have to ask: Should they be running the place? What's the real purpose of the chief of mission? And if the purpose is just to perpetuate an ongoing journey, as opposed to getting to the destination, then career people win hands down. But if the goal is to get in and get something done, the appointees are going to win every time.

For this reason, political appointees, especially those from the business world, are a direct threat to the current system. They are not overly concerned about hierarchy and protocols as career people are. These types also like to talk to anyone who could potentially help with a problem they are trying to solve or a deal they are trying to close. Successful businesspeople with a limited appointment can and will pick up the phone and call cabinet members, senior White House leadership, corporate CEOs, or just about anyone who can help them get their job done, including the president. Career people either feel constrained or may in fact be constrained from doing so depending on circumstances. They generally must reach these people through some channel.

Political appointees are used to "closing" a deal, not working on it endlessly. They like to measure results. The career bureaucrats believe a meeting was successful if it resulted in the scheduling of another meeting. The appointees generally want to know what the next step is necessary to finalize the objective, and they also tend to have greater immunity to localitis, which can plague career FSOs. "Localitis" refers to a foreign service officer's tendency to absorb local culture and analyze issues from the host country's viewpoint, causing them to lose sight of US interests. Career FSOs are also sometimes seen as unwilling to push on contentious points for fear of alienating their host country. This is one of the reasons FSOs are frequently rotated to other regions and countries, where they have to start at square one establishing relationships and gaining access.

Don't get me wrong, there are many smart and hardworking members of the career Foreign Service. The problem lies not with the individuals but with the system. Simply put, there are just too many people, and not only from a cost standpoint. It's about effectiveness and not having folks tripping over one another.

Diplomacy has two aspects, but forget expertise and communication—I'm talking about sales and marketing. Marketing is the promotion of the United States' "brand" through goodwill gestures, events, parties, exchanges, fellowships, etc. Sales is the act of convincing one's interlocutor to see things the way we see them, to buy into that US brand, and to get that interlocutor and his or her government to take appropriate action as soon as possible. Sales generally takes a back seat to marketing. Marketing is fun, easy, and no one gets "hurt." Sales is tough. It requires persuasion, beginning gently but sometimes elevates to arm twisting. All too often it requires the direct use of leverage to further the US agenda. Career folks tend to shy away from this activity as it is seen as a "rocking of the boat." It's much easier to have cocktails on the veranda of the ambassador's mansion and make friendly small talk than to tell a foreign power that we intend to tariff or sanction them if our companies or our people are going to continue to be mistreated by a supposed friend.

Here are two suggestions to make this system work more effectively:

First, cut down on the total number of people in the system. Give those who remain clear, tangible objectives. Forget tallying how many meetings you attended or how many cables you wrote. How did you tangibly advance the interests of the United States as articulated by the incumbent president, often referred to as the foreign policy agenda? Note: I said the president's foreign policy agenda, not a personal or groupthink perception of what the US agenda should be.

Second, the president sets the agenda. He or she decides which countries are currently in favor, who is on the outs, and also which leaders we support and which leaders we do not support. That is why the president was elected—from whatever party they represent. If the voters don't like the policy, elect someone else next time. Give your best advice, but once the president has decided, salute smartly and execute or resign. Don't undermine, leak, bad-mouth, slow roll, or do any number of things that are done each and every day by unelected bureaucrats who think they are "saving" the country from a misguided or out-of-touch administration.

July 9, 2018. It is my first legal day on the job. After a flag-raising ceremony in front of the EU Mission, I present my credentials to Donald Tusk, president of the European Council. Presenting credentials involves handing over your letter of credence from the president, and also the letter of recall of your predecessor. Tusk strikes me as stiff and humorless. He's the guy who said about Europe working with the US, "We realize that if you need a helping hand, you will find one at the end of your arm."[3] I try to break the ice by telling him my father's family came from the same town, Danzig, Poland (now Gdansk), as his family. He looks at me disbelievingly. Why would I walk in and lie about something like that? To me it was just an indicator of his animus towards the president; I was trying to be nice, to find a point of commonality, but he did not like Trump, so no surprise, he didn't seem to like me either. Oh well. I tried.

As much as I'd considered it before I arrived, the ceremony drove home for me the gravity and wide scope of my role. The ambassador is both the chief of the diplomatic mission and the president's personal representative to the host government, local businesses, and civil society. As the chief of mission (COM), an ambassador oversees all departments with the assistance of a deputy chief of mission (DCM). Each COM is under general supervision of the US secretary of state, but ambassadors exercise a wide degree of authority. According to the Foreign Service Act of 1980, the chief of mission (COM) has "full responsibility for the direc-

---

3   Megan Specia, "E.U. Official Takes Donald Trump to Task: 'With Friends Like That' ..." *The New York Times*, May 16, 2018, https://www.nytimes.com/2018/05/16/world/europe/europe-donald-tusk-tweet-trump.html.

tion, coordination, and supervision of all Government executive branch employees in that country."[4] Amidst the complex relationships and duties I was introduced to in my first days at post, upon arrival, I also received a little laminated wallet card, the kind a college kid would get with important campus phone numbers and reminders. My card included the line: *When in doubt say "no" or call "home" to consult.* Good, simple advice that I tried to follow—but often when I called, it seemed the person on the other end of the line was distracted.

I was eager, ambitious, and had established a direct line to the president. It was time to hit the ground running. My office at the mission was on the fourth floor. The hardware in my office looked like stuff that belonged in a museum—and this is in Brussels. Who knows what kind of equipment they have to deal with in Djibouti or Dakar. I insisted (over much objection) that I be allowed to bring my cell phone into the office with appropriate safeguards. Every morning I was handed an agenda by my assistant. Great, nice list. What is the objective of each item? I made sure that staff could articulate the point of everything scheduled. I then spent my time not just being reactive to things on this list but being proactive—determining the subtext of each bullet point and what the president's agenda would indicate he wanted done, even it wasn't written down in 12-point Times New Roman on a piece of paper. For instance, I knew that the National Security Council (NSC) intentionally excluded ambassadors from important policy meetings in DC. Their attitude was to treat us like mushrooms: keep them in the dark and feed them shit. We wouldn't be included unless we put it upon ourselves to suss out what was going on and to get involved.

A few times a week, we had a small executive committee meeting in my office or in the SCIF (sensitive compartmented informa-

---

4   "Foreign Service Act of 1980 (P.L. 96-465)," United States Department of State, Section 207, accessed July 31, 2020, https://www.usaid.gov/sites/default/files/documents/1868/fsa.pdf.

tion facility, a secured space within a building or a building itself where only people who have appropriate clearance can enter). I'd then host a non-classified country meeting with forty to fifty people. It was my goal to bring foreign service officers of all ranks into the process. These were the subject matter experts and careerists that had information that would take me years to acquire, and it was essential to tap into that knowledge. In the cafeteria, I didn't want to sit off on my own in some cloistered corner. I grabbed my tray, waited in line for whatever was on the menu that day, and then sat down wherever I found a spot.

One thing I emphasized at the EU mission was making our radio and TV studio and our press department as robust as possible. Yes, I was a bit of a media whore. Not because I like the way I look under bright lights but because I wanted our mission to have significant exposure. The more exposure we had, the more recognizable we became, and so the more access we created. The US-EU mission was always being mentioned somewhere in the European press, and I considered that a very good thing.

The NATO summit in 2018 was certainly well covered. Before it ever began, the media expressed expectations that ranged from low to abysmal. There was a genuine concern that Trump had flown to Brussels to announce a US withdrawal from the alliance—though it didn't happen that time, it may well still come to pass, despite the fact that NATO has bound North America and Europe since the end of WWII. NATO has historically seen its mission as threefold: (1) deterring Soviet expansion, (2) preventing the return of nationalistic militarism in Europe, and (3) encouraging European integration. If the European Union is the primary driver of economic and political unity on continental Europe, NATO covers the security dimension. Key to the agreement is Article 5, stating that an attack against one member of the alliance is an attack against them all. This security umbrella helped provide Europe the opportunity to rebuild itself after World War II, while linking it to the United States and securing democratic values. During the Cold War, NATO was a pivotal carrot for the United States to ensure countries remained in its orbit.

If you look at the three goals of NATO as I just stated them, they all remain very important. But the way the alliance is funded and structured is hugely problematic. NATO members have formally committed to allocating at least 2 percent of their GDP to national defense and 20 percent of their budget towards procurement or research and development. However, in practice, very few members have met these stated goals. In 2014, only three allies hit the 2 percent number, and the Obama administration did next to nothing about it. When President Trump took office, he emphatically restated the goals and started to demand action. By 2019, nine allies met the 2 percent minimum, and another sixteen allies met the 20 percent benchmark. Sixteen allies have submitted plans to meet the 2 percent and 20 percent goals by 2024. Much to Trump's consternation, and fueling much of his public jabs at then-Chancellor Angela Merkel, Germany is one of the largest holdouts. Despite being Europe's largest economy, Germany only spends about 1.38 percent of its GDP on defense. When Trump insulted Merkel, what he was really voicing was frustration about Germany's reluctance to make good on its promises to NATO and its willful blindness to Russia's malign intentions.

Besides the problems inherent in the fact that NATO members contribute in varying degrees to funding the coalition, another source of irritation is incongruity. NATO's military exercises rarely go smoothly because of the patchwork nature of the alliance: every country has its own regulations and standards affecting all manner of things, from weight restrictions on roads that inhibit tank movements, to entry requirements at borders that prevent swift entry, to noise restrictions that limit aircraft activity. I get that you can't have a bunch of tanks rolling through a Bavarian village at 2 a.m., but the restrictions make it extraordinarily difficult to coordinate any kind of NATO exercise—and what's more, the restrictions are often motivated by emotion instead of pragmatism. Many European countries hold fiercely to their sovereignty but simultaneously want to be under the umbrella of EU protection. When you cede control to an organization and then try to reclaim it...this is what makes the relationships within and with the EU inherently complex. What gets lost in the complexity is the ability to be nimble and the willingness to use their collective size and weight to interact with a country like the US. The overriding raison d'être of the EU is peace. But in some sense, that peace itself is a squandered opportunity—it should be utilized, along with the strength and might of a combined bloc of twenty-seven countries in alliance with the United States, to neutralize mutual enemies like China and Russia. To coordinate this would take a committed and tough-minded president, one who is ready to focus our relationship with the EU as a partnership that can be utilized to great positive ends for us both.

In 2018, President Trump and Secretary of State Pompeo wanted to use the NATO summit as an opportunity to address the inequality in defense spending and burden sharing between the US and Europe, but what they really wanted to drive home was the imbalance in the transatlantic trade relationship more generally and how it needed to change.[5] I didn't disagree.

The economic relationship of the United States and the EU is a cornerstone of the global economy. Trade between the United States and Europe accounts for one third of global GDP, forty trillion dollars of combined GDP, sixteen million jobs, and $5 trillion in two-way foreign direct investments. Europe is an economic

---

5   Louis Nelson, "Trump criticizes NATO members ahead of summit," *Politico*, July 9, 2018, https://www.politico.com/story/2018/07/09/trump-criticize-nato-summit-702296.

powerhouse, and yet it still wants to cling to the way our trade relationship was created in the immediate aftermath of WWII, when Europe's economies were in shambles, and we were willing to help them with the vast undertaking of recovery. Now they repay us with trade protectionism and draconian data privacy policies, not to mention their embrace of China and lax response to its Belt and Road Initiative. China's Belt and Road Initiative (BRI) "is one of the most ambitious infrastructure projects ever conceived. Launched in 2013 by President Xi Jinping, the vast collection of development and investment initiatives would stretch from East Asia to Europe, significantly expanding China's economic and political influence."[6] Basically, it's China's plot to assert itself as the world's single most powerful superpower, and Europe is doing little to stop it.

Seventy years after we bailed them out, we have 13.7 percent of the EU market, and they have 22.5 percent of ours. Europe creates regulatory barriers that block entry for US goods and services. In fact, EU standards and technical regulations impact 92 percent of the value of goods exported to the EU from the United States. This creates roadblocks that disadvantage American producers. Instead of facilitating innovation, Europe is now focusing on new regulations needed to "contain" digital innovations—showcasing their ever-present presumption that regulation is always necessary. This philosophy has real consequences for EU businesses, investors, and consumers, as well as for our trade relationship with Europe.

When Trump said that the EU is acting like a cartel, part of me agrees. They're no longer the struggling nations of the post-WWII era. Their population is bigger than ours, their economy is robust, and they no longer need to be protected by us, fiscally or militarily. Trump's lens was financial. He zeroed in on the fact that they want

6   Andrew Chatzky and James McBride, "China's Massive Belt and Road Initiative," Council on Foreign Relations, January 28, 2020, https://www. cfr.org/backgrounder/chinas-massive-belt-and-road-initiative.

to have primacy in regulating food and drug safety. They want us to adhere to their standards in order to do business with them, and this has created a trade deficit. It's thinly veiled protectionism, nothing more than that. Protectionism, shielding domestic goods by taxing imports, buffers your market from competition initially, but it also stifles innovation and ends up being detrimental to any country's economy in the long run. European countries are especially effective at disguising protectionism as consumer protection, but the fact of the matter is that they enjoy their trade surplus and will do what it takes to maintain it. So I'd say to them, cut the crap and stop with the emotional appeals. And I'd say to us, let's close our market in industries with a big upside to them, like cars, and make it clear what it would take for us to reopen them. Clearly, it will take pressure from the European private sector against the EU leadership to convince them to negotiate all of the issues, including agriculture, in good faith.

It's a shame that we need a bazooka to kill a fly, and yes, Europhiles will be shocked at my suggestion, but it seems that incremental leverage doesn't move the European bureaucracy to action. It's only when a European head of industry calls their elected leaders and says, "Your policies are killing our business with the Americans," that things begin to happen.

My point is that the Trump administration began executing on what they said they were going to do from the time Trump took office. The Europeans may protest that his straightforward, transactional style (pay your NATO dues, now!) was ungentlemanly; it's simply not the way things are done. This was where the resentment about Trump really comes from. It's not about his bad manners or his late-night Twitter rants. It's that he's not willing to continue playing the game of wait and see, of protocols, empty handshakes, and niceties about our long-standing friendship with the Europeans. Trump's view was not that it's all part of a never-ending continuum; the inertia and the imbalance is something we can fix. His style is to go from asking nicely to asking firmly, to asking very firmly, to threatening, and then to following through on the threat.

Sometimes things just need to be said, whether they seem too direct, unpopular, or harsh. Donald Trump is certainly no Ronald Reagan, but at times when I listened to his straight talk with other world leaders, Trump's style brought to mind a moment that Reagan made famous in his speech at the Brandenburg Gate on June 12, 1987. With Peter Robinson, Reagan's speechwriter, Reagan went back and forth about including the famously endur-ing line, "Mr. Gorbachev, tear down this wall!" (Outtakes included, "Herr Gorbachev, bring down this wall." Doesn't quite have the same ring to it…) Secretary of State George Shultz reviewed the speech and balked at the line, which he felt was too much of an affront. Others at the State Department agreed. In the limo on the way to the Berlin Wall, Reagan smiled. He had made his decision. "The boys at State are going to kill me," he said, "but it's the right thing to do." So he gave the speech, delivered the line addressed in his impassioned, evocative manner, and made history.

So let's try acting more boldly when the moment calls for it, for instance, when really making a move on correcting our trade imbalance with Europe. If closing our markets to them is too extreme, let's start by eliminating barriers to trade, by dropping needless regulations. If after we do so, the trade imbalance is still there, then this becomes an internal US economic issue or a private sector problem—indicating that the US is not competitive enough to absorb opportunities in the European market. In other words, if there is still a trade deficit after Europe drops its nontariff barriers, that's our problem, not Europe's. Let's try it and see what happens.

In my first week while starting to figure out the true state of affairs regarding the major issues in my purview, I also start to settle in at the residence on Avenue de Myrtille. Side note: it always irks me when ambassadors or their spouses refer to the residence as "my house." It's not yours; it's the American taxpayers'. Ambassadors are just passing through. Ambassadors should be told that the homes they occupy overseas are public property and need to be used for public purposes. There are too many COMs who use them as their personal fiefdom instead of a place for hosting and entertaining. In the case of my house, its design and furnishings did not lend itself to being a true representational space for the USA, and I set out to fix that.

The residence is located in a leafy but less-than-ideal location in the suburb of Uccle, about thirty minutes south of the center of Brussels where the embassy is located. On most mornings, I would get up at about 5:30. At least, that's when I would get out of bed. Anyone who knows me well knows that I would have been awake for at least an hour already, reading and watching the news. I could tell as soon as I arrived that the house was overstaffed, but I usually would make my own coffee in the morning. The talented chef, Fabrice, would then make breakfast if I wanted it, which more often than not I didn't (he tried his best not to get offended). My driver, who had a wonderfully dry sense of humor, would pick me up in an armored suburban or BMW, and we'd be on the road to the embassy by 8:00. Sometimes, if we were stuck in traffic or running late, the driver would turn on the blue lights and hop the car up onto the train tracks. Let me tell you, riding to work in an armored car might sound cool, but in reality, it's the opposite. It feels like being in a coffin. The bulletproofing makes the air totally static and stifling, and everything is muffled. In tow, we'd have three Belgian federal police officers in their own car. These officers were paid for by Belgian authorities as a courtesy to the US. They protected the three American ambassadors in town (the ambassador to the EU, the ambassador to Belgium, and the ambassador to

NATO) and the Israeli ambassador, but no other foreign dignitaries permanently stationed in town had such a detail.

Back to the residence. It was an unusual house—with lots of what realtors call "quirks" and everyone else calls "issues." It was built by an oligarch who was paranoid about his personal safety— he had a panic room in the basement. There were umpteen locks on the bedroom door. And guess what? Poor guy was assassinated before he ever got to move in. The layout featured ten or eleven bedrooms on three floors, a basement, an indoor pool, and a large garden. None of it was in terrific shape. What really bothered me was the kitchen, which was impersonal and utilitarian with big commercial appliances. The place wasn't fit for hosting guests, so I requested updates to make it so. Unfortunately, they were only completed about two or three months before I had to leave post.

I also got lambasted in the press over the so-called renovations, but what I really had to deal with was years of deferred maintenance on the residence. It had been left vacant for close to two years, and when I arrived, none of those basic systems worked properly. This was a $12 to $15 million home left to fester and decay, and so a lot of money was spent was just putting it back into serviceable condition. Walking down the hall, I noticed one bedroom that was completely sealed off. Why? Because the bathroom attached to it wasn't functioning correctly. And guess what? The whole house stank. Literally, when I showed up, the place had smelled like sewage. The housekeeper of thirty years told me that had always been the case, and that no one had ever been able to figure out why. During my "needless renovations," the contractors discovered an issue with the plumbing, and I made sure they addressed it. At least the next ambassador could entertain in a residence that no longer smelled like shit.

A couple of days in, and it is dawning on me that I was right: this is a *really* consequential job. All kidding aside, if I play my cards right, I am in a position to really help move the needle on the administration's agenda to lower the trade deficit, drop onerous protectionism by the Europeans, and create a closer and more secure relationship between the two largest western democracies. Only one problem. I need access to the top of the EU. In this game, nothing else counts. Access is what I need to help me establish credibility and to start making headway to accomplishing goals.

After my positive first impression on POTUS, I now had a direct method of communicating with him when necessary or desirable. Now I have to figure out how to gain the same access to the EC's president, Jean-Claude Juncker. I had heard that he loved to drink, was a chain-smoker, and not in the best of health, but he was a formidable, if affable guy, if you could break through to him. He was no amateur; he had made the rounds in EU politics and knew the ropes. He also had an attack dog in Martin Selmayr, secretary-general of the European Commission, whom I came to distrust and dislike for reasons I'll get into later. I knew Juncker wasn't a formal guy, unlike Tusk.

Here is the challenge. EU presidents just don't meet with ambassadors. Rank means everything, and a president meets with a president, not a lowly ambassador. At least that's what my staff tells me one morning during my first week when I ask about a one-on-one with JCJ. OK, I think. But I am not just any ambassador.

The ambassador of the United States of America is and should be in a completely different category than any other when it comes to the EU and to most countries. I'm not talking about me, Gordon Sondland, but about the office that I held. Given our extraordinary relationship with Europe in terms of finance, defense, politics, and shared values, the US should and must be treated extraordinarily. The same should hold true for the EU ambassador to the United States when he or she comes to Washington; he or she should be treated with the same deference and respect.

"So. When can I see Jean-Claude?" I ask my staff. The response is dead silence. Imperceptible eye rolls. I am sure the unspoken "groupthink" in the room went something like this: "Don't you get it, ambassador? He ain't gonna see you." I try again, more direct this time. "Please call President Juncker's office and ask his staff if he is available to see President Trump's representative at three p.m. tomorrow." Now there are perceptible eye rolls. The outward answer is a "Yes, sir."

After about an hour, the staffer who was tasked to make the call comes back into the room, looking a bit chagrinned. "Mr. Ambassador, President Juncker is unable to see you at three p.m. tomorrow." I open my mouth to respond. "He will meet you at four p.m. instead." Wait. What? That crazy son of a bitch just asked for a meeting with the president of the European Commission and got it. Just like that.

But that's not what actually happened. I did not get the meeting. The United States of America got the meeting. I was just the messenger.

Mission accomplished? No. Now I actually have to prepare for and attend this meeting. This involves a full briefing by at least a dozen staff the next day. "Mr. Ambassador," I'm informed, "you will go with five members of your mission, and President Juncker will be accompanied by five members of his staff." I just want to go and talk to the guy for an hour. Shoot the shit. Get to know him. Find out what's *really* on his mind and how I can bring he and POTUS closer on a number of key issues. I know he is scheduled to come to the White House in a few weeks for a trade discussion, so I figure I'd talk to him about what Trump really wants: to figure out how to cut the trade deficit and open the US and EU markets to each other's products, to accept each other's systems and regulations. When I mention to my briefing team that I am hoping for a low-key one-on-one, I again get the *perceptible* version of the eye roll. Don't push your luck, Ambassador Sondland. You got an extremely rare meeting. You're going to a one-plus-five meeting. One-plus-five. NOT one-on-one. Now, Mr. Ambassador, shut up and pay attention to the remainder of the briefing, which goes something like this.

Head to the thirteenth floor of the Berlaymont building. (The Berlaymont building is like the Harry S. Truman building that houses the Department of State—it was designed decades ago and is constantly trying to keep pace with a growing role.) You must walk to this spot. Greet him as "Mr. President." Turn for the camera. Be seated at the long table set with flags, place cards directly across from the president. You will have a list of talking points. He will have a list of talking points. It already sounds like a sure-fire way to avoid getting into some meaty issues that could actually result in some progress.

The next day I'm driven to the Berlaymont building in my armored BMW trailed by a police car and a handful of armed body-guards. I have on my best dark "serious" ambassador suit.

I walk towards the designated spot where I am supposed to meet President Juncker in front of the cameras, and an idea occurs to me. We are still about twenty feet apart, and I muster a big smile and open my arms as if to prepare for an embrace. "Jean-Claude!" I say loudly. He immediately responds with "Gordon!" and his arms outstretched. I could tell the staff on both sides are apoplectic. I had just called the president of the European Commission, a man I had never met, by his first name. Instead of shaking hands, I gave him a bear hug. We have our pictures taken, with his hands on my chest in friendly gesture like rubbing a Buddha. When the photographer finishes, I say, "Thanks so much for squeezing us in on such short notice. Could you and I perhaps chat for a moment before we begin the big meeting?" He replies with a gleeful smile that tells me that he too wants to dispense with the formality *and* the staff as much as I do. "Of course Gordon." He turns to the assembled large group, points to the next room, and says, "We have refreshments and snacks just over there, please make yourselves comfortable." Before anyone can protest, Jean-Claude Juncker and I are together in his large office, alone. He takes his shoes off, lights a cigarette, and we begin a conversation that lasts nearly an hour. In the end, the Big Meeting never even took place. Juncker was now an ally, one that was ready to vouch for me as someone who had credibility and influence. Access.

CHAPTER FIVE

"DIPLOMACY IS THE ART OF SAYING 'NICE DOGGIE' UNTIL YOU CAN FIND A ROCK."[1]

After a few months, I'm starting to hit my stride. Every morning as I arrive at the front door of the embassy, the marines salute me. It feels a bit strange at first. I've never been a military man (I find civilian rules hard enough to follow), but I always stopped to salute back to the marines. I also made a point to stop and look the men and women at the gate straight in the eye. These were the people who would fight and die for those of us inside the embassy if it were ever attacked, and that wasn't lost on me, nor was my own responsibility and sense of duty. After all, since Vietnam, more ambassadors than generals have been killed on the job. Not that Brussels was anything resembling a hardship post—but the world is a volatile and unpredictable place. You never know what might happen.

---

1   This quote is most often attributed to Will Rogers.

I now have a good handle on the issues under my purview and how to maneuver around some of the obstacles and personalities in my way. One of the most important elements I'm dealing with as ambassador, as I alluded to in describing dealings with NATO, is trade.

When people talk about a conflict and they say, "It's actually not about the money," it's always about the money. The same holds true when it comes to our dealings with Europe. Much has been made of our special relationship with the EU and all the history and shared values we have. Yes, those things are important. But when it comes to trade, the EU has been a fair-weather friend. As I said before, we helped them get them back on their feet, out of the ashes of WWII; we paid to repair and rebuild their economies, industries, and infrastructure. Now eighty years on, when we ask to rebalance the relationship in order to get rid of our trade deficit with them, the response is, "Eh, we don't feel like it." Of course they don't, because the status quo benefits them. Long before I arrived in Brussels in summer 2018, Trump was getting rightfully frustrated with the EU's foot-dragging, given that the deficit is pegged around $150–200 billion per year, depending on the math. Not exactly small change.

Europeans balk that we would ask them to do anything about righting the deficit. They say it's based on consumer spending, valuation of the dollar versus the euro, and a host of other reasons. The fact remains that we buy more from Europe than they buy from us—mostly because they make it really difficult for our businesses to "comply" with their "standards," which are stringent and occasionally irrational means of covering for their hugely protectionist policies. They want to have dominance in global regulation. They want to set all standards for data, privacy, and food and drug safety. They want us to adhere to these standards they create as a prereq-

uisite in order to do business with them. This is especially true of
the French, who believe they run the EU show—and often, they do.

Enter Trump and his desire to cut to the chase. After multiple sessions with Cecilia Malmström, the EU commissioner for
trade, Bob Lighthizer, our smart and capable US trade representative, reported back to the boss. The news was not good. The EU
was, as usual, unwilling to make any material concessions to help
reduce the deficit. One of the biggest offenders was and has long
been cars, more specifically, German cars. We buy a lot of them.
More than a fifth of all imported cars in the United States are from
Europe, and[2] Germany accounts for about 55 percent of all EU
auto exports, especially from the Volkswagen Group (which also
owns Audi, Bentley, Porsche, and Lamborghini), BMW, Mercedes,
and Continental, the tire manufacturer.

As I said, it's about the money, but it's not only the money.
The Department of Commerce reported in 2018 that foreign auto
imports pose a threat to US national security. The reason? Keeping
up with "breakthroughs in automobile technology is necessary for
the United States to retain competitive military advantage and
meet new defense requirements."[3] Protected markets in Europe
lead to a decline in the global competitiveness of US automakers
and a flood of inexpensive foreign auto parts that cost us domestic manufacturing jobs, which in turn means less funding here
for research and development. The end result is a serious risk to
American innovation.

So, what to do? Trump has an idea—an offbeat one, as usual.
Let's go directly to the German car makers and do a deal with them.

2   Jack Ewing and Ana Swanson, "Trump May Punt on Auto Tariffs as
     European Carmakers Propose Plan," The New York Times, November
     11, 2019, accessed July 24, 2020, https://nyti.ms/2rs9CuK.
3   Donald Trump, "Adjusting Imports of Automobiles and Automobile Parts
     Into the United States," White House, May 17, 2019, accessed May 24, 2022,
     https://www.federalregister.gov/documents/2019/05/21/2019-10774/
     adjusting-imports-of-automobiles-and-automobile-parts-into-the-united-states.

Let's tell them we want to bypass the EU and its red tape and regulations. Same with the German government. We'll ask Mercedes, BMW, and Volkswagen simply to move as much of their production to the US as possible. *That* will help with the trade deficit and will royally piss off both Germany and the EU.

Germany has a "save and protect" mentality when it comes to finances, despite being the largest economy in Europe. They don't like to spend. Being savers is a good thing only to a point—if everyone's saving and no one's spending, who's subsidizing all the retailers, the car manufacturers, and the service industries? Money needs to circulate, and the Germans are loathe to allow it to do so. It's in their DNA after the conflicts of the past 200 years to always have some money socked away under the mattress. That "save, save, save" ethos pervades their entire society from individuals to the government. Going back to funding NATO—it's one thing to go to a struggling country and say, "Hey, you're not spending two percent of your GDP like you should be!" but in the meantime, all of that country's bonds are in default, and their people are starving. Germany is not in that category at all, obviously, and yet they are one of the worst offenders.

Trump knew he was poking the Germans in a sore spot when he chose the car industry as a way to go after them. His approach was to hit them where it hurts, right in the fender. The ambassador to Germany, Rick Grenell, and I start hatching plans in Brussels. We arrange and join an under-the-radar dinner to discuss it with the Secretary of Commerce Wilbur Ross and three CEOs of leading German automakers, Herbert Diess, Dieter Zetsche, and Nicholas Peter.

Wilbur has over fifty-five years of investment banking and private equity experience, and he has been chairman or lead director of more than one hundred companies in more than twenty countries. Along the way, he's mastered the art of dispassionately conveying bad news. This time, he delivers the message with the salad course. It went something like this: "We are looking into tariffs against your cars, which will kill your business. We have no choice because the EU won't engage in meaningful discussions." He continues by suggesting, "How about you move a significant portion of your production to the US and we can avoid all of this unpleasantness?" (Oh, and by the way, these guys showed up in Brussels at the drop of a hat once they got an inkling that tariffs were on the menu. Merkel was pissed that they were even talking to us, but they were worried about their business—they wanted to have a pragmatic and reasonable plan rather than an emotional, political plan.)

The car guys soberly take in what Wilbur said. After that first dinner, we have a series of discussions and set up a visit for all three auto chiefs to come to Washington in December 2018 to meet with Lighthizer, Mnuchin, Grenell, and me in order to move the conversation into the tangible deal phase. The meeting is set for the Executive Office Building (EEOB), next to the White House. The French Revival-style EEOB sticks out like a wedding cake dropped from the sky among most of Washington's sober classical buildings. President Truman called it "the greatest monstrosity in America."

Inside, each executive is ensconced in their own meeting room, waiting to take their turn discussing their particular business objectives in private without their other two competitors listening in. Everything is going well. All of a sudden, Lighthizer's cell rings. It's Trump. Lighthizer takes the call in the hallway. Apparently, Trump had discovered that there was a big meeting going on with a bunch of world-famous CEOs, and he wants in on the action. We hadn't notified him, figuring we had not moved the deal far enough along to warrant presidential attention. "How come you guys are meeting without me?" he asks Lighthizer. "Bring everyone over to my office, and let's continue the discussion."

So over to the White House we go. Trump is in effusive host mode, holding court in the Oval Office. He shows the Germans around, posing for pictures. I'm sure they were wondering how the busiest guy in the world has time for this laid-back hospitality.

We then head to the Roosevelt Room. Trump is in his element. He is telling stories, asking questions, and completely putting these guys at ease. It's like watching Leonard Bernstein conduct the New York Philharmonic. Then we get down to business. "I need you guys to help us solve the trade deficit problem. I want you to bring your factories to the US. We'll take great care of you. We'll get you quick permits, grants, whatever you need, and you'll make more money here, you know that." The music stops. The Germans' heads are spinning. Here they thought they were coming to Washington for mundane technical meetings, and all of a sudden, they are being entertained by the president of the United States. To the untrained eye, the whole thing looked like cacophony. In my view, it was a brilliant choreography on the part of Trump.

After a silence, the Germans respond tentatively. Slowly, they start to warm to the idea. Volkswagen says after the meeting, "From our perspective, the US position is understandable. They want more investment in the US. Now it is up to the governments and the European Union to find a solution that benefits all parties. As Volkswagen Group, we are committed to encouraging stable trade relations between the US, Germany, and the whole European Union."[4] It seems like things are on track, and then Trump says, "Guys, I like your cars, but I hate the seats." The Germans look at each other in befuddlement. WTF is he talking about? Zetsche, the CEO of Mercedes, bravely wades in. "I'm not sure what you mean Mr. President." "The seats, the seats," Trump says insistently.

"What about the seats?" inquires Dieter. Trump responds, "There's too many damn buttons and knobs to get the seat to the

4   Darlene Superville, "Trump, German auto executives meet at White House," *AP News*, December 4, 2018, https://apnews.com/article/f176ceed069a4e18a634a4be12efafa5.

right place. What's wrong with the old-fashioned grab bar, under the seat? Forward. Back. That's all you need!" Awkward silence. Zetsche comes to the rescue again. "Don't worry Mr. President, we will shortly have facial recognition in all of our cars. You won't need to adjust the seat at all. It will know who you are and will automatically adjust when you sit down." "OK, OK". Trump seems satisfied with this response.

Despite appearances, there is method to this madness. Trump gets three titans of the global auto industry just off kilter enough to think: (1) Trump is crazy, (2) Trump is crazy enough to put us out of business if we don't play ball, and (3) Trump is also crazy enough to help us get a sweet deal in the US, which will allow him to take credit for fixing a chunk of the deficit and, for our part, we could actually do better here than in Europe.

After the meeting, I follow Trump back into the Oval Office alone, uninvited. He glances at me skeptically. "How do you think that went?" (I don't know why I do these things, but I responded honestly.) "It went great until you started in on the seats," I tell him. He looks at me and grimaces. "What the fuck do you know, Sondland? Get out of here." I turn and leave the Oval Office, smiling.

Wilbur's gambit was far from the first or the last time the Trump administration wielded the threat of tariffs. He regularly used them as leverage in trade agreements; it's part of his negotiation strategy. In this case, it yielded results: German carmakers are quietly promising to increase their investments in their US factories, which will help create an additional 25,000 jobs in the United States.[5]

From the very beginning, in his first presidential campaign, Trump promised to renegotiate trade deals he viewed as unfair— and he delivered on those promises. He renegotiated several chapters of NAFTA, now known as the United States-Mexico-

---

5   Ewing and Swanson, "Trump May Punt on Auto Tariffs."

Canada Agreement (USMCA); withdrew the US from the Trans-Pacific Partnership, a poorly conceived regional trade agreement; extracted auto concessions from South Korea by reopening elements of the US-Korea Free Trade Agreement,[6] and opened bilateral trade negotiations with the United Kingdom and Japan.

But dealing with the EU has proved particularly thorny, in part because the stakes are so high. The economic relationship between the United States and the EU is a cornerstone of the world economy and a major, if not the major, factor in the transatlantic relationship. Most people think of China as the top trade partner of the United States, but US exports more than three times the goods to the EU ($337 billion in 2018) as to China ($107 billion). In terms of investment, half of all global investment into the United States in 2019 came from Europe, while 61 percent of US global investment flowed into Europe. The number one partner for the EU in the trade of goods is the US and vice versa—but in 2019, the US imported $515 billion in goods from the EU, while US exports to the EU amounted to $337 billion.

It's true that the US-EU trade dynamic has become sharper in recent years and that Trump's goals and his style had something to do with that, but so does a stronger, more aggressive European Commission trade agenda. Between auto tariffs, real and threatened, and an ongoing dispute with Airbus that resulted in World Trade Organization-authorized tariffs on EU goods from wine to cheese to whiskey, the US-EU trade relationship has become contentious.[7]

6   Donald Trump, "President Donald J. Trump is Fulfilling His Promise on the United States – Korea Free Trade Agreement and on National Security," White House, September 24, 2018, accessed May 24, 2022, https://trumpwhitehouse.archives.gov/briefings-statements/president-donald-j-trump-fulfilling-promise-u-s-korea-free-trade-agreement-national-security/.
7   Tim Hepher, "Airbus offers subsidy concession to end US tariffs," *Reuters*, July 24, 2020, https://www.reuters.com/article/us-wto-aircraft-airbus/airbus-offers-subsidy-concession-to-end-u-s-tariffs-idUSKCN24P0GR.

Trump changed the US-EU trade dynamic from the soft touch, multilateral, and globalist approach that Obama favored to one that's more direct, bilateral, and transactional. Obama pursued large, sweeping, and ill-fated trade deals like TTIP. In fourteen rounds of talks that took place over five years, neither side could reach agreement on a single one of its twenty-seven chapters. Trump officially and rightly killed it. While the US and EU bicker over one trade deal for years and years, China has accelerated to unprecedented levels of growth, flouting international laws and norms in the process.

Trump was unafraid to confront Europe and countries elsewhere over imbalances in the trade dynamic. He was right to go hard after China's flagrant intellectual property abuses. And his no-nonsense approach worked: he increased the number of manufacturing jobs in the United States by about half a million jobs.[8] During his administration before COVID, the economy was strong, with low unemployment and a strong dollar. The pandemic was obviously enormously challenging for trade and the global economy—that would have been the case no matter who we had as commander-in-chief. Disrupted supply chains and stunted growth and productivity have produced one of the most profound economic disruptions in history, a situation no single leader could have avoided.

Other than cars, another big bee in Trump's bouffant when it comes to trade is agriculture. It's no surprise, as agriculture is traditionally the largest hurdle to transatlantic relations. It's a complicated subject impeded by a few main issues, a primary one being the laws, regulations, and standards that relate to the use of hormones or additives in food, drinks, or fodder for animals. Culturally, there is a huge divide between the US and EU when it comes to the treat-

---

8   Kate Trafecante, "The myth of the manufacturing jobs renaissance," *CNN Business*, February 8, 2020, https://www.cnn.com/2020/02/08/economy/manufacturing-jobs/index.html.

ment of food. For instance, US law allows for the use of a small amount of antimicrobial rinse in cleaning and preparing chicken for transport—and by the way, this practice in the United States reduces prevalence of salmonella from 14 percent in controls to 2 percent. EU chicken samples typically have 15-20 percent salmonella.[9] I don't know about you, but I'd take a minute dose of antimicrobials over a bout of salmonella any day. Nevertheless, Europeans are appalled at this practice, and the European media loves to refer to the horrors of "chlorinated chicken" coming from the United States. Biotechnology is another point of contention. Yes, genetically modified foods are more prevalent in US food production. No, no one has proven that they are dangerous. Geographical indication (GI) protection, another major barrier to free trade between the US and Europe, refers to products from a specific region that are highly regulated. (Think champagne, parmesan, and feta cheese.) Champagne, from an EU agricultural perspective, can only refer to a beverage created from grapes grown in the Champagne region of France—so all US companies producing sparkling wine beverages have to use a different product name or indicate on the packaging that, in fact, this is not genuine champagne. To be fair, the US has some GIs with strong interest groups; for instance, Idaho potatoes or Florida oranges. But Europe far and away has many more GIs. (I'm looking at you, France. Again.)

Back in the summer of 2018, the good old days when our biggest domestic problems included Chipotle's bad burritos and banning plastic straws, I was part of a White House trade meeting between then-European Commission President Jean-Claude Juncker and President Trump. Trump really wants to push the fact that our markets are more open to the Europeans than theirs are to us. He

---

9   Julia Glotz, "Chlorinated chicken explained: why do the Americans treat their poultry with chlorine?" *The Grocer*, June 12, 2020, https://www.thegrocer.co.uk/food-safety/chlorinated-chicken-explained-why-do-the-americans-treat-their-poultry-with-chlorine/555618.article.

proposes to Juncker that both the EU and the US drop all tariffs, non-tariff barriers to trade, and subsidies on goods and services coming from either side.

I'm not sure how far Trump will get with Juncker, who was no neophyte to the negotiation game. During his tenure as president of the European Commission, the EU weathered Greece's economic crisis and the near extinction of the euro, over a million refugees and migrants flooding into Europe, the UK's angst-inducing decision to leave the union, and growing populist movements in many EU member states. Any one of these events could potentially have unraveled the European project, but Juncker held the union together. He drew on his decades of experience to weather multiple major crises and in doing so maintained a largely positive image in the eyes of the public.

In other words, JCJ is no pushover. He knows how to toe the line between placating Trump and not pissing off Emmanuel Macron and Angela Merkel irrevocably. On the day of the White House meeting, we need to draft a statement ahead of Juncker and Trump's press conference. One major goal is to break the barrier around agriculture; it is a touchy topic, for all the reasons I just mentioned, but we want to find a way to bring it to the table in our trade talks. The Europeans always make it clear that agriculture is one of their sacred cows, an area on which they aren't going to budge, and that makes Trump even more determined to break the logjam.

The day before Trump and Juncker are set to meet, I have a terse conversation with the ambassador of the European Union to the United States, David O'Sullivan. O'Sullivan tells me the only thing Juncker plans to discuss are soybeans and liquefied natural gas (LNG). I say, "The president is expecting to do a substantive deal. If all he wants to discuss are soybeans and liquefied natural gas (LNG), you should just go home because Trump doesn't want to talk about small change. We need to talk about agriculture, cars, big stuff." O'Sullivan just looks at me dismissively. But the next day, he takes me aside. "OK, OK," he says. "There are maybe a couple other things we can bring up."

We head to the Oval Office a few minutes before the Juncker-Trump press conference is supposed to begin. JCJ comes in from the Roosevelt Room, where he's been holed up with his team. He says to Trump, "Donald, I need a favor from you." "Right here," he points at his paper. "I need you to change this one word from 'agriculture' to 'farmers.' Using the word 'agriculture' will just piss off Macron," he explains, "but if we could substitute the word 'farmers,' the meaning would stay the same but the change would be enough to placate Macron and avoid conflict." Secretary of Commerce Wilbur Ross is listening, standing off to the side shaking his head, no, no! He knows the implications. Director of the United States National Economic Council Larry Kudlow knows it's a mistake too, and he steps in. "Don't do that Mr. President," he warns. Trump sort of shrugs, as if to say nah, whatever; it's fine. Implying, we're among friends. JCJ and I get each other; if he wants me to do this, sure. I trust him. Well, they deliver the remarks—including an announcement of the formation of an executive working group to reduce transatlantic barriers to trade. The responses are positive, even though we didn't get much out of the actual statement but the aforementioned promises to buy more of our soybeans and LNG. But what do you know, days later, Juncker is back in Europe. He goes out and makes a statement to the effect of "Hey, guess what everybody. I didn't budge on agriculture! Read the remarks, you'll find nary a mention of the word!" A not so subtle wink and a nod in Macron's direction. You can imagine Trump's reaction. Thus began the tariff war.

After Juncker leaves Washington on July 26, 2018, Martin Selmayr is tasked with continuing the discussions with the White

House. He and Kudlow begin speaking directly and cutting me out of the loop. An email is sent about another potential meeting between Juncker and President Trump, and I am copied. I weigh in and say I don't think the meeting should take place so soon after their last meeting where Juncker had worked us over and that I think more work should be done on fleshing out the trade issues before meeting again. Kudlow replies to me, incensed. How dare I make my opinion known? He calls me and says, "All policy is made at the White House, and ambassadors are supposed to be seen and not heard. Go back to giving parties." I tell him that isn't what I had signed up for. Over time, Kudlow began to realize that I was more effective than he thought and that I went out of my way to be more inclusive. We met halfway. Towards the end of my tenure, we became good friends and colleagues, and I respect him a great deal. Selmayr, on the other hand, turned into a huge problem. He and EU ambassador to the US David O'Sullivan were hugely anti-Trump and took every opportunity to disparage the president instead of solving issues. When I attended a meeting with Selmayr and Brian Hook, the special envoy to Iran, to discuss our withdrawal from the Joint Comprehensive Plan of Action (JCPOA), Selmayr began to pontificate and argue with Hook. It was fine for him to make his position known, but he was quite insulting and questioned the US's motives and integrity, to which I took great offense. He had a habit of pissing a lot of people off. Diplomats regularly referred to him as "Voldemort—he who must not be named" or "the monster of Berlaymont," and eventually he was shoved aside after controversy erupted when he was being fast-tracked for a promotion to secretary-general.[10]

Some key figures I've already mentioned who were involved in negotiating trade during my tenure included US Trade

10   Hans von der Buchard, "Martin Selmayr: 'Monster of the Berlaymont' or committed European?" *Politico EU*, July 16, 2019, https://www.politico.eu/article/martin-selmayr-monster-of-the-berlaymont-or-committed-european/.

Representative (USTR) Robert Lighthizer on the American side and EU Commissioner for Trade Cecilia Malmström, who was succeeded by Phil Hogan. The Office of the US Trade Representative is responsible for "US international trade, commodity, and direct investment policy," as well as overseeing trade negotiations. The USTR is a member of the cabinet and is "the president's chief trade advisor, negotiator, and spokesperson."[11] Lighthizer was previously a key trade negotiator for President Reagan.[12] He's an extremely pragmatic guy, a frequent critic of China, and has an affinity for vulgar language and filthy humor that sometimes throws people off.[13] In other words, we get along swimmingly. He's also one of these guys that I would trust with anything, including my wallet. Lighthizer believes trade policy should not be linked to geopolitical goals but instead focus on liberalization. He acknowledges the Trump administration's trade policies have been targeted, aggressive, and uncouth at times, but also emphatically believes, as I do, that "fear of rocking the diplomatic boat cannot be an excuse for inaction."[14]

The EU's top trade role, the equivalent of the USTR, was held by Cecilia Malmström from 2014 to 2019. Malmström was an effective and shrewd negotiator, quietly winning many key trade victories for the union, such as a trade deal with Canada, Japan, and Mexico, while going toe-to-toe with China and the Trump admin-

11   "Mission of the USTR," Office of the United States Trade Representative, accessed September 4, 2020, https://ustr.gov/about-us/about-ustr.
12   Zeeshan Aleem, "Why Trump's pick for US trade representative, Robert Lighthizer, is a big deal," *Vox*, January 3, 2017, https://www.vox.com/policy-and-politics/2017/1/3/14152712/trump-robert-lighthizer-trade-representative.
13   Matthew Korade, Adam Behsudi, and Louis Nelson, "Trump picks Lighthizer to serve as US trade representative," *Politico*, January 3, 2017, https://www.politico.com/blogs/donald-trump-administration/2017/01/robert-lighthizer-us-trade-representative-trump-233116.
14   Robert E. Lighthizer, "How to Make Trade Work for Workers," Foreign Affairs, July/August 2020, https://www.foreignaffairs.com/articles/united-states/2020-06-09/how-make-trade-work-workers.

(above) A little soiree with Ivanka Trump, Charles Michel, Jared Kushner, and Josep Borrell. This is truly kitchen diplomacy. It took an act of congress to get our EU friends to take off their jackets and ties (Borrell was a lost cause in this regard), however, it really made the discussion warm and substantive. Photo credit: Collection of the author.

(above) Dan Brouillette, myself, Maroš Šefčovič, and DOE official Mark Menezes in front of Air Force One on May 14, 2019. This is the way to travel: Air Force One complete with President Trump's personal microwave Chef. Photo credit: The White House.

(above) In the Oval Office with Romanian presidential advisor Bogdan Aurescu, Klaus Iohannis, President Trump, and National Security Advisor John Bolton on a Bilateral meeting. As you can see, Bolton and I are sitting on extreme opposite corners of the sofa. This picture speaks volumes. Photo credit: The White House.

(above) We are in Crawford with George H.W., George W., and Jeb Bush. Photo Credit: Collection of the author.

(below) Me, Sean Penn, Gov. Ted Kulongoski. Photo credit: Collection of the author.

(above) Let's go have a burrito, guys. The so-called Three Amigos, Kurt Volker, Rick Perry, and me. Photo credit: Collection of the author.

(above) Presenting my credentials to Donald Tusk, president of the European Council. Photo credit: Collection of the author.

(above) President Trump and Amb. Sondland at the Oval Office. When I could get Trump's undivided attention, he became an extraordinarily effective boss. Photo credit: The White House.

(above) President Trump arriving for NATO. This is where I warmed my way into a one-on-one meeting with Trump by pleading sore balls. Photo credit: The White House.

(above) President Trump's handwritten notes on my testimony. Photo credit: The White House.

(above) The residence of the United States ambassador to the European Union in Uccle, Belgium. Photo credit: Collection of the author.

(above) With Federica Mogherini, the EU's former high representative for the Common Foreign and Security Policy. Photo credit: Collection of the author.

(below) With Mike Pence at a White House meeting in the vice president's office. Photo credit: The White House.

(above) With incoming president to Ukraine, Volodymyr Zelensky at his inauguration in Kyiv on May 20, 2019. We quickly determined that Zelensky is the real deal. Photo credit: Collection of the author.

(above) With Kay Bailey Hutchison, United States permanent representative to NATO, Jay Leno, and Tod Wolters, supreme Allied commander Europe. Photo credit: Collection of the author.

(above) With my embassy colleagues at the US mission to the EU. Photo credit: Collection of the author.

(above) With Secretary of State Mike Pompeo and incoming President of the European Commission Ursula von der Leyen. Ursula gave me the highest compliment by telling Mike that his EU Ambassador speaks German in complete sentences. Photo credit: Collection of the author.

(above) With Mitt Romney during his presidential 2012 campaign. Photo credit: Collection of the author.

(above) Phil Reeker, Kurt Volker, me, and Ana Birchall, Romanian minister delegate for European affairs and later vice prime minister, on board the USS Donald Cook in Odessa, Ukraine. Photo credit: Collection of the author.

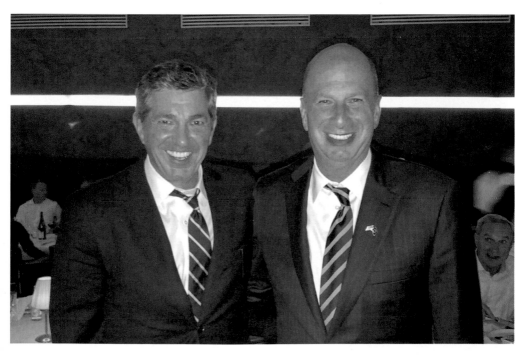

(above) With Stavros Lambrinidis, the EU Ambassador to the US. Stavros, who has become a good friend has the right touch with US-EU relations. As a practicing lawyer in the US for many years, he really "gets us." Photo credit: Collection of the author.

(above) Apples Tim Cook stopping by to see if he can help on the EU's overburdensome regulations and double taxation. Yes we can! And we did. Photo credit: Collection of the author.

(above) With PM Benjamin Netanyahu in Jerusalem. We discussed nudging the EU into a position of greater solidarity with the US when it came to the Abraham Accords, the US Embassy move to Jerusalem and sidelining those who would stand in the way of peace and trade with the Arab nations. Amb. David Friedman was our host and he is a diplomatic stud! Photo credit: Collection of the author.

(above) According to Assistant Secretary of State Amb. Phil Reeker, this unique dinner probably had some profound consequences with the respect to Ukraine's conflict with Russia. I was lucky to get key players such as Poland's President Duda seated to my right to spend some time that evening with Zelensky and other leaders which gave Ukraine a friend when in need. I asked everyone to exchange personal phone numbers and be on a first name basis that evening. The career staff cringed but it seemed to work! Photo credit: The White House.

(above) A lighthearted goodbye hug to Ukraine's President Petro Porochenko. Petro lost the election to Zelensky, had some corruption issues but was still a great friend of the US. Photo credit: Collection of the author.

(above) With Finish President Sauli Niinesto and our very effective US Amb to Finland Bob Pence (no relation to the VEEP). We, along with Gen. Tod Wolters, the NATO Supreme Allied Commander Europe (SACEUR) tried to encourage Finland to join NATO. Sauli was not ready to make that jump quite then, although we knew he was seriously considering. After Russia's invasion of Ukraine, the Finns (and Swedes) wisely made a fast pivot and their applications are in to the NATO "membership committee." They will each be incredibly accretive to NATO. Photo credit: Collection of the author.

(above) Well, at least US Amb. to Germany and then acting DNI Ric Grenell cuts a dashing figure. We were headed to a meeting that required both of us to twist some German arms to stop Nordstream 2 and to treat the US more equitably on automobile trade. Needless to say, Ric is an amazing arm-twister. Photo credit: The White House.

(above) I had to bring in the varsity team in my good friend Jay Leno when we held President Vladomir Zelensky's introduction to the EU leadership event post his inauguration. Jay would have been an incredibly effective Ambassador, but probably does not want to quit his day job. Photo credit: Collection of the author.

(above) Headed to meet an arriving European leader. The Trump "brief on the fly." By the time we walked another five hundred feet or so, POTUS knew enough to make most of these leaders feel like they were his old friends. He did cut to the chase quickly. Sometimes it actually worked! Photo credit: The White House.

(above) Enroute to Finland with Gen. Tod Wolters. Tod has an incredible combination of IQ and EQ. He would make a superb political leader. Photo credit: Collection of the author.

(above) Aboard Air Force One with EU-VP Maros Sefcovic. We are working on selling a little American "freedom gas" to the Europeans so they don't get hooked on the Russian stuff. Maros was a real champion of European energy independence. Too bad it took an invasion of Ukraine to get the Germans to figure this out. Photo credit: The White House

(below) Secretary Rick Perry and I in Normandy with Trump for the D-Day anniversary remembrance. Rick is an extraordinary salesman and was a really effective Energy Secretary. Photo credit: Collection of the author.

(above) EU Commission President Jean-Claude Juncker was a kisser. Jared wasn't having any of it (Ivanka might be jealous), however, the President said "lean in" so…. Photo credit: Collection of the author.

(above) With Mike Pompeo during happier days. Contrary to popular belief, I really like and respect Mike. I just wished he had been in the foxhole alongside when the partisan knives appeared. Photo credit: The White House.

(above) Secretary of the Treasury Steven Mnuchin, Vice President Mike Pence, and my wife Katherine Durant participate in my confirmation as the twentieth United States Ambassador to the European Union. Photo credit: The White House.

(above) Ukrainian presidential advisor Andriy Yermak, Ukrainian energy minister Oleksiy Orzhel, Rick Perry, me, and Ukrainian finance minister Oleksandr Danylyuk. Photo credit: Collection of the author.

istration.[15] She was succeeded by Phil Hogan, an Irishman known for being a political bruiser. His appointment as trade commissioner sent a clear message—the EU was toughening up for a fight. However, his tenure as top trade negotiator for the EU was short-lived; he resigned after the press accused him of flouting COVID-19 rules when he attended a large golf gathering in Ireland.[16]

These were some of the key policy figures I interacted with, but I also made a point to connect with my own kind, i.e. business leaders. In spring 2019, I led a meeting of the European Round Table for Industry (ERT), whose membership consists of the presidents of leading EU companies. I ask how many attendees owned property in the US: vacation homes, second residences. Most of them laugh and raise their hands. I ask how many of them flew their beef over with them, had their cars shipped here while they vacationed, or feared taking aspirin from an American pharmacy when they got a headache. Again, laughter.

One member of the committee, the head of a large multinational firm, says what everyone else is thinking: limiting US goods in Europe isn't about American products not performing up to European standards—it's about European protectionism. They are worried that with our production efficiencies and our lower prices, our huge agribusinesses would flood their markets and put all the little French farmers out of business. Macron and Merkel will never go for removing tariffs and non-tariff barriers, the ERT members say. France would never allow $2/lb. American GMO tomatoes to enter and land on the shelf next to $10/lb. organic French grown ones, offering the choice over to the consumer. Germany was more than happy to protect their auto market to our detriment.

15   Ryan Heath, "Cecilia Malmström: Trade commissioner, European Union," *Politico*, 2018, https://www.politico.com/interactives/2018/politico-power-list-women-to-watch/cecilia-malmstrom/.

16   Pat Leahy, "The rise and fall of Phil Hogan: How his hard work was undone by arrogance," *The Irish Times*, August 29, 2020, https://www.irishtimes.com/news/politics/the-rise-and-fall-of-phil-hogan-how-his-hard-work-was-undone-by-arrogance-1.4341077.

The European business leaders knew, as I've told you, that the EU policy was ultimately all about trying to maintain the EU's trade surplus. It's been that way for a long time: hedge, avoid, and continue squabbling over the smaller issues in order to obfuscate the bigger problem. We can't do that anymore. Now, perhaps, there's an opening for big changes; COVID has challenged so much about our way of life, including the way we do business. It's also created unprecedented opportunity to reimagine the way things work, multinational trade included. There's no better time than now to act on removing barriers to trade between the US, EU, and UK. Why don't we ask the EU again to open access to their markets without hiding behind the old "standards" arguments? *This* is a real moment of need, for us and for them. So let's call upon that old friendship and see it made real. We have the best products and highest safety standards on the planet—and now is the time when we should show both economic and psychological solidarity.

If their markets are made fully accessible and a deficit continues to persist on our side, fine. In that case, we can see that it's the result of things like consumer preferences, price, and exchange rates as they claim, not the result of protectionism. Then it's on us to refashion American products to make them more appealing to the European market; we would meet the challenge of providing customers with what they want. And I have no doubt that our American ingenuity, a quality that the president also believes in and values highly, will allow us to rise to the occasion.

If either side feels significantly disadvantaged, we can tweak the arrangement or revert back to the status quo. In either instance, we'll have key information that will help us improve the relationship between the US and EU as trade partners and as allies.

Energy is another huge and sometimes contentious issue in our dealings with the EU—and another cornerstone of the transatlantic relationship. We've long encouraged the EU to diversify its energy sources, and one place where we were having a modicum of success was in regards to liquefied natural gas (LNG). Former Energy Secretary Rick Perry, a huge supporter of the president's policy to boost US LNG exports, enlisted me to help sell the EU on institutionalizing exports of American LNG to the EU. The goal was to give the Russians a run for their money. This was both in our strategic and our economic interests. We had huge excess LNG capacity, and Europe had a need. Plus, the Europeans needed to wean themselves off of a dependency on Russia. That said, it's really hard to compete when we have to ship our product across the Atlantic and the Russians simply need to turn a valve.

Some EU states are still reliant on coal and are trying hard to shift away from it, but nuclear power is still a tough sell in Europe, especially in France, and renewables are not yet able to make up the difference. So for the time being, gas remains a key part of the EU's energy composition. The problem is that Russia has long been a key supplier of their natural gas: in fact, about 70 percent of Russia's gas exports in 2018 were bound for the EU.[17] The threat of Russia using energy for political coercion cannot be overstated. Putin and Gazprom would have no problem whatsoever interrupting supply if it served their ends. In fact, Russia has weaponized Europe's dependency on its gas before: Moscow shut off the pipelines midwinter in 2006 in order to extract concessions from Ukraine, effectively leaving Europe out in the cold. Europe needs to divorce itself from its energy dependence on Russia and diversify routes and supplies, especially in light of Russia's inexcusable actions in Ukraine and its plans to bring online the Nord Stream 2 pipeline, a major concern at the time.

The Nord Stream 2 pipeline would have transported Russian gas directly to Europe, bypassing Ukraine and making it a huge

---

17   "European Energy Security: Options for EU Natural Gas Diversification," Congressional Research Service, February 26, 2020, https://crsreports.congress.gov/product/pdf/R/R42405.

geostrategic concern. Nord Stream 2, if activated, would have doubled the capacity of Russian gas transported to Europe, which would only serve to further enmesh Europe's energy needs with Russia's supply. The project also represented a deeper political and economic connection between Russia and Germany, who would have been the single largest recipient of Russian gas in the EU—and no surprise, was also the European country that most heartily supported the pipeline's completion—prior to the Russian invasion of Ukraine in February 2022. It was incredibly shortsighted of Merkel not to recognize that Russia could use this pipeline as a political noose to hang around the neck of their economy, the EU's largest. Germany has now finally abandoned the project. The Germans, realizing that Nord Stream 2 was a bad idea and abandoning their support for it, were the missing piece for so long; finally, they have come to their senses. It seems like Nord Stream 2 is definitely "dead in the water," so to speak, but Nord Stream 1 is still online and generating a lot of money for Russia, despite sanctions.

The US was right all along to warn against it since it made Europe more dependent on Russia. Opposition to Nord Stream 2 always existed from many EU officials, especially those from Poland, Denmark, and the Baltic states, and obviously the Ukrainians. Right now the EU has a once-in-a-generation opportunity to loosen Russia's energy chokehold on parts of Europe. The United States can be a major and immediate part of the solution. We are the world's largest producer of natural gas and are on track to be the third largest exporter of LNG, after Qatar and Australia.

Some used to posit that the US only opposed Russian pipelines to line our pockets—that we wanted to stymie the Russians only so we could export more of our own LNG to Europe. This conclusion is limited and wrong. The US has long been a vocal proponent of the EU having a diverse array of energy sources: it's in Europe's own best interests economically and for security reasons—and yes, it also so happens we have an excess of LNG, which we welcome the chance to sell to the Europeans. Why wouldn't they want to buy gas from a friend rather than an enemy? Seems like common sense to me.

In order to make headway on this issue, I befriend Maroš Šefčovič, a Slovakian diplomat and vice president of the European Commission, the highest ranking energy official on the EC. Maroš had been the ambassador of Slovakia to Israel. He was then appointed to be the first permanent representative of Slovakia to the EU from 2004 to 2009 shortly after the country joined the union. After holding multiple positions within the EC, he became vice president for the Energy Union and European Space Policy under Juncker. I make a point to seek him out, and we hit it off. After discussing the LNG issue with him several times, I learn that Trump is going to do a ribbon cutting at a new LNG terminal in Hackberry, Louisiana. The facility would allow the United States to ship American natural gas all around the world and employ 7,000 people. It would have the capacity to export fifteen million tons of LNG annually, an amount that could supply over 40 percent of the natural gas that Germany imported from Russia in 2017, or 25 percent of all of the LNG imported by the EU in 2018. This is from one plant. Going on the trip will be a great opportunity for me to bring attention to the deal and encourage more of that ilk.

I call up Šefčovič. "Hey, Maroš," I say. "If I can get you on Air Force One on May 14, do you want to come with me and talk about energy as a key component of the US-EU partnership?" He says, "Yes please." Translation: hell yes! So I make a few phone calls. Access to foreigners aboard AF1 is extremely restricted for under-standable security reasons. So here I go again. I know that foreign dignitaries from places like Russia, China, and North Korea are just not allowed on board, full stop. Maroš being from Slovakia is... maybe kinda questionable. What if the person we're talking about is a VP of the European Commission and the highest ranking EU energy official, I ask? Well…maybe. Instead of waiting around and getting nowhere, I call one of the White House's deputy chiefs of staff whom I know and like. "Dan," I explain, "I want to get my buddy Šefčovič on AF1 for this trip. Can you help me out?" He tells me he'll take a look at the manifest and see what he can do. He calls me back a few minutes later. "Sure," he says. "I'll take three of the low-level tagalongs off and put your guy on." Great, step one complete. But it's not as if we were climbing the air stairs quite yet.

It's obvious why getting on AF1 is a source of difficulty and envy, even if the destination is rural Louisiana. Air Force One is the ultimate diplomacy tool: everyone wants to ride because by definition, the president is aboard and it gives passengers a great opportunity for access. White House staff are notorious for scooping up empty seats and planting themselves on board even when they are not at all needed or relevant. It's a great junket and an opportunity to spend some time with the boss. But just try and get a high-ranking European official aboard to fly with POTUS when he's visiting one of our largest LNG export terminals to demonstrate to the EU and the world that the US stands ready with safe, reliable, and conflict-free energy…. This, of course, is a challenge that required haggling on my part and that of Secretary Perry, who also puts in a call on Šefčovič's behalf.

Off the plane goes a few hangers-on and on the plane goes Šefčovič, accompanied by me and Deputy Secretary of Energy Dan Brouillette (who later became the secretary of energy after Rick Perry's departure). Dan Brouillette is an effective and smart deputy for Rick, and he really makes Šefčovič feel welcome. On board, Trump has a different protocol from Obama. According to AF1 crew members, Obama wanted everyone in the back of the plane, far away from his suite and office at the front. As soon as the plane is in the air, Trump wanders out of his quarters back to the conference room and sits down. And he's pretty much in the conference room for most of the flight, hanging out, going over the schedule, chatting with whoever happens to be on the plane.

One thing about AF1 that I'm sure transcends administrations is that the food is terrible. This is a plane that costs an insane amount of money per minute to operate. Despite this, the government is worried about giving anyone on board a "free meal" out of an abundance of political correctness. So as you board, they collect ten bucks or so per person for a meal—I'm not kidding. And it's a desiccated sandwich or something, paid for by lunch money you dole out like you're in grade school. So as you eat your cardboard sandwich, Trump holds court over a meal that involves something like deep fried prawns with ketchup or a burger with fries.

Our first leg of the day's journey takes us to Hackberry, Louisiana, where we tour the new Cameron LNG export facility. Afterward, Trump gives a speech to a large and supportive crowd. This is his corner of the country, and campaigning for the 2020 presidential race is kicking into high gear. There is lots of enthusiasm for the president and plenty of jokes from him about the crowded Democratic field of potential nominees. But the thrust of Trump's speech is about making America a leader in energy supply and giving jobs to American workers. He does give me and Maroš a shout-out, saying, "We have some of our big people from all around the world, because you're going to be selling energy all around the world. Louisiana starts here and then it goes around the world." After that stop, AF1 continues on to New Orleans, where Trump gets off to attend a campaign fundraiser at a private residence. Some of his staff deplanes with him, but the rest of us stay on AF1.

When we land late that night at Andrews Air Force Base, about 11 p.m., a sanctimonious young staffer comes into the conference room where VP Šefčovič and I are sitting along with several senior US senators and congressmen. He tells us in no uncertain terms to deplane in the rear of AF1, as the president would deplane alone down the main airstairs. I feel his tone to be a bit imperious given the room is (other than me) filled with VIPs. Everyone shrugs and says fine, although it seems like a bit of a downer after a full day of POTUS treating the delegation, particularly Šefčovič, like royalty. As we make our forced march to the back of the airplane, I turn around in the darkened cabin to see what I first think is an aide lumbering quickly down the long aisle behind us. As he gets closer, I realize it is actually President Trump. "Stop you guys! Where do you think you're going? You are all very important people. You deplane with me. Who the fuck told you to leave out the back door?" he shouts. Boy, does that leave an impression with everyone, particularly Šefčovič. Laughing, we all do an about face. As I pass the truculent aide on my way to the door of honor, I can only smile and thank him for his warm and gracious hospitality.

And by the way, National Security Advisor Bolton, who was not on the trip and had no clue whatsoever as to the purpose of my inclusion or Šefčovič's (a frequent occurrence when one's ego and hubris control one's behavior), believed that the whole event was yet another joy ride by the recalcitrant Ambassador Sondland, as Bolton claimed in his book. In truth, Perry and Brouillette were extremely pleased, and off Šefčovič went, back to Europe, singing our praises and arranging for more US LNG to make its way to the EU.

There were lots of reasons that it sucked to leave post the way I did (by being recalled—in other words, fired—in the wake of the impeachment trial, which I'll get into later), but one of the things I most regretted was not being able to finish some of the business I had begun. Even so, it's satisfying to see some of the projects with which I was involved continue to develop and find success. One such issue was my support of the use of small modular reactors

(SMRs)[18] in Europe, again to help them extract themselves from Russian influence and diversify their sources of energy. Nuclear power has long been a hot-button issue among Europeans—supposedly for safety reasons but more for optics—but in either case, SMRs are an intriguing alternative. These nuclear reactors are far smaller in size, way cheaper to produce, and pose far fewer risks than their larger counterparts but can still generate significant amounts of electricity (up to 300 megawatts).[19]

SMRs require less initial capital investment and can be rapidly installed; they don't have the huge infrastructure demands of traditional nuclear power plants, which can cost more than $10 billion and about eight years on average to build. Rather than constructing a single large reactor, a cluster of SMRs can begin operating as soon as they are assembled. (Think of taking a cluster of AA batteries together to produce power instead of using one clunky car battery.) SMRs are safer as they are less likely to overheat due to their small cores, easier to cool, and are designed to automatically shut down before any kind of catastrophe occurs. Ease of transportation and installation also means SMRs can be used in remote or underdeveloped regions without a lot of infrastructure.[20]

I hosted an EU-US high-level forum on SMRs in October of 2019, which was a great success. US Secretary of Energy Rick Perry was there, and the goal of the session was to look at the nexus of technology, government, and regulation to see how SMRs could be implemented on a large scale, and how to fund such projects. This event turned into a series of working conferences that continue to this day to bring SMR technology forward.

---

18   "Small Modular Nuclear Reactors: Status and Issues," Congressional Research Service, August 24, 2017, https://crsreports.congress.gov/product/pdf/IN/IN10765.

19   "Small modular reactors," International Atomic Energy Agency, accessed August 28, 2020, iaea.org/topics/small-modular-reactors.

20   "4 Key Benefits of Advanced Small Modular Reactors," Department of Energy, Office of Nuclear Energy, May 28, 2020, https://www.energy.gov/ne/articles/4-key-benefits-advanced-small-modular-reactors.

Worldwide, there are about fifty SMR designs and concepts in various stages of development. These are rapidly becoming more viable, which is a good thing since many of the traditional plants are just as rapidly aging.[21] In fact, in late 2020, the US Nuclear Regulatory Commission (NRC) completed phase 6 review—the last and final phase—of the certification needed for the first SMRs, meaning the technical review and approval of the SMR design is now complete. With almost no new nuclear construction completed in the US over the past three decades, this is promising news for us and for the rest of the world. This is one issue that I've continued to watch since I left post, bolstered by the knowledge that despite how my ambassadorship came to an abrupt end, the work I did in Brussels was not all in vain.

---

21   Lois Parshley, "The countries building miniature nuclear reactors," *BBC News*, March 9, 2020, https://www.bbc.com/future/article/20200309-are-small-nuclear-power-plants-safe-and-efficient.

CHAPTER SIX

DINNER PARTIES
AND DESTROYERS

I've been at post for nearly a year and have attended countless events. Most of them were forgettable, perfunctory. Many were also enjoyable enough, but I sometimes found the meeting and greeting part of my job tedious—I had little appetite for standing around chatting while eating chèvre and cornichons. As the months have gone by, the time spent away from my family has grown more challenging. I wish circumstances would have allowed me to have a partner by my side at the endless stream of events, but I also knew it is vitally important for Katy to be back home in Portland overseeing the business, which has hit a few road bumps through no fault of hers. A partner of ours is showing his true colors in my absence, and they aren't good. I also miss being able to drop in on my kids or see them easily on college breaks. I find I am also uncomfortable being away from the corner office for so long.

I also regret that the renovations at the ambassador's residence are taking so long that I can't host events more often myself, something I really enjoy. But I have an idea. One mainstay of the Brussels social calendar for the diplomatic set are national days. These celebrations of each EU country are held in Brussels at the embassy or the residence of the ambassador. They are usually somewhat boring "check the box" evenings—people go say hi, make the rounds quickly, and go home to watch TV.

The prospect of hosting a national day that few people cared about and even fewer would enjoy sounded lame. If we can really make a splash, the event can be more than fun and memorable; if we can get some high-level attendees, we can use it as a means to meaningfully advance the US agenda. My staff suggests a goal of raising $25,000 from corporate sponsors. We raise about ten times that much. The aim is to get the attention of the top leadership of the EU—ambassadors and others of that ilk rather than only deputies or staff. I also want to leverage the entertainment to motivate some foreign leaders to leave their formidable bubbles in order to help showcase my latest project, which was raising the profile of Volodymyr Zelensky, the newly elected president of Ukraine. He was not yet well known to Europe's cognoscenti, and I figure I can help him and help us (us as in the US) if I help pave the way for him to make some key connections.

I meet Zelensky at his inauguration in Kyiv on May 20, 2019, which I attend as part of the official delegation from the United States. Vice President Pence was originally set to attend but couldn't, so Energy Secretary Rick Perry is asked to lead the group. Others on the trip include US Special Representative for Ukraine Kurt Volker and Director for European Affairs for the United States National Security Council Alexander Vindman, who had essentially written himself into the delegation. Despite doing so, he later refuses to attend a meeting with his fellow delegates where he could have voiced any of his concerns about our dealings with Ukraine. In hindsight, I see that he wanted to do no such thing because he wanted to maintain a plausible deniability about anything that would be said. I know the press has painted him as an honorable hero, but in my opinion, that's far from the truth.

He intentionally hid in the weeds and built a storyline for himself while refusing to engage in a way that would have brought his concerns out into the open where they could have been addressed. Also, I didn't learn this until much later after his book came out, but apparently National Security Advisor John Bolton (who didn't attend the meeting in Kyiv) repeatedly tried to remove me from the delegation. Bolton didn't know what I was doing or why I was going, but he was too arrogant to inquire. Pompeo was fine with me talking to the president; he just wanted to be kept informed. Bolton, on the other hand, was extremely insecure and didn't like anyone to have the kind of access he thought should be reserved for people of his ilk.

Zelensky and I hit it off. I can see that he is funny and sharp. He is a younger guy and has the kind of no-nonsense attitude and demeanor that make me think he'd get along well with President Trump. That's why I am pretty disappointed when Trump tells me later that he doesn't give a shit about Ukraine. But I'll get to that.

I like Zelensky. And I want him to know that I want to help him out, so I impress upon him that I'll be talking to POTUS about Ukraine. The Trump administration needed to start paying more attention to Ukraine's unique geographic and political import. Ukraine is a bulwark against Russian influence, so it's of key importance to US strategic interests—and Europe's, a fact that has been made abundantly clear in the couple of years since all of this took place.

Basically, I want to do whatever I can to act as convener. The president would catch on to Ukraine's importance in due course, and by that point, I'd already have a good relationship with Zelensky. We'd be teed up to make progress on issues like energy security and corruption. On the other side, I can help Zelensky connect with European officials that would help him with things he wanted: he needs to get in good with Poland to avoid getting screwed by the Russians on energy; he needs to make good with the EU on a number of security issues, and so on. I can help.

I knew Zelensky was a comedian in a past life so I decide to ask Jay Leno, a friend from past work on charity events, to come host the national day celebration for the US in Brussels on June 4. Zelensky is a big fan, and Jay is a terrific person—no prima donna stuff, no artifice, and just really funny. One of the best in the business. Leno is the hook. But beyond that, I really want to create an important diplomatic event—I use the prospect of Jay's headlining to invite multiple EU presidents and prime ministers to see him perform and meet him afterward.

As any event planner worth their salt knows, a bit of sleight of hand is required when making invitations. Call it chicken vs egg diplomacy: everyone who's asked to attend always wants to know who else will show up of equal or higher rank. "President X, President Y is joining me for dinner with Jay Leno—can you move your schedule around to join us?" (Never mind whether you know yet if President Y is available. They are *always* booked). Then the second call: "President Y, President X would like to see you if you can move your schedule to join us." God forbid a single president shows up, and there are only ambassadors and commissioners milling about. Talk about a crisis!

The strategy works. Andrzej Duda from Poland, Viorica Dăncilă from Romania, Volodymyr Zelensky from Ukraine, High Commissioner Federica Mogherini, President of the European Parliament Antonio Tajani, Georgian Prime Minister Mamuka Bakhtadze, and others show up. Senior US leaders in attendance included Secretary of Energy Rick Perry, Senior Advisor to the President Jared Kushner, Counselor of the Department of State Ulrich Brechbuhl, Acting Assistant Secretary of State for European and Eurasian Affairs Philip Reeker, US ambassador to Belgium Ronald Gidwitz, and US ambassador to Poland Georgette Mosbacher.

As the dinner begins, I tap my water glass and give an informal introduction. Then I insist that everyone present drop the formalities and refer to each other by first names, not country or position. "Let's make it like an extended family dinner," I suggest. I also ask people to exchange cell numbers and stay in close contact with each other afterward, especially with Zelensky, the newcomer. Objectively, the dinner is a big hit. The principals actually speak to one another off the record, people are standing in corners talking about deals, and leaders linger and enjoy themselves. Mission accomplished. The US facilitated an embrace of Ukraine, and I used the correct utensil during each course. Win win.

When I was in Kyiv to attend Zelensky's inauguration, I made it a point to lay a wreath in the Maidan, Ukraine's independence square and the site of uprisings against the corrupt government of Viktor Yanukovych, who wanted to move the country away from integration with the EU and toward Russia. His people were not supportive of this, to say the least. Violence erupted in April 2014 as Russian-backed militants began encroaching on cities and towns in eastern Ukraine. Ukraine's government and volunteer forces pushed back against attempts to overtake these territories. Unlike Crimea, which Russia outright claims as theirs, Moscow still at that time recognized the eastern Ukraine areas as Ukrainian sovereign territory and officially denied supporting militants in the region, although this is patently false. The peak of the previous conflict in eastern Ukraine was in 2015, when Yanukovych was forced into exile. Though the intensity of the violence subsided afterward, there were still 25,000 Russian-backed fighters in the region as of February 2020,[1] and then the world watched in horror as Russia launched a full-scale invasion of Ukraine two years later.

---

1   "Ukraine: Background, Conflict with Russia, and U.S. Policy," Congressional Research Service, April 29, 2020, https://crsreports.congress.gov/product/pdf/R/R45008.

The conflict in Ukraine showcases a lack of coordinated action between the United States and the EU. Before the Russians invaded in 2022, there was no immediate or domestic drive for US intervention in Ukraine—though in Europe, energy concerns of an emboldened Russia were always far more immediate—but an unchecked and aggressive Russia is not in the long-term security interests of either the United States or Europe. Many EU member states are economically intertwined with Russia and fear upsetting the Russian bear by coming out too stridently in support of Ukraine. After all, the distance from Berlin to Kyiv is about the same as New York City to Chicago.

A lack of EU action empowered Russia to act as an aggressor, which it will continue to do long after the latest conflict in Ukraine subsides. Russian troops are still supporting the Syrian government. The occasional Russian submarine ventures into territorial waters of European countries, pushing the limits to see how far it can go before being spotted. Recent uprisings in Belarus had many concerned Russia might send troops to support the embattled government, which has long been seen as a crony of Moscow. The 2020 US presidential election was surely affected by election interference; we should have a deep concern about covert Russian attempts to influence domestic US politics.

With issues like these in mind, the national day celebration wasn't meant to just be a fun soireé but an opportunity to connect with people who could help me advance the points of commonality in the agenda of the US and EU. One of the VIPs who came to the event and could help with that (theoretically) was Federica Mogherini, the EU's high representative for the Common Foreign and Security Policy. The high representative is a relatively new position; only one person held the position before Mogherini (it is now held by Josep Borrell from Spain, who was a previous president of the European Parliament).

The high representative is a big deal, responsible for the European External Action Service (EEAS). Individual member states conduct their own diplomacy, but the high representative and EEAS execute the foreign policy of the EU basically the EU's Secretary of State. Mogherini was something of a young hotshot; she went from being a member of the Italian Parliament from 2008 to 2014 to becoming Italy's youngest foreign minister to coordinating the foreign policy of twenty-eight countries.

That said, Mogherini's legacy as high representative is dubious. Her crowning jewel of foreign policy was the Iran nuclear deal, which was dismantled by President Trump and is now being discussed for revival in a new form by the Biden administration. The Joint Comprehensive Plan of Action (JCPOA) was a multilateral attempt to constrain Iran's development of nuclear weapons. The United States, the United Kingdom, France, Russia, China, and Germany—known as the P5+1—negotiated a deal with Iran that would ensure that their nuclear program would only be used for peaceful purposes. In turn, the United States, EU, and UN would lift sanctions on Iran, allowing their faltering economy to reenter the world market. The Obama administration, as well as the other P5+1 negotiators, all claimed that the JCPOA was the best way of ensuring Iran would never obtain nuclear weapons and would only use nuclear stockpiles for peaceful purposes.[2]

The Trump administration did not share this view. Trump believed the sanctions relief would allow Iran to grow its economy and continue to seek other advanced weapons, such as its ballistic missiles programs, which were not part of the JCPOA. There were reports that Iran was still developing nuclear weapons in secret and that regulators inspecting sites in Iran were not given full access. Some of the evidence for this is found in publicly avail-

2   "Iran Nuclear Agreement and U.S. Exit," Congressional Research Service, July 20, 2018, https://crsreports.congress.gov/product/pdf/R/R43333.

able reports. In any event, the inflow of investment and businesses into Iran, a massive market with a burgeoning middle class, was a boon to then-President Hassan Rouhani. On May 8, 2018, President Trump announced the United States would withdraw from the JCPOA and the sanctions would be reapplied.

The fallout was swift and severe. The other members of the P5+1 opposed this decision. The EU in particular opposed it, as the EU and US were the two chief negotiators. EU officials saw the JCPOA as a deal they brokered in cooperation with the United States, so they saw our withdrawal as an affront.

Relations with Iran increased in intensity. The Trump administration declared the Islamic Revolutionary Guard Corps (IRGC) a Foreign Terrorist Organization—the first time an official state military force was designated a terrorist organization. Reports of an attack by Iran on US installations led to the deployment of the USS *Abraham Lincoln* Carrier Strike Group to the North Arabian Sea. In turn, Iran escalated tensions through attacks on oil tankers in May and June of 2019. At one point in mid-2019, there were genuine concerns that the ratcheting up of tensions would lead to an outright conflict between the United States and Iran. Many pundits cited a phantom plot within the IRGC to stoke a fight and combative elements within the Trump administration, seeking to drum up approval ratings through a military conflict.[3]

We knew the EU was not going to withdraw from the agreement because it had too much invested in an economic relationship with Iran but at the same time knew Iran was violating elements of it. Still, we could have found some way to play good cop (EU)-bad cop (US) to pressure Iran in a way that could have achieved our shared goal: to get Iran to stop the uranium enrichment, stop the assassinations, and stop funding terrorism. Instead, the EU (in an action

---

3   "U.S.-Iran Conflict and Implications for U.S. Policy," Congressional Research Service, May 8, 2020, https://crsreports.congress.gov/product/pdf/R/R45795.

helmed by Mogherini in January 2019) created the Instrument in Support of Trade Exchanges (INSTEX), a legal agreement known as a special-purpose vehicle (SPV) that would allow countries to do business with Iran without operating under the sanctions, essentially a work-around undermining the efficacy of US sanctions. When I heard about it, I gave a strongly worded interview saying that countries could choose to do business with Iran or with us, but not both. Given how much more money is at stake in countries' dealings with us, that made the choice pretty clear.

At the end of the day, Iran is a mortal threat to Israel, the latter being one of our key allies and the only true democracy in that part of the world. Iran also funds, plans, and executes malign activity all over the world. I saw the intelligence firsthand: if Iran gets intercontinental ballistic missiles (ICBMs), it will not hesitate to hold us all hostage to its demands. At least when it comes to countering the influence of Russia and China, what holds the US and EU back is that we have misalignment of strategy. This we can work on and fix. When it comes to dealing with Iran, the US and the EU do not see eye to eye. We want to sanction them to force them to come to the table. The EU wants to placate and cajole them to do so. And now the Biden administration, in true "undo everything Trump did" knee-jerk fashion, is trying to reinstate the JCPOA, even as Biden's own US Special Envoy for Iran Robert Malley says, "You can't revive a dead corpse," referring to the agreement.[4]

Mogherini and I did not agree on many policy issues. I knew this was likely to be the case even when I first arrived at post since she was a primary architect of the JCPOA, and I knew the US jettisoning that agreement was a blow to her. But I contacted her without any preconceptions to see if I could establish a personal connec-

---

4   Arshad Mohammed and Humeyra Pamuk, "U.S. envoy says Iran nuclear deal effort is at 'critical phase,'" *Reuters*, October 25, 2021, https://www.reuters.com/world/middle-east/us-says-push-revive-iran-nuclear-deal-is-critical-phase-2021-10-25/.

tion and a good working relationship. I discovered firsthand that she could be charming and friendly, but perhaps not completely trustworthy. Instead of just looking you in the eye and saying, "I can't help you on that particular issue, but we are still allies and friends," she would pander to whomever it was she was speaking with if it served her interests. One example: in July 2019, Pompeo and I meet with her in his office in DC to discuss various issues of importance (mostly classified stuff I can't discuss further). But one issue is the fact that we need to address that Iran, pissed off at the US reinstating sanctions, has been harassing ships in the Strait of Hormuz after the JCPOA fell apart. The Strait of Hormuz is an area of key strategic importance: a critical chokepoint through which 30 to 35 percent of the world's maritime oil trade passes. When Iran attacks or prevents ships from sailing in the Strait of Hormuz or threatens to close it completely, this has an outsized impact on the world market because all of the world's big oil or natural gas importers—including the United States—depend on shipping that passes through the strait.

In this meeting with Mogherini, Pompeo suggests that the US and the EU need to significantly increase our presence in the strait and to do so in a bold fashion, with lots of ships passing up and down it to give a visual assertion of our power. This would send a clear message to Iran that we weren't going to back down on sanctions and that they couldn't act like an aggressor. He is suggesting something akin to a FONOP, a freedom of navigation operation, where, in essence, the military sends a reminder that it is in international territory and doesn't need an invitation to be there by sailing or flying through contested territory in a display of force. For instance, the US sailing around the South China Sea to challenge China's claim to several island chains in the area. As we discuss the idea, I ask her, "Federica, do you have any assets that you might be able to help us with?" She sits for a moment, then mentions that the EU has a couple of ships down in the Horn of Africa doing drug interdiction. Maybe she can ask that they be redirected up to Hormuz for a while to help. "I'm not sure," she says, "but let me look into it." And so Pompeo says, "We'd really appreciate that. That would be great." There were no promises made, but it seemed like she was interested and willing to help—because she was sitting in front of the secretary of state.

A few weeks later, Jim Jeffrey, the special representative for Syria, is over in Brussels. We go together to a meeting in Mogherini's office. The meeting begins in a friendly enough manner, and then I say, "Federica, by the way, did you ever hear anything back on the ships that we discussed with S?" Federica looks at me with daggers in her eyes. "What ships?" she asks. I say, "Remember, you said you were going to check and see if we could move some ships up from the Horn of Africa to the Straits of Hormuz to help with the Iranians." She looks at me and says, "This meeting is over." And she gets up and leaves. I tell Jim Jeffrey the story. I wasn't pressuring her or accusing her of reneging on any promises. I was just checking to see if she had made any progress—after all, she was the one who had volunteered to look into it. She must have either never meant to do so, or she had asked for permission to move the ships and had her hand slapped by somebody. Either way, her response was disingenuous. Initially, I thought she would be a reliable partner in a lot of things. In the end, she wasn't. She was always unavailable or unreliable, and Pompeo understandably came to really dislike her because of that.

Another issue that came up in my dealings with Federica and other European officials had to do with data privacy and security. The Europeans regard data privacy as almost a sacred right. They are willing to sacrifice safety and security in order to maintain it. We look at it more pragmatically. We say, "Yes, we want our citizens' data to be protected. But if law enforcement needs to pull that data in order to prevent or explain death or injury, then they should be able to do that." For instance, the information documented when preserving the passenger record after a flight lands can help trace a terrorist several years after the fact. Look at how much we learned about the 9/11 hijackers since then. By the time we were learning about them yes, it was too late to stop those attacks, but it is incredibly helpful information to have for the future. If there is a pattern that happens like that again, we know what to look out for. By contrast, Europeans insist that flight manifests should be destroyed immediately on landing—so all of that valuable intelligence would be lost.

Though it's gotten more complex and important in recent times, data privacy has been a major thorn in the side of US-EU relations for decades. The US and EU have fundamental differences in their approach to data privacy and legal regimes. The EU has the strictest, highest regulatory walls around data privacy and sees itself as the standard-bearer of data regulation. This often leads to clashes with the major tech firms in the United States, low public support among Americans for greater privacy, and contrasts with the US belief in the free flow of data, which leads to greater economic opportunities. We weren't as aggressive as we should have been when the Europeans were setting up mechanisms for data regulation in the Bush and Obama eras.

The Safe Harbor Agreement was the first major US-EU privacy deal, instituted in 2000. It allowed US companies to meet EU standards on data protection and allowed for the transfer of personal data across the Atlantic. This agreement remained in effect until October 2015, when the Court of Justice of the European Union stated that it did not meet evolving EU data protection standards. This impacted about 4,500 US companies that were operating in Europe at the time and created massive uncertainty. It was seen by most as a direct response to revelations about US surveillance programs tracking and listening in on EU citizens that rocked transatlantic relations in 2013.

In June 2013, leaks by Edward Snowden helped reveal that the US National Security Agency (NSA) had been collecting data on EU member states and leaders. This was a serious blow to our relationship with the EU, and we still have not recovered. Major US internet, telecommunications companies, and technology firms had been helping the US government collect data on allies via cell phones. The US had engaged in direct surveillance of phone calls by world leaders.[5] The revelations were far reaching and damning. To this day, many Germans refer back to this incident as a major sign of the untrustworthiness of the United States.

After the invalidation of Safe Harbor, the EU-US Privacy Shield became the de facto data-sharing accord since 2016. In July 2020, the Privacy Shield was invalidated as well by the European Union Court of Justice. Unlike the Safe Harbor invalidation, this ruling only applies to personal data, not other forms of data flow.[6] Secretary of Commerce Wilbur Ross stated the Privacy Shield still applies for the time being, and 5,300-plus US companies will still need to abide by it until a replacement mechanism can be devised.[7] But a lack of clear regulations on data will impact jobs and companies, making them less willing to operate in Europe.

The other noteworthy data privacy regulation that impacted America was the institution of the EU's General Data Protection Regulation (GDPR), one of the most expansive data protection laws

5   James Ball, "NSA monitored calls of 35 world leaders after US official handed over contacts," *The Guardian*, October 25, 2013, https://www.theguardian.com/world/2013/oct/24/nsa-surveillance-world-leaders-calls.

6   Daniel Hamilton, "Europe's new privacy ruling will help fragment the global economy," *The Washington Post*, July 22, 2020, https://www.washingtonpost.com/politics/2020/07/22/europes-new-privacy-ruling-will-help-fragment-global-economy/.

7   "US Secretary of Commerce Wilbur Ross Statement on Schrems II Ruling and the Importance of EU-US Data Flows," US Mission to the European Union, July 16, 2020, https://useu.usmission.gov/u-s-secretary-of-commerce-wilbur-ross-statement-on-schrems-ii-ruling-and-the-importance-of-eu-u-s-data-flows/.

in the world. Remember in the summer of 2018 when you received dozens of emails from companies and websites stating they had updated their terms of service and wanted to convey their policies of managing data? That was the GDPR coming into effect. It sent massive ripples across the tech world, as companies had to quickly adapt to this new law restricting their use of data. In practice, the GDPR raises data security standards and data breach notification requirements, as well as requires any organization or company holding your personal data to notify you if it is moved or transferred.[8] Companies that violate the GDPR can face fines of up to 20 million euros (about $23 million), and there are cases of GDPR violations impacting international companies operating in Europe.[9]

We have failed ourselves by allowing things to progress as far as they have without checking them. When you check something at its inception, you can respond with a lower level of alarm. With data protection more generally and the GDPR more specifically, if the US had started off by saying, "This is not happening. Europe, you are not controlling the playing field; we are setting it up together," we would have had a very different outcome. But we are not allowed to raise our voices in protest to such behavior because of the power of elitist Europhiles, who are endemic to the US diplomatic corps. We treat the EU as if they have some childlike innocence, but in reality, the French and Germans and others are wicked smart, manipulative, and self-interested. They surely don't treat us with any special kindness or kid gloves, and we shouldn't be the suckers who do so with them. We should have a straightforward relationship that benefits us both instead of acting naïve and unsophisticated while being taken advantage of.

---

8   Stephen Mulligan and Chris Linebaugh, "Data Protection and Privacy Law: An Introduction," Congressional Research Service, May 9, 2019, https://crsreports.congress.gov/product/pdf/IF/IF11207.

9   Hamilton, "Europe's new privacy ruling."

Ultimately, for now, the EU is the one leading the charge on data protection, and they are doing it for the same reason they like to whine about our food standards: they want to be the arbiters. Frustratingly, Washington seems to show little interest in leading the way when it comes to setting standards regarding data privacy, and in the absence of clear US leadership, the EU emerges as the frontrunner. When we do push back against European protectionism, we often get a gasp of faux disbelief, a wide-eyed "Moi? Surely you can't mean that" response. But it's time to get past this. And the true test of the EU's data laws will be China, notoriously a black box of data practices—their system tracks citizens and assigns them scores that impacts their social standing, impinges on human rights, and is a frightening look at what's to come for all of us if we allow them to keep at their plans to install a network of 5G hardware around the world—it will make us dependent on and vulnerable to them.[10]

China's rise as a global player more generally has many in Washington and Brussels worried. Rightfully so. China steals intellectual property, threatens its neighbors in the South China Sea, and persecutes its ethnic and religious minorities. It's been buying up ports across southern Europe to extend its influence into the European market. The internet of tomorrow is being built on Chinese hardware, which they are installing at an alarming rate around the globe. We need to stop pussyfooting around and stand up to China's global aggression. Trump is actually dead-on accurate in his instincts on the need to stop this. I believe China would be scared if the US and the EU acted together: if we threatened to kick Chinese students out of our universities, if we got rid of Chinese infrastructure and hardware, and if we decided to stop buying

---

10   Nicole Kobie, "The complicated truth about China's social credit system," *Wired,* June 7, 2019, https://www.wired.co.uk/article/china-social-credit-system-explained.

Chinese products in the unthinking way we do now—that would make a real impact.

Huawei is both a proxy and example of China's current largesse and prowess. The giant telecommunications company has been enormously successful in China, but its leadership structure is murky. Some of their top brass have extensive connections to the Chinese Communist Party (CCP) and the Chinese military, meaning the CCP could easily tap into Huawei networks to spy on countries. As a result, the US banned the use of Huawei equipment in 2012, and President Trump has imposed further restrictions on interacting with the company.

Huawei came into the limelight in the last few years over its implementation of 5G infrastructure. Put simply, Huawei has the cheapest 5G equipment and became the default company to install the network for many countries in Europe. As European countries flocked to Huawei for their telecom's needs, the United States has put pressure on European allies to block Huawei components in their infrastructure. The UK announced in July 2020 that they will remove all Huawei equipment by 2027.[11] That's far too little action taken far too late. By then, the damage will be done.

China develops a product, provides the related services, and comes up with the financing—we haven't done that with 5G. We need to divert some of our budget into doing so, and this would be not only a good investment but would also help us protect friends and allies from malign influence. There are already European companies in the 5G game, such as Ericsson, based out of Sweden, or Nokia, a Finnish company. Together, those two companies, if united, could have a comparable share of the 5G market as Huawei. So let's box out China and create a 5G network using US and EU technology and hardware.

---

11   "Britain bans new Huawei 5G kit installation from September 2021," *Reuters*, November 29, 2020, https://www.reuters.com/article/us-britain-huawei/britain-bans-new-huawei-5g-kit-installation-from-september-2021-idUSKBN28A005

That said, decoupling from China will not be easy. We are deeply entangled with them economically, and that's all the more reason we need to do something about it now before it gets even more complicated. The *Economist* noted that "lost revenues in China, the expense of moving factories out of the country and compliance with the Chinese and American technospheres' diverging standards could cost global technology firms \$3.5trn over the next five years."[12] The moves will not be painless, but they are more than necessary, and they need to be made now. More on China a bit later on.

Although I made it a point to dispense with protocol to focus on substantive issues like these whenever possible, at times I could not ignore it. Protocol was taken really seriously by some people in the State Department, not the least of whom was the person whose entire job revolved around it. I get it: place placards and seating arrangements may seem like small stuff, but the implications of a misstep when world leaders are involved can be significant. The chief of protocol is the title held by the official in charge of receiving lines, hosting foreign dignitaries, and appropriate treatment of the flag—anything at all having to do with etiquette, formalities, ceremonies, major events, the presentation of credentials when foreign ambassadors arrive in the US, and the like. It makes sense to have a hard-ass in the position of chief of protocol. That seat was held by Sean Lawler when I was in Brussels. He fit the bill, perhaps a bit too well—he was a former military guy and was known for having a bit of a temper and for being territorial.

That style did not sit well with me, and it ended up being his undoing. When Jean-Claude Juncker departed after a summit with Trump on July 25, 2018, there was a lot of grumbling in the back-

12 "The Trump administration wants a US-China commercial split," *The Economist*, August 15, 2020, https://www.economist.com/business/2020/08/13/the-trump-administration-wants-a-us-china-commercial-split.

ground. Juncker was not prepared to make any major concessions on any trade issues, Trump was frustrated, and the whole thing did not achieve the hoped-for outcomes. Lawler was accompanying Juncker and the ambassador of the European Union to the United States, David O'Sullivan, to the airport. Supposedly, he overheard Juncker and O'Sullivan talking about what an idiot Trump was, how they were glad Juncker had come out of the meeting without concessions, and on and on. Lawler was highly offended. You have to imagine that overhearing things like that, as a chief of protocol, is probably not highly unusual. But Lawler took it to heart and decided unilaterally to do something about it. He took it upon himself to downgrade the diplomatic status of the EU ambassador to the US during what he later characterized as a "routine review." Since the EU is considered an organization or a group and not a country, their ambassador doesn't automatically have the same rank as that of a bilateral ambassador. But the US recognizes the key importance of the EU (our biggest trading partner!—bigger and more important than any single European country) and so has long afforded the ambassador from the EU to the US the same status as any bilateral ambassador.

When Lawler downgraded the EU ambassador, he did it clandestinely. The first time anyone notices something amiss is when O'Sullivan shows up at George H. W. Bush's funeral on December 6, 2018. He's seated in the nosebleeds. He is the very last person to be called up to pay his respects. Naturally, he later inquires as to what the hell is going on. That's when he finds out about the diplomatic downgrade—it was like a key player being sent to the farm leagues and told to sit on the bench. To their credit, the EU brass handles it well. They don't want to make an international incident, but they make it known they want the issue resolved. Quickly. I do too, because I don't want there to be any kind of retribution. If they decide to retaliate, guess who is going to get kicked to the curb—most likely, the American counterpart to the EU: me.

I call Sean and calmly asked him to explain the situation. He gets very defensive. He argues that the EU should have never had bilateral status in the first place. I just listen. I want to understand what his rationale was, and I also need to learn whether anyone else had approved what he had done. After he finishes blowing off steam (and saying nothing consequential), I call Lisa Kenna, Secretary Pompeo's extremely smart and hardworking chief of staff. I ask her, "Lisa, can I do anything about this?" She says, "Let me talk to S."

Lisa calls me back a few days later and says, "Nope. S didn't approve this." I say to her, "We have so many more legitimate issues with the Europeans that picking a fight over this stupid thing is shooting ourselves in the foot. It's just going to give them all the excuse they need not only to downgrade us in Europe but also to just get pissy about a lot of other bigger and more important things. We have fights that actually matter in terms of achieving something. This squabble gets us nothing." She responds, "I completely agree with you. Let me look into it."

In the meantime, I call Lawler and tell him that I am coming to DC for meetings and would be stopping in on him. We meet in his conference room a week or so later. I am very respectful; I simply say, "Sean, help me out here." I tell him that I had heard that his action was in response to the conversation between O'Sullivan and Juncker. I tell him, "I would be pissed too. I don't like when the Europeans and others talk smack about the president, but this is not a fight we need to pick right now. Can we work this out? We have a lot of other arguments going with the Europeans about things with much higher stakes." He says no. In no uncertain terms will he budge on reversing the downgrade. I tell him that it was too bad that we can't come to an agreement but that I am going to see it reversed immediately. And I do. I prevail upon Pompeo to reverse this, which he immediately does. Sean is very angry about it, and not long after, he ends up getting fired. It wasn't only over this, but I do think it contributed to his problematic reputation for "aggressive" incidents in the workplace.

In the end, the problem is solved. O'Sullivan was reinstated to his rightful rank—meaning more importantly, the EU is restored to its position in Washington. And my seat at the table is safe. The EU was grateful for my efforts, and O'Sullivan and I became much closer and were able to make progress on substantive US-EU issues.

Another event I hosted on a much smaller scale could have had a lot of impact if the 2020 impeachment trial hadn't totally derailed the forward movement it initiated. I work hard to convene an intimate dinner party with Charles Michel, the former prime minister of Belgium who was to become the President of the European Council after Tusk, Jared Kushner and Ivanka Trump, and Josep Borrell, a foreign minister from Spain who became the high representative/vice president (HRVP) after Mogherini. I set the date for September 23, 2019 when I knew we'd all be in New York for the UN General Assembly meeting. It is an unprecedented event for this type of group, and it explicitly does not follow protocol. Presidents meet with presidents, COMs with other COMS, etc. I deliberately mix that up a bit. Instead of following the rules and inviting a group of people with perfectly matched titles, I want to gather a select group at the table that I knew would make things happen. I use whatever political capital I have to explain my objective: a reset of the US-EU relationship as Michel prepares to take over as president of the European Council, and Borrell to become the new HRVP.

Here's a funny story about Charles Michel: he's a bit of a straightlaced guy. Once early in my tenure, I was in the VIP lounge at the Brussels Airport waiting for a cup of coffee before my flight.

A guy walks up to me, and he's wearing slacks and a shirt with the sleeves rolled up; he has round glasses; he looks a bit nerdy like an accountant or something. He says hello to me, and I politely respond. Then he says, "It's nice to see you," and asks me how things are going. I say, "Well, they're going pretty well. We've got some tough issues to solve...." I'm trying to keep the conversation at surface level while racking my brain to try and figure out who this person is before I say something that lets him on to the fact that I have no clue who he is when apparently I should. He says, "Yeah, I know what you mean. We're in a tough spot on some of these things," and he starts going on and on. Finally, I stop him and reach out for a handshake. "I'm Gordon Sondland," I say, and he stiffens. "I know who you are." "I'm sorry," I say. "What was your name?" He goes, "I'm Charles Michel, the prime minister of Belgium." Oops. A few months later, he becomes the president of the European Council, and I pay him a visit to congratulate him. "Who are you again?" I joke. He starts to laugh.

It was nice to have that connection established with Michel because I could tell it's hard to break through with him. And Tusk, the previous EC president, had really hated Trump and was very vocal about it. Pompeo and Mogherini disliked each other vehemently. I decided we should have a small dinner party: no agenda, very casual, and no aides around, a gathering where we could relax and get off on a new track together. I asked Jared and Ivanka if they would be willing to host.

Jared is very smart, highly effective, and highly criticized because of envy. He quietly but effectively used his leverage in the family across the interagency writ large. The beauty of his position was that very few people knew whether it was Jared speaking or the president, and they really didn't want to find out. Not to imply that Jared didn't faithfully follow the president's direction; he did. The Middle East deal is a gamechanger, thanks largely to Jared, someone with no previous White House experience. I began working with him in late 2018. He'd been around for a year and a half and had a remarkable command of a broad range of interests. He would have been a great hire for a Republican administration or even a Democratic one, for that matter, even if he had no familial ties to the president.

Some called Jared "the second-most-powerful man in the White House," and I wouldn't disagree. I met him at one of the fundraisers in LA when Trump was running for president in 2016 and was immediately impressed by him. Once I took office as ambassador, I made a point to look for opportunities to communicate with him. Jared Kushner wields an enormous amount of political leverage, especially considering he's young and unelected. As senior advisor to the president, he achieved a historic peace deal in the Middle East, was instrumental in reforming the criminal-justice system, took a key role in building Trump's border wall with Mexico, conducted diplomatic outreach with China and Mexico, and played a key role in Trump's 2020 campaign, including fundraising, strategy, and advertising.[13]

Negotiating this dinner between our five schedules was a monumental task. It took quite a bit of finagling and patience. To her credit, Ivanka was the one who really made it all come together schedule-wise—and she was also gracious enough to offer the use of their Park Avenue apartment. I was grateful for her help. But I also suggested we keep it simple and informal. Let's skip all the servers, I said. We don't need an army of people cooking an elaborate meal. Let's have it like a small family dinner around the kitchen table.

When everybody shows up, I take my jacket off. I take my tie off. Jared does the same, and so does Michel. Borrell won't do it—he's an old-school guy. Fine. But we do sit down at a small table,

---

13   Brian Bennett, "Inside Jared Kushner's Unusual White House Role," *Time Magazine*, January 16, 2020, https://time.com/5766186/jared-kushner-interview/.

not in a formal dining room, and we talk for several hours. It is an amicable and casual evening. We all call each other by first names, and there is a level of candor and confidence among the five of us that would have been impossible in a larger, more formal gathering. That's the kind of convening that Bolton would never think to do. He's so self-important it would never occur to him to jettison a formal meeting with a showy display of importance in order to do the kind of kitchen-table diplomacy that can really help move the needle on delicate issues.

I was hoping that the dinner, and especially the connection to Jared, would pave the way for Josep, Charles, and the new head of the EC, Ursula von der Leyen, to get into the White House to discuss issues like Huawei and China, correcting the trade deficit—real substantial issues. And I got some nice kudos from people for making the dinner happen as a setup for exactly that sort of progress. In the end, it was frustrating to see that great opportunity go to waste. As it turned out, two days later, a phone call permanently altered not only my plans for my ambassadorship, but my life in general, and would also have repercussions for America's political process. But apart from that phone call, the opportunity also fell victim to the problem of process. I can tell you, ambassadors all over the world, political appointees, have created their own similar opportunities and have reached out in vain to the State Department or the National Security Council to say, "Okay, I've met prime minister so and so, or this or that king. We hit it off and we're going golfing or hunting or whatever next weekend. Now we need to go in for the kill on whatever the issue is." And in the end, the potential connection is never acted upon in the way it should be. It disappears into the ether because everyone's so busy with the process and the cables and all the time-sucking stuff that nobody cares about that they can't capitalize on rare opportunities like this. We have to allow political appointees to pave the way but then be ready to act upon openings like this one.

It turned out that this was a sort of Last Supper for me, demarking a bright line between "before" and "after," as my world was about to be turned upside down—and many would stand ready to call me a Judas. Anything that seemed important or stressful in my life up to that point, any preoccupations I had, large or small—I'd just tell my former self: you ain't seen nothing yet.

CHAPTER SEVEN

WHAT'S THE MATTER WITH UKRAINE?

It's a warm afternoon in Brussels in late July 2019. At home in the finely appointed residence, my dog is being groomed by a PhD foreign policy expert while I nibble on canapés prepared by my private chef. The phone rings. "Hey Gordon," the president says. We chat for a few minutes. Then POTUS stops with the niceties.

"I just had a call with the new guy, Zelensky. I want you to drop all the trade, energy, security stuff, eating escargot and fromage, whatever you're doing over there. I want you to get on a plane to Kyiv." OK, I say, is there some kind of party? "No, no, and I also don't care about their political problems or Russian encroachment or any of that. I don't give a shit about Ukraine really. I just want you to go over there and dig up any dirt you can find about Joe Biden's son so that I can use it to rig our upcoming election. And I'm gonna cut off any aid we're giving these guys until I get what I want. M'kay? Oh, and why don't you look for crooked Hillary's old server from 2016 while you're there too."

So I hang up, finish my hors d'oeuvres, and hightail it to the airport where I procure a military escort and a fighter jet to take me to Kyiv. Then I bumble my way around Ukraine and DC on and off for the next several months on my secret mission from the president, a lone wolf trotting along, inviting myself along to meetings where I had no business, colluding with Rudy Giuliani—or occasionally cooking crack with him in dark alleys, all in an attempt to try and bring down Hunter Biden in order to smear his dad and ensure Trump a second term.

OK, OK. I'm sure you get the picture. This is fictional hyperbole, but it's the story the press developed of me: a meddlesome EU ambassador with no foreign policy experience goes to Ukraine (which isn't even in the EU, mind you) and mucks around; the only reason he's ambassador in the first place is that he's a longtime buddy of Trump's who wrote a massive check for the president's inauguration, and then Trump is such an ignoramus that he puts this guy in an important and sensitive position. Now Trump is trying to investigate his political rival so he directs his shill to consort with Giuliani to dig up dirt in Ukraine on the Bidens. In the meantime, I'm in on the fact that military aid for Ukraine is going to be withheld until they give us the info we need. The takeaway was that I was a flunkey for the president, responding to his beck and call, willing to work outside the confines of diplomacy or even the law to do whatever the president wanted in order to fulfill his desire to win the 2020 election.

It's a great story, and it all fits together quite neatly. The problem is it's completely false. If you pull at it a little and look at the evidence used to support all of these fantastic plot points, you'll soon see that the story falls apart and the truth about what happened becomes quite unsexy. Not uninteresting though...

From the very beginning of my ambassadorship, before I ever arrived at post, Ukraine was on my radar. This was not because of any prurient interest on my part. When I was first handed my briefing book at the Foreign Service Institute's ambassador school, there was a section on Ukraine. The fat binder had several hundred pages of information on issues of all kinds: country-by-country issues, recent developments, key events, and the lay of the land according to the preexisting team at the embassy. One of the many items in that book was an overview of the US relationship with Ukraine and the importance of the US and EU working together to support Ukraine's independence and the prevention of further Russian incursions.

To be crystal clear, Donald Trump never asked me to go to Ukraine—directly or indirectly. Not ever. Not once. In fact, from what I learned, President Trump seemed to believe anyone dealing with or going to Ukraine was a complete waste of time. I, however, as I mentioned before, saw a lot more to be gained by a US-EU relationship with the country, and not to be smug, but I believe time has proven my point. My career staff at the mission also confirmed this. The US-EU relationship vis-à-vis Ukraine is a vital one that needs lots of attention and cultivation. Ukraine is a young democracy, and it has looked to the United States for leadership since gaining independence from the failed Soviet Union in 1991. Clearly, it's in the interest of the United States to encourage a partnership so we can ensure Ukraine does not fall into old modes and align itself with Russia—or be pulled under by Putin. For both the US and the EU, the country is of key strategic importance, sandwiched in between the European continent and Russian territory. It's a populous but poor country (a little smaller in size than Texas, but with a population of 41.9 million, larger than that of California), which makes it even more prone to influence by those who would woo its leadership for their own ends. For the US, beyond the political relationship, it's not insignificant that over 900,000 Ukrainians live and work in the United States and over two million Americans can trace their heritage to Ukraine.[1]

---

1   "History and modern context of Ukraine-U.S. relations," Embassy of Ukraine in the United States of America, accessed August 19, 2020, https://usa.mfa. gov.ua/en/ukraine-and-usa/political-issues-ukraine-and-usa.

Russia hasn't given up hope that it can suck Ukraine back into its sphere of influence, or even its empire. We've all seen this play out in an abhorrent fashion since the invasion in February 2022. But Russia fired some warning shots in 2014 when the country annexed the Crimean Peninsula, Ukrainian sovereign territory. This illegal annexation of territory through military force violated international law, and there was widespread bipartisan support in Congress for Ukraine and condemnation of Russian aggression. The United States sanctioned Russia over this aggression and provided defensive weapons to Ukrainian forces fighting in the east, but obviously, this wasn't enough.

Another huge problem in Ukraine is corruption. A small group of oligarchs, most of them in the energy sector, control much of the country and have stunted economic growth over the decades. Working closely with European allies, the US has worked to strengthen Ukraine's defense capabilities and energy security and has pushed for economic and social reforms to strengthen the rule of law in the country. What will come of all of this in light of the most recent conflict remains to be seen.

For decades, the EU and NATO have eyed Ukraine as a prospective member, especially after the historic Euromaidan Revolution to oust former President Yanukovych in 2014. Ukraine has had an Association Agreement with the EU since 2017. Under this agreement, Ukraine is undertaking reforms on foreign policy, justice, education, and trade to be in line with EU standards, with the ultimate goal of joining the union.[2] Ukrainian citizens no longer need a visa to access to the EU's Schengen area. However, Ukraine still faces numerous domestic challenges (again, see corruption) before it can be considered for membership. I believe Ukraine

---

2   Rikard Jozwiak, "After Four Years Of Drama, EU-Ukraine Association Agreement Comes Into Force," *RadioFreeEurope/RadioLiberty*, August 31, 2017, accessed August 19, 2020, https://www.rferl.org/a/eu-ukraine-association-agreement-goes-into-force-after-four-years-drama/28708426.html.

should be let into the EU immediately, given what took place in February 2022. There's no time to waste. Does Brussels honestly expect the Ukrainian government to implement more than 80,000 pages of rules and regulations while it fights Russia? Ukraine will come around on environmental standards and food hygiene, but as I write this, cities are being bombed, and innocent civilians are dying. When you have the opportunity to take in a new EU member whose leaders and citizenry have demonstrated their yearning for Western values by literally putting their lives on the line, you act. What downside is there for the EU compared to the tremendous loss Ukraine is experiencing?

As far as NATO goes, for many years, Ukraine sought to remain nonaligned but still contributed troops to NATO peacekeeping operations. After the Russian invasion in 2014, Ukraine's parliament revoked its neutrality and voted to cooperate with NATO. However, as long as the conflict in eastern Ukraine remains unresolved, full membership in NATO is a tough hurdle for Ukraine to clear. From Russia's perspective, such an action would represent a march right up to its border in clear escalation and challenge.

It is clearly in the interests of both the United States and EU for Ukraine to be a strong, prosperous democracy. I have no doubt Ukraine will eventually become a member of both the EU and NATO eventually. But it won't be an easy road, and the past few years have only made it more winding.

My job while at post was not so much to deal with Ukraine directly but to create commonality between the EU and the United States in our support of Ukraine and its independence: its energy independence, its political independence, and its independence from corruption. It's not like I ever thought I was a key point person on Ukraine. There were plenty of other capable experts dealing with the country, people who had devoted their lives to study and work on its issues: for instance, former US Ambassador to Ukraine Marie Yovanovitch, who I found to be an excellent diplomat despite her unceremonious ouster, and her successor, Chargé d'Affaires William Taylor, who I also thought was a highly competent official. Other experts involved in Ukrainian issues included Special Envoy Kurt Volker, another experienced diplomat who had a special remit to address the ongoing conflict in eastern Ukraine and Crimea. Volker is extraordinarily smart, and more than that, his heart is in the right place; he has a lot of respect for and from the Ukrainians, and his relationships there transcend local politics. Phil Reeker was another expert who was active on Ukraine as assistant secretary in the Bureau of European and Eurasian Affairs. He and Volker had known each other for decades and saw eye to eye on most issues. Then there was the National Security Council crowd: John Bolton, then the head of the NSC; Fiona Hill, coordinator for European, Ukraine, Russia, and Near Eastern affairs, also the most senior point person at the NSC for me next to Bolton; and Alexander Vindman, an NSC director for Eastern European, Caucasus, and Russian affairs. For any of these individuals, Ukraine was a far more central part of their portfolio than it was for me.

Because of what happened with the impeachment inquiry, Ukraine unfortunately became synonymous with corruption in households across America, despite all efforts the country had made to combat exactly this negative image. The geopolitical importance of Ukraine got lost in the frenzy of breathless coverage of President Trump's interactions with Ukrainian President Zelensky. What's more, Zelensky was a huge fan of the United States and a young, energetic, and dynamic president ready to work hard to achieve these aims. In the aftermath of the impeachment trial, there were very few in the diplomatic world who wanted to do anything with Ukraine. After the Trump impeachment trial shenanigans, headlines went from portraying Ukraine as a promising, newly reinvigorated country on the rise to a troublesome quagmire of political intrigue. And frequently lost in the noise of domestic debate in the United States is the plight of nearly forty-two million Ukrainian people whose country have been at war in some fashion for over eight years. Thankfully, the situation has changed, albeit for the worst reasons. As Russia grows increasingly expansionist and aggressive, refusing to back off territorial claims in eastern Ukraine, and continuing to manipulate, coerce, and bribe people of influence in the country, it is more important than ever that we look for ways to counter Russian influence and to build up our alliances in the region.

During my very first days in Brussels, I asked my staff to arrange meetings with all kinds of people—those who I identified as important or potentially important and those who they thought valuable for me to meet based on their own expertise. I met with the EU ambassador from Canada. I met with the president of the American Chamber of Commerce (AmCham). Brief aside on AmCham. AmCham in Europe has a huge group of multinational corporations on their board. Despite this, it's not a very effective organization...though I'm not supposed to say that aloud. Part of it is the comparison with the Chamber of Commerce in the US, which is very powerful—when those members decide they want something from the Hill or the White House, their lobbyists and CEOs take action and make sure they are listened to. AmCham EU is not a serious advocacy organization in the same way. For instance, at one point, Exxon was in trouble with the European Parliament over an environmental issue and had their Parliament building passes revoked. When the Exxon leadership went to AmCham to ask for help, they were told that an appointment to discuss the issue would be arranged with Klaus Welle, secretary-general of the European Parliament, in two and a half weeks. What? One of the most valued companies in the world was supposed to wait almost three weeks before their issue was even discussed? I got ahold of Klaus Welle's phone number (I'd met him once or twice before). I asked, "Klaus, why would you block Exxon from the building and piss them off? You don't want us blocking European companies from doing business in the US, do you? Because that's what this amounts to, or will result in." Two and a half hours later, the Exxon guys got their badges back. And while we are talking about inefficiency, if not ineptitude, consider this about the European Parliament itself: its official seat and the venue for most of the plenary sessions is Strasbourg, France; parliamentary committees have their meetings in Brussels, Belgium; and Parliament's secretariat, the staff, is officially based in Luxembourg. This means the entire organization shleps back and forth between Brussels and Strasbourg (a distance of 200 miles) every single month for meetings, costing the EU €114 million per year. Imagine if our Congress held some meetings in Philadelphia and others in Washington, DC. Even less would get done.

Some of my other early meetings when I arrived at post were with officials and dignitaries from Ukraine, including Pavlo Klimkin, the foreign minister of Ukraine under President Petro Poroshenko, and an official from Naftogaz, the national oil and gas company of Ukraine. Both of them wanted to talk about gaining more US help in pursuing Ukrainian energy independence. They also wanted help pressuring the Russians to renew contracts that kept Russian gas flowing through Ukraine; this setup created fees that were an important part of the Ukrainian government's revenue. These meetings were suggested and arranged by career staff.

I wanted to form a substantive relationship with the key players that would help the US and EU gain a foothold in Ukraine and to make ourselves known as an ally to the Ukrainian people. The way I saw it, a very good reason to make nice with the Ukrainians was to show Russia that the US and EU were totally aligned in acting as allies to Ukraine and to show Ukraine, when struggling with economic or corruption issues, that they could turn to us for help instead of their neighbor to the east. One of the things that intimidates Putin the most is when there is no daylight between the US and EU on an issue important to Russia. If there's unequivocal agreement between the US and EU, if we have France and Germany and all the rest of the European bloc standing next to us, it's very hard for Russia, or anyone else, to stop us. We're just too big. When you combine the US military and the militaries of the EU member states with NATO assets, we create a very formidable front of Western democracies. The problem is we don't stand together nearly enough—not close enough together, anyway. Our squabbles and catfights prevent us from flexing our muscle.

So I was told from the start: the issues under your purview include some that involve Ukraine. The country was not central to my mandate, but I felt I could play a key role in fortifying the US-EU relationship with the country. So in February 2019, when a request came in for someone from the EU to travel to Odessa and join President Poroshenko and Ambassador Yovanovitch to talk about Russian aggression, I asked to go. At that point, Russia was still holding twenty-four Ukrainian sailors hostage after a clash in November 2018 in the Kerch Strait—the narrow waterway between Russia and annexed Crimea and the entry into the Sea of Azov.

Three Ukrainian ships were traveling from Odessa to Mariupol when they were attacked by the Russian coast guard. Russia then positioned a freighter under the bridge, essentially blocking access to the Sea of Azov and asserting full control over the body of water. Russia seized the three vessels and twenty-four Ukrainian sailors, claiming the Ukrainian ships violated territorial waters even though the waters are jointly administered by Ukraine and Russia thanks to a 2003 treaty. Ukraine claimed it was an act of aggression. The Ukrainian sailors were held by Russia until September 2019. [3]

In response to this incident, under Operation Atlantic Resolve, an ongoing US effort to counteract Russia's aggression in Ukraine, we sent several destroyers to the region for maritime security operations (read: show of force). The USS *Donald Cook* entered the Black Sea on February 19, 2019, the second time the US sent a vessel into the Black Sea that year. [4]

The best response would be to have the US and EU show up in Ukraine together in a joint show of force—an obvious middle finger to Putin. When you combine our forces, our economic might is alarming to him; it intimidates him. The pairing of delegates could have been Juncker with Trump and Mogherini with Pompeo, but this is a last-minute request, and no one of that stature is going to drop what they are doing to fly to Odessa on short notice. So it winds up that Jean-Christophe Belliard, former EU deputy secretary-general, goes, along with me, Special Envoy Kurt Volker, and Phil Reeker. A Romanian official, Vice Prime Minister Ana Birchall, comes with us. Romania was holding the presidency of the EU Council at the time and was also materially interested in the energy issues. We get a military jet and fly to Odessa and stand together on the USS *Donald Cook*. A lot of media is there; President Poroshenko comes. We know this visit would get some play in Moscow—they'd see us there together and think the US and the EU are conspiring to strengthen Ukraine. That is exactly what we wanted them to think—and it works. The Russians, based on our sources, are pissed that we were there. In fact, they were so pissed that I had some extra security for a while once I got back in Brussels.

3   Andrew Roth, "Kerch strait confrontation: what happened and why does it matter?" *The Guardian*, November 27, 2018, https://www.theguardian.com/world/2018/nov/27/kerch-strait-confrontation-what-happened-ukrainian-russia-crimea.

4   Ben Werner, "Destroyer USS Donald Cook Enters Black Sea for Second Time this Year," *USNI News*, February 19, 2019, https://news.usni.org/2019/02/19/uss-donald-cook-enters-black-sea.

While I am in Odessa, I meet with then-US Ambassador to Ukraine Marie Yovanovitch and discuss internal dynamics and energy issues. Historically, most Russian gas destined for European markets has had to pass through Ukraine. But in 2011, the first Nord Stream pipeline came online, connecting Russian gas directly to German markets. Since then, only 40 to 50 percent of Russian gas exports have gone through Ukraine, greatly reducing the gas transit revenues that significantly contributed to the Ukrainian economy. The second Nord Stream pipeline would further cut into Ukraine's transit revenues, another reason the United States was opposed to its activation beyond those I described in earlier chapters. So while I am in Odessa, I talk with Yovanovitch about Nord Stream 2 and how the EU and US can work to stop it.

And I do my thing with President Poroshenko: our interaction is cordial if not friendly, and we establish a rapport that leads us to be in direct contact with one another. We continue talking occasionally over the next few weeks, and it comes out that he wants what every Ukrainian president wants: an Oval Office meeting. I tell him I will look into it, knowing it was a long shot. When I inquire, the National Security Council wisely says let's wait to see the results of the upcoming Ukrainian presidential election.

The elections were held in late April of 2019, and to the pleasure of the US and the EU, Volodymyr Zelensky unseated Poroshenko. Zelensky had widespread recognition in Ukraine: he starred in a popular TV show about a schoolteacher who unexpectedly becomes president. Zelensky found himself at age forty-one the new president of Ukraine, tasked with combating corruption, negotiating a ceasefire with Russia to end a five-year conflict, and restoring faith in Ukraine's institutions.

We liked Zelensky because he was a young guy with a fresh vision of what Ukraine could become. He wasn't a career politician or bureaucrat. He also had a sense of humor and a style that made me think he could get along well with President Trump. As I described in the previous chapter, I traveled to attend his inauguration in Kyiv on May 20, 2019. Three days later, I am in DC with Secretary Perry and Volker briefing President Trump and key aides at the White House about our trip. We emphasize the strategic importance of Ukraine and our impressions of President Zelensky as a reformer who received a strong mandate from the Ukrainian people to fight corruption and pursue economic prosperity. We ask the White House to arrange a congratulatory working phone call from President Trump to Zelensky and to start talking about a White House visit.

The meeting doesn't go over well. The president is in a pissy mood, and he brushes us off, saying the Ukrainians are crooked and that we should talk to Rudy Giuliani about our request. I am disappointed but also a bit surprised—what the hell does Rudy Giuliani have to do with the US-EU relationship with Ukraine?

I am a bit deflated, but I am not deterred. Back I go to Brussels to see how I can continue to make progress. My next encounter with Zelensky is at the national day celebration I host at the embassy in Brussels on June 4. The evening is a resounding success. The headline in the *Financial Times* the next day reads, "Ukraine's president Volodymyr Zelensky reassures European backers: Former comedian distances himself from controversial oligarch and attacks Russia's ambitions."[5] This is exactly the point. We want Ukraine to take anti-corruption measures and to align itself with the EU once and for all. The article goes on to quote Zelensky saying, "Ukraine in the EU is the death of the Russian imperial project...it is a powerful blow against Russian authoritarianism." Phil Reeker sends an email saying, "This headline underscores the importance and time-

---

5   Roman Olearchyk and Michael Peel, "Ukraine's president Volodymyr Zelensky reassures European backers," *Financial Times*, June 5, 2019, https://www.ft.com/content/4c942a46-8791-11e9-a028-86cea8523dc2.

liness of Zelensky's visit to Brussels, and the critical—perhaps historic—role of the dinner and engagement Gordon coordinated."[6]

Great. It feels like we are on the right track. I am surer than ever
that Zelensky and President Trump need to meet face-to-face: I can
tell there would be a like-mindedness, a chemistry there. So what is
the problem, I wonder? I reach out to Secretary of State Pompeo to
see if he can help me make headway on arranging the meet. Soon
afterward, Perry convenes a conference call with myself, Volker,
and Bolton. I chime in when necessary, but Perry is largely the
talker. We fill Bolton in on our previous meeting with Trump
on May 23. We tell him, "John, the president hates Ukraine. But
we really like Zelensky. We think Zelensky should come to the
Oval Office, and here's what we're going to do to make that happen.
We're going to work with Giuliani in order to figure out what the
president wants. We're going to circle back and tell you about our
progress." We lay out our intentions for the next steps. Here's the
exchange that followed:

> **June 10, 17:45 Gordon Sondland:** John, Thanks
> for the support and good conversation. We all feel
> much more comfortable with the direction. Rick
> [Perry], Kurt [Volker] and I will stay on point...

> **June 11, 0:26 John Bolton:** Thanks—stay
> in touch. [7]

No "cease and desist." No "I disagree with your tactics," "let me
and the others handle Ukraine," or "you're an idiot, back off." I hear
nothing of the sort from John Bolton, Fiona Hill, or Alexander
Vindman. Apparently, they couldn't tell me this sort of thing to
my face but had no problem stating or insinuating such things to

6 Email from Phil Reeker, June 5, 2019.
7 Email from John Bolton, June 11, 2019.

the Committee on Intelligence or to the international news media in the months to come.

Back in DC on July 10, 2019, with the express and advance invitation of Bolton, I join White House meetings that include Oleksandr Danylyuk, secretary of Ukraine's National Security and Defense Council, and US NSC officials, including Bolton, Secretary Perry, and Volker. There is a follow up phone call the next day, and it emerges that there is a difference of opinion between Secretary Perry, Volker, and myself on the one hand and the NSC on the other: we three favor promptly scheduling a call and meeting between Presidents Trump and Zelensky; the NSC does not. Bolton thinks the call should wait until after Ukraine's parliamentary elections on July 21, and others of us disagree. But still, everyone is speaking and coordinating. Fiona Hill later inaccurately testified that this was a pivotal meeting that resulted in me offering the Ukrainians a meeting with President Trump in exchange for some investigation. She also later went on to say that I didn't respect her because she's a woman. It had nothing to do with her gender. I didn't respect her because she's a whiner. She's a highly intelligent person and could be an excellent subject-matter resource, but she is not a decision maker. She was not, nor she should be, a manager running a department. Her answer to any suggestion was always "No. We can't do that." She always had a reason. I don't think she could negotiate her way out of a paper bag.

All of that aside, the meeting was a positive step toward accomplishing our shared goals. Then came the infamous call on July 25, 2019 between Zelensky and Trump, which later triggered the whistleblower complaint that led to efforts to impeach Trump. I was not on the call. I never saw a readout of the call until it became public a few months later. I was actually in Ukraine on a trip arranged by Volker at the time it took place. The meetings I attended in Ukraine had been set up well before the call was planned and were not connected with Trump's discussion with Zelensky. The only thing I saw about the phone call between the two of them was the summary, which was a very short paragraph that said the president of the United States and the president of Ukraine had a cordial call. It sounded completely anodyne, and I was just glad that it happened, as it seemed to me to be a step forward in the two of them solidifying their relationship. Again, no one said a word to Perry, to me, to Volker, or to the ambassador in Ukraine about this supposedly disastrous call, where President Trump apparently asked Zelensky to dig up dirt on the Biden family as "a favor," while threatening that the US wouldn't play nice with Ukraine if Zelensky didn't do as he asked.

In the meantime, while I was in Ukraine, I had my own perhaps more colorful phone call on July 26 that will also live on in infamy, if not quite in history. Mine had a lot more comedic potential though, as *Saturday Night Live* was quick to point out, because it involved a soliloquy on a rap star and mention of Trump's ass.

I want to make it clear: it's the height of disingenuousness to claim that on one hand, what was said on the phone call between Zelensky and Trump was beyond despicable and had awful implications and then on the other hand, to have an entire team of officials—including a cabinet secretary and a special envoy involved—not say a word to me or anyone else directly about how awful it was. No note, no follow-up. In the meantime, people are allegedly running around the White House, lawyers for the president are worried, and there's chaos unfolding behind the scenes—but no one bothers to tell me, Kurt Volker, or Rick Perry, a member of the president's cabinet, who is taking the lead on this issue?

If someone thought there was any collusion going on, we should have been fired immediately. If there was a shadow of a doubt that we were complicit in something illegal, someone—Bolton, Hill, Vindman, whoever—should have stepped in and said so. That's why in the end, I truly believe the whole Ukraine issue was a red herring. This was nothing more than a hatchet job, an attempt to entrap various people one by one in a chain that led up to the president. To generate enough press froth and fervor to whip the country into a state where they could push through an impeachment of President Trump.

My goal was to keep the focus on strengthening Ukraine's relationship with the United States and the EU, and so I had little interest in dealing with Giuliani, who seemed totally tangential to the issues that mattered to me. In fact, as Foreign Service Officer David Holmes later said in his testimony, "Someone wondered aloud about why Mr. Giuliani was so active in the media with respect to Ukraine. My recollection is that Ambassador Sondland stated, 'Dammit Rudy. Every time Rudy gets involved, he goes and f——s everything up.'"[8]

I can't say I recall those exact words coming out of my mouth, though it sure does sound like me. All I knew was that the president refused to discuss Zelensky and Ukraine with me, and so I did as Trump requested, and I called Giuliani to see if I could figure out what was going on. I had my first phone conversation with Giuliani in early August of 2019. The two of us don't know each other before this call; I'd only interacted with Giuliani once briefly, several years before becoming ambassador. In our conversation, Giuliani does mention the name Burisma, but to me the company is just one of many examples of Ukrainian companies run by oligarchs. I thought the reference to Burisma was made in light of anti-corruption efforts we were seeking to support. And by the way, this phone call, my first contact with him as an administration official, happened months after the supposed drug deal we were cooking up together.

---

8   "Holmes recalls Sondland saying "Rudy f---s everything up,"" *CNN*, November 21, 2019, https://www.cnn.com/politics/live-news/impeachment-hearing-11-21-19/h_22189ff1e2 67fdf4a38ef93bec7ac8f6.

August meanders on, and I hear rumors that Trump is planning to withhold aid that has been promised to Ukraine. I don't know much about what we had promised to Ukraine; that is Ambassador Bill Taylor's purview. Once the rumors bear fruit, Taylor asks for my help in elevating the issue. I try to make it clear to him: you're the ambassador to Ukraine, not me. This has nothing to do with the EU; they aren't the ones holding up Ukraine's aid. If you'll recall, the media narrative later said that I kept inserting myself and meddling in the Ukrainian issues. But in fact, I was asked repeatedly to get involved, this time because I had access that Taylor didn't have, and he wanted my help. I do ask around in the State Department, contacting Phil Reeker as well as Pompeo's assistant and right-hand Lisa Kenna, what the deal is with withholding the aid, but no one is clear or wants to say.

In the end, given the many versions of speculation that have been circulating about the security aid, I call President Trump. I ask directly, "What do you want from Ukraine?" The president responds, "Nothing. There is no quid pro quo." He repeats "no quid pro quo" multiple times. It is a very short call. President Trump is in a bad mood. I don't press further.

In truth, though I was annoyed that the aid was being withheld, it was because it was disrupting what should have been a simple transaction I was trying to conduct. Having met Zelensky and knowing Trump, I thought if they got together at the White House, not just for the photo op but sitting one-on-one together in the Oval Office, they would really like each other. And once Trump likes someone, things happen. Everything I wanted to accomplish between the EU and Ukraine would have been doable. The ball would start rolling. I could feel it. So my goal was very singular. I just wanted to get Zelensky a date to meet the president in Washington, and that was it.

In the meantime, I had a lot of other things going on. The NYC dinner with Ivanka Trump, Jared Kushner, Charles Michel, and Josep Borrell took place on September 23. On September 25, I was at the United Nations General Assembly (UNGA) in New York. The US presence at the UNGA summit was sparse. President Trump's speech at the UNGA summit didn't have anything to do with Ukraine; instead, he restated his administration's policies on Iran, North Korea, China, mass migration, and the deteriorating situation in Venezuela.[9]

Venezuela has been in a state of political and economic disarray since 2013. When Hugo Chávez died in 2013, he was succeeded by his right-hand man, Nicolás Maduro. Under Maduro's watch, the economy of Venezuela has completely collapsed due to widespread corruption and the drop in global oil prices, prompting nearly five million people to leave the country. After the 2018 elections, opposition leader Juan Guaidó declared himself interim president in January 2019. Although more than fifty countries, including the United States, recognize Guaidó as the legitimate leader of Venezuela, the military remains loyal to Maduro, effectively creating dueling governments.

President Trump and Zelensky do finally meet briefly face-to-face on the sidelines that day. I breathe a sigh of relief when I see the two of them begin to banter with each other—just as I hoped and expected. Zelensky even cracks a joke about the White House meeting that has been the subject of so much speculation and fervor. He says, "You invited me. But I think—I'm sorry, but I think you forgot to tell me the date."

That night, I'm at an official dinner with Pompeo and others at the Palace Hotel. I get a text from a White House lawyer asking

---

9   Donald Trump, "Remarks by President Trump to the 74th Session of the United Nations General Assembly," White House, September 25, 2019, https://trumpwhitehouse.archives.gov/briefings-statements/remarks-president-trump-74th-session-united-nations-general-assembly/.

me to call immediately, so I step out into the foyer. That's when I first learn about the whistleblower report: In a letter dated August 12, 2019, an unnamed intelligence official described what he had learned about the July 25 phone call between Zelensky and Trump. The report intimated that the president of the United States was trying to solicit foreign interference in the upcoming 2020 presidential election.

The report was pretty thorough in describing recent high-level engagement by United States officials on Ukrainian issues, so it's no wonder my name appeared—four times to be exact, but none of these mentions were negative or accusatory. To me, the whistleblower's main concerns were Rudy Giuliani's involvement in US-Ukraine relations and Trump's allegedly inappropriate requests in the July 25 phone call to Zelensky.

The next day, I meet with Secretary Pompeo in New York in his SCIF, where we call Ambassador Volker to discuss the whistleblower complaint. We all agree that nothing improper occurred and that the complaint is completely off base. Even so, it doesn't look good.

To me, there could be no greater validation in my growing belief in the presence of the Deep State. When I say "Deep State," I'm not talking about a highly organized shadow government or anything so well defined. Instead, I think of the Deep State as a group of highly partisan, left-wing career bureaucrats who believe they have divine right to determine US policy, no matter who is sitting in the White House. They have a lot of tactics they use to "slow roll" anything from the president of the USA that they don't like. When there's a president in office who bureaucrats, who are very progressive, are against, they deploy every tactic they have to intervene. One favorite move is to accuse effective people of doing illegal things, when in fact the aggrieved bureaucrat is just miffed to be left out of the process—incidentally, revealing that they are unneeded, like the emperor with no clothes. The Deep State members like to set people up, lodge complaints, and take down those who don't share their liberal, progressive agenda, and they have a huge discomfort with any type of diplomacy that's a departure from the norm. I disrupted the "business as usual" approach more than most do in the State Department, and a lot of the career people were appalled by me calling leaders on their cell phones, referring to officials (to their face) by their first name, and making personal connections with people who helped achieve policy aims. The gall! What they failed to note was how often it worked in moving the ball forward.

As I mentioned, the first I heard of the whistleblower report was on September 25, the day before it was publicly released. But the House had been notified by the inspector general of the report's existence and had launched an inquiry into Rudy Giuliani on September 9.[10] On September 19, 2019, the still-unreleased whistleblower complaint was linked to Ukraine and to a specific ask of President Zelensky, according to an exclusive by the *Washington Post*.[11] Nancy Pelosi then announced a formal impeachment investigation into the president on September 24, 2019, stating that Trump's communications with Ukraine presented a "breach of his Constitutional responsibilities."[12] From that moment on, there was no escaping the train wreck that was the Trump impeachment trial.

10   Elizabeth Janowski, "Timeline: Trump impeachment inquiry," *NBC News*, October 16, 2019, https://www.nbcnews.com/politics/trump-impeachment-inquiry/timeline-trump-impeachment-inquiry-n1066691.

11   Ellen Nakashima, Shane Harris, Greg Miller and Carol D. Leonnig, "Whistleblower complaint about President Trump involves Ukraine, according to two people familiar with the matter," *The Washington Post*, September 19, 2019, https://www.washingtonpost.com/national-security/whistleblower-complaint-about-president-trump-involves-ukraine-according-to-two-people-familiar-with-the-matter/2019/09/19/07e33f0a-daf6-11e9-bfb1-849887369476_story.html.

12   Heidi Przybyla and Adam Edelman, "Nancy Pelosi announces formal impeachment inquiry of Trump," *NBC News*, September 24, 2019, https://www.nbcnews.com/politics/trump-impeachment-inquiry/pelosi-announce-formal-impeachment-inquiry-trump-n1058251.

The White House argued that this was an illegitimate investigation and an overreach by House Democrats. From the White House's perspective, in order for the inquiry to be valid, the House needed to (1) hold a full vote to formally begin impeachment proceedings, (2) allow Republicans to issue subpoenas, and (3) grant the White House the ability to cross-examine witnesses and have access to evidence. So, yes. The Democrats kinda skipped several steps.

I don't want to, but I begin preparing to testify. Many of the people around me are receiving summons, and I know it is just a matter of time. Then I am told neither the State Department nor the US Department of Justice will represent me. I have to find my own lawyer. I know I need not a good one but an outstanding one—and I also know who to call for advice. I first met Karl Rove during the early years of George W. Bush's administration. (Bush affectionately referred to Rove as "Turd Blossom." I am also privileged to have a disparaging Bush nickname: "Gordo.") Karl is one of the kindest and smartest people that I have ever had the privilege to know. He helped my Democratic friend Governor Kulongoski develop his relationship with the Bush administration; he also created a multitude of opportunities and introductions for me. Because Karl is a born, selfless connector, I greatly value his opinion on the best lawyer in town when I am summoned for my appearance before the House Intelligence Committee. Without hesitation, the only person he recommends is Bob Luskin.

Luskin is one of the best known and most highly regarded litigators in Washington, DC and has represented clients in virtually every high-profile matter in DC over the last three decades. He has represented a cabinet officer and senior White House officials of both parties in criminal investigations by independent counsels and the Department of Justice, and I knew he would have great credibility with Democrats. Luskin's extraordinary skills and abilities were on ample display later during the trial, not just as my counsel but as someone who clearly knew how to maneuver in dealings with the committee.

I know things are heating up significantly when Volker resigns in late September, and then he spends more than eight hours testifying on Thursday, October 3. Subpoenas have also been issued to Pompeo, Giuliani, and many others. Sure enough, I receive a request to testify voluntarily before the House Intelligence Committee, the House Committee on Oversight and Reform, and the House Committee on Foreign Affairs (collectively referred to as "the House"). They tell me the session will be a closed-door deposition scheduled for October 8, 2019.

I put a halt to everything I am working on at post and fly from DC to Brussels. Back home in Portland, people were getting riled up about my appearance; small groups picketed outside some of our hotels with signs like, "Sondland Tell the Truth," as if I planned to do something otherwise. Then Oregon Congressman Earl Blumenauer said that people should boycott all Provenance properties, which was not only jerk move but also an illegal thing to do. There is a prohibition against members of Congress seeking reprisal against a presidential administration official, and clearly his making such a statement would do economic harm to my business and me. My friend and lawyer Jim McDermott shot back with a press release pointing to such: "Congressman Blumenauer would do well to learn and understand the laws that Congress has passed before he makes reckless and destructive threats that would only economically injure hardworking Oregon employees." [13]

A little after midnight on the morning I'm supposed to testify, Bob Luskin gets a voicemail from a State Department official instructing me not to appear for the deposition. Bob Luskin issues a

---

13   Jeff Manning, "Earl Blumenauer calls for boycott of Gordon Sondland hotels," *The Oregonian*, October 10, 2019, https://www.oregonlive.com/politics/2019/10/blumenauer-calls-for-sondland-hotel-boycott.html.

statement: "As the sitting US ambassador to the EU and employee of the State Department, Ambassador Sondland is required to follow the Department's direction. Ambassador Sondland is profoundly disappointed that he will not be able to testify today. Ambassador Sondland traveled to Washington from Brussels in order to prepare for his testimony and to be available to answer the committee's questions."[14] Disappointed, perhaps. Relieved, certainly.

Later that day, the White House refuses to turn over internal documents on Ukraine. The President tweets, "I would love to send Ambassador Sondland, a really good man and great American, to testify, but unfortunately he would be testifying before a totally compromised kangaroo court, where Republican's rights have been taken away, and true facts are not allowed out for the public to see."[15]

My reprieve is only hours long. A subpoena is issued for me the next day. The letter accompanying the subpoena calls for me to appear in person for a deposition on October 16 and turn over relevant documents by October 14. The letter, signed by the three chairmen—Adam Schiff, chairman of the House Permanent Select Committee on Intelligence; Elijah Cummings, chairman of the House Committee on Oversight and Reform; and Eliot Engel, chairman of the House Committee on Foreign Affairs—warns that failure to comply with the subpoena, "including at the direction or behest of the president, the White House or State Department," will "constitute further evidence of obstruction of the House's impeach-

---

14   Kyle Cheney, "Democrats subpoena Gordon Sondland after Trump inter-
      venes," *Politico*, October 8, 2019, https://www.politico.com/news/2019/10/08/
      trumps-eu-ambassador-ordered-to-not-give-deposition-in-impeachment-probe-000278.

15   Donald Trump (@realDonaldTrump), "I would love to send Ambassador Sondland, a really
      good man and great American, to testify, but unfortunately he would be testifying before
      a totally compromised kangaroo court, where Republican's rights have been taken away,
      and true facts are not allowed out for the public to see. Importantly, Ambassador Sondland's
      tweet, which few report, stated, 'I believe you are incorporating President Trump's intentions.
      The President has been crystal clear: no quid pro quo's of any kind.' That says it all!" Twitter,
      October 8, 2019, https://twitter.com/realDonaldTrump/status/1181560708808486914.

ment inquiry and may be used as an adverse inference against you and the president."[16]

Shit is getting real.

The foregone conclusion is that what the whistleblower said is true. I am cast as unethical, treasonous, and nefarious, and all before I can utter a word in court. My testimony is going to be my first and perhaps my only chance to clear my name, right the record, and move on with my job and my life. I hope. Once again, I need to get prepared.

I also have to keep doing my job. I'd been working on a few of the things on in the meantime: on September 30, 2019, the US mission to the EU hosted its annual Rentrée event, a celebration of the transatlantic relationship, friends, and colleagues of the US mission of the EU in Brussels. At the beginning of October 2019, the State Department announced Poland was being approved for the Visa Waiver Program, allowing visa-free travel for Polish citizens for up to ninety days. A highly sought-after program for countries, it is a legitimizing act and is only granted after years of controlled and consistent adherence to US visa rules. On October 9, the European Commission published a major report on the risk assessment of 5G networks, with which my staff and I had been consistently involved. The situation in Venezuela was heating up, and I met with some South American officials to discuss how the US and EU could help. As with Ukraine, Venezuela is obviously not in the US ambassador to the EU's portfolio. But in today's increasingly complex and globalized world, these matters tend to spill over into other people's backyards. Guaidó was pushing EU countries to support him in Brussels, which involves me as the

16   Rebecca Shabad, "House Democrats subpoena E.U. ambassador after State Department blocks testimony," *NBC News*, October 8, 2019, https://www. nbcnews.com/politics/congress/house-democrats-subpoenas-eu-am-bassador-after-state-department-blocks-testimony-n1064026.

chief US diplomat in the city. So with all this going on, it's not as if I am sitting around, biding my time while waiting to testify.

Even so, the specter of what I have to face in DC on October 17 is certainly hanging over me. Again, I fly back to Washington. Again, Kwame Manley and Bob Luskin prep me for testimony. They do a terrific job. In the span of three weeks, they cram in what would normally be about six months of work on a case, and without a bunch of the documentation or records that they would normally have at their disposal.

One of Kwame's main points to me was to know when to STFU. He had this little hand motion like someone tying a bow, which he would use when I started to say too much. As soon as I saw him start to do it, I knew what it meant: shut your mouth. As he calmly reminded me, the most common mistake in a crisis is to leap into a sprint before knowing where you are going. Crisis brings out panic, and panic causes mistakes. It's the typical fight-or-flight response: you sense danger and immediately start running wildly toward anything that looks like a door. And what looks like a door when you're running like a frantic animal might actually be a hole. There's no better way to get deeper into the hole than continuing to speak when you don't need to.

Since my previously planned testimony on the 8th, a few things had changed or emerged: Former US Ambassador to Ukraine Marie Yovanovitch had testified on October 11, detailing what she saw as a smear campaign to ruin her reputation and remove her from office at Trump's behest. Fiona Hill had testified on October 14, giving a totally skewed and largely inaccurate perspective on my involvement in Ukrainian issues. The White House continued to refuse to cooperate with the impeachment inquiry. Multiple subpoenas had been sent but ignored, including to Energy Secretary Rick Perry, Pence, Giuliani, Defense Secretary Mark Esper, and two businessmen who used to work with Giuliani—Igor Fruman and Lev Parnas. But my counsel told me I had no choice but to appear. I had no agenda to undermine the Trump administration or to opine on the actions taken by the president or others. I did not want to be involved in the impeachment proceeding at all. This is in contrast to numerous other career officials who, in my opinion, testified with an agenda designed to undermine the Trump administration, Secretary Pompeo's management of the Department of State, and my own involvement as ambassador.

So off I go to the Hill on the morning of October 17. It is a bit surreal: all of the reporters chasing me down the hall, the cameras snapping, and people yelling their questions at me. Like getting made in the mob, some people joke that you've only made it in DC once you've gone through your first media firestorm. While the humor masks fear and anger, the quip isn't far off. Involvement in an incident worthy of a high volume of media attention suggests you're a matter of some significance. But that is a small consolation in the middle of a crisis, when your actions or behavior become the subject of scrutiny and devastating criticism, and where the stakes are incredibly high, professionally and personally. The Trump impeachment trial was pretty much all the media could talk about for several months straight, and they made it into a total three-ring circus, where I was portrayed as one of their favorite clowns. This was not a fact-finding exercise, undertaken in order to reveal the truth at all costs, no matter whom it favored. This was a takedown mission on the president.

I do my best to shut it all out when I go to enter the room where I spend almost ten hours testifying in front of the House Intelligence Committee. As a *NYT* source correctly reported, I do not try to shield my conversations with President Trump from the investigators. I answer questions from both Democrats and Republicans as truthfully as I can—though without the benefit of documents that I could have used to prepare my testimony (which the State Department refused to allow me access). A fulsome recollection of every in and out and every conversation that had to do with Ukraine is difficult, to say the least.

Much of what I said in my testimony has already been described here, and the rest of it is in the public record if you're so inclined to go read all 379 pages. So here's the briefest summary: In my statement and in response to questioning, I reiterated that Ukraine was part of my portfolio and that I received the blessing of Secretary Pompeo to work on Ukraine policy from my vantage point in Brussels. I outlined a clear chronology of my work relating to Ukraine. I then covered key points that I knew were of interest to the committee, mentioning the following:

1. A public embrace of anti-corruption reforms was a precondition for securing a White House meeting with Zelensky. Nothing about this raised red flags, and it seemed to me solid and standard US policy to make such a request.

2. I made it clear that I had very limited interaction with Rudy Giuliani and had spoken with him seldomly and briefly.

3. Based on my recollection, in our conversations, Giuliani did not mention the Bidens but did raise Burisma—this did not strike me as unusual since Burisma is an example of one of many Ukrainian companies run by oligarchs and prone to corruption.

4. I regularly kept the National Security Council and State Department apprised of my activities on Ukraine and received no warnings or condemnations of any kind.

5. I clarified that some of my texts had been misinterpreted—when I ask people to call me, it's not because I

want to hide any record of our conversation but simply because I prefer to talk rather than to text.

6. I was not initially aware of any discussions about withholding US security assistance from Ukraine in return for assistance with the 2020 reelection campaign.

I come out of it alive, still standing. The media reaction overall is positive, if somewhat skeptical. I want to get back to Brussels, to get back to work, but I know this isn't over yet. On October 22, Ambassador Bill Taylor testified, and then on October 31, it was NSA adviser Tim Morrison's turn. In reading their statements, I recall some important details I know I need to add to my own testimony. It's not that I am purposefully trying to shield information from the committee. It's like when someone says, "Do you remember when we ate dinner at that Italian place, and I was sitting under that fiscus tree, and you splattered spaghetti sauce on your blue shirt?" And all of a sudden, you start to piece together additional details about the evening and your dialogue with this person that you would have otherwise forgotten—that's the sensation that arose in reading what they and the others had to say in court. I realize that, in a few instances, the way I had phrased things in my testimony could have been construed as a false statement—when I heard someone testify about where we were together and what we said and so on in detail, I recalled with more accuracy what had happened. And I want to correct my testimony to be accurate and complete. I make the amendment in writing, which is totally permitted under committee rules (within a certain period of time, if you have additional things to add, you can make an affidavit and file it). So I amend my testimony, adding details that I recalled about when, where, and how I had learned about Giuliani's involvement and about the resumption of aid to Ukraine being predicated on Zelensky's statement into the resumption of investigations into Burisma and anti-corruption measures. Of course, after Bill Taylor's testimony doesn't immediately line up word for word with mine, the media immediately starts crying out that I am lying, covering something up, colluding with the president's henchmen to protect him, and on and on.

My only goal in any of this mess was to secure the meeting between Trump and Zelensky. Because I said I would. Because I thought it would help advance the US-EU agenda. Because it would aid Ukraine's pursuit of energy security and political independence. That's it. For the record, once and for all, Trump didn't send me to Ukraine, I wasn't there to investigate Biden or his son, and I had nothing to do with Giuliani and his reported activities. Ukraine didn't need to be a big or important part of my portfolio; I had twenty-eight other countries, those that were actually in the EU, to worry about. Ukraine should have been a drop in the bucket in terms of the volume of work I did related to it or the attention I paid it versus other countries in my purview. Unfortunately that trickle turned into a tsunami.

CHAPTER EIGHT

FRONT ROW
AT THE TRUMP
IMPEACHMENT SHOW

I hope that if you've read this far, you have a good sense of who I really am. But I'm assuming that when you started reading, the only reason you likely had heard of the words "Gordon David Sondland" was because you had associated me with three other words: "quid pro quo."

Those three words explain how a son of immigrants, a hotelier from Washington, ended up with my name in the headlines across the globe for a few days in November 2019. It wasn't about me; it was that the fate of the American presidency that hung in the balance. So what is it about this innocuous phrase that transformed my life forever, that caused so much commotion that many thought a president would be impeached over it?

Quid pro quos aren't nefarious by nature. The meaning in Latin, "something for something" or "this for that," referred to an equal and voluntary exchange between two parties. Relationships are based on exchanges, and exchanges, in turn, rely on confidence. I have to trust you to deal honestly with me when we engage in a trade. In rare instances, you can appeal to a sense of magnanimity and ask me to give you something for nothing. But it doesn't often work that way in the real world—and sometimes people are offended by the idea of a handout. And of course, who loves a transaction better than Donald Trump?

In that infamous July 25, 2019 phone call between Trump and Zelensky (the one that the president called "perfect" and millions of others called "impeachable"), Trump set out a quid pro quo for the Ukrainian president: "I'd like you to do us a favor...." He continued,

> I would like you to find out what happened with this whole situation with Ukraine, they say CrowdStrike...I guess you have one of your wealthy people...The server, they say Ukraine has it. There are a lot of things that went on, the whole situation. I think you're surrounding yourself with some of the same people. I would like to have the Attorney General call you or your people and I would like you to get to the bottom of it.... Whatever you can do, it's very important that you do it if that's possible.[1]

Since Zelensky was a comedian in his former career, he'd likely appreciate what Jerry Seinfeld said about favors:

> There's two types of favors, the big favor and the small favor. You can measure the size of the favor by the pause that a person takes after they ask you to "do me a favor." Small favor, small pause. "Can you do me a favor, hand me that pencil?" No pause at all. Big favors are, "Could you do me a favor..." The longer it takes them to get to it, the bigger the pain

---

1   "Full Document: Trump's Call with the Ukrainian President," *The New York Times,* October 30, 2019, https://www.nytimes.com/interactive/2019/09/25/us/politics/trump-ukraine-transcript.html.

it's going to be. Humans are the only species that do favors. Animals don't do favors. A lizard doesn't go up to a cockroach and say, "Could you please do me a favor and hold still, I'd like to eat you alive." [2]

Zelensky was sure to know that whatever followed this phrase, big pause or small pause, it was in his best interest to do it or see it done. At least he was being asked rather than eaten.

This is what Trump was getting at, as *Politico* explained[3]: The president wanted Ukraine to investigate the cybersecurity firm—CrowdStrike—that determined the Democratic National Committee had been hacked by Russia. Trump told the Associated Press in 2017 that he thought CrowdStrike was "Ukraine-based" and "owned by a very rich Ukrainian." The firm was actually founded by a Russian American and is based California. Trump went on later in the conversation to mention how little he thought of Ambassador Yovanovich, and he brought up Hunter Biden and the fact that he wanted to restart the investigation into him that Yovanovitch had supposedly helped to halt. So there was a lot packed into Trump's "do us a favor."

But back to quid pro quo for a moment: gradually the phrase came to mean "this *instead* of that," which could end up being a pretty bad trade. In the 1500s, when people went to the apothecary and ended up with a substitution—that type of quid pro quo could kill you. Nowadays, the phrase is shorthand for when someone in a position of power strong-arms the weaker party into an unfair exchange. It has connotations of being hustled or cheated, fleeced or betrayed. (So in a way, this entire book is a quid pro quo. You give me your time and your $27.95, and I'll tell you a story....)

2 "Semantics," http://site.iugaza.edu.ps/mtarabin/files/2019/09/
   Semantics-Pragmatics-Discourse.pdf.
3 Kevin Collier and Donie O'Sullivan, "What is CrowdStrike and why is it part
   of the Trump whistleblower complaint?" *CNN Business*, September 26, 2019,
   https://www.cnn.com/2019/09/26/tech/what-is-crowdstrike/index.html.

And yes, quid pro quos happen all the time. They aren't bad; they're just the way things get done in business, in politics, and sometimes in personal interactions. Just look at the studies that show when married men pitch in and clean the bathroom, they have more sex.[4] If that's not a "this for that," I don't know what is.

After my private testimony on October 17, I flew to Brussels to get back to business. It was a relief to burrow back into my work, even though I knew I was far from off the hook. There was a lot of activity on 5G, set off in earnest by a new EU report on 5G vulnerabilities. Based on the findings, we had even more reason to push hard on European allies to remove Huawei-designed equipment from their infrastructure.[5] In late October, I hosted an EU-US high-level forum on small modular reactors (SMRs) at the European Commission. As I mentioned earlier, many countries in Europe have a strong cultural bias against nuclear energy, but SMRs are a breakthrough: the technology is a way to harness the promise of nuclear energy as an alternative to large gigawatt reactors—a scalable source of power generation with far less risk and environmental impact. The conference was a success; Rick Perry came. It has now turned into an annual event and SMR development has progressed tremendously in the past few years. Soon I believe the technology will be a gamechanger in meeting the needs of the transatlantic economy. Another thing that happened around that time: On November 5, Secretary Pompeo formally provided the required one-year notice that the US was withdrawing from the Paris Climate Agreement, which caused quite a kerfuffle in the EU.[6] Trump had made it known we would eventually leave the

---

4   Susan Kelley, "Want more sex? Split the household chores," *Cornell Chronicle*, August 2, 2016, https://news.cornell.edu/stories/2016/08/want-more-sex-split-household-chores.

5   "The 5G Future: Incredible Promise, Significant Risk," Department of State, accessed May 24, 2022, https://cl.usembassy.gov/5g-technology-incredible-promise-significant-risk/.

6   Michael R. Pompeo, "On the U.S. Withdrawal from the Paris Agreement," U.S. Department of State, Press Statement, November 4, 2019, https://2017-2021. state.gov/on-the-u-s-withdrawal-from-the-paris-agreement/index.html.

agreement, but I had to do damage control with people about the issue as best as I could. So in other words, I was plenty busy.

In the meantime, the impeachment trial lurched on, the testimonies kept coming, and my name kept popping up. The White House was sticking to their story that there was no quid pro quo. In former Ambassador to Ukraine Marie Yovanovitch's testimony, she claimed President Trump had personally pressured the State Department to remove her, based "on unfounded and false claims by people with clearly questionable motives."[7] Fiona Hill claimed Giuliani and I circumvented her and the National Security Council to run a shadow foreign policy on Ukraine. This shadow foreign policy was a national security threat, according to Hill. Vindman testified that he had repeatedly raised allegations of the mishandling of Ukraine policy to his superiors; he also said that he had confronted me directly about my support of the supposed quid pro quo—this alleged screaming match between us never happened. I would remember, and so would many others, if Lt. Col. Vindman and I, an appointed ambassador, had gotten into a loud and heated discussion. It just never happened.

Another troubling and ridiculously absurd (but more accurate) recollection came from David Holmes, a career foreign service officer in Kyiv. When I was there on July 26, after the bilateral meetings that had been planned long in advance, I had lunch with Holmes and a couple other State Department staffers. Holmes testified that I had placed a call to Trump at the table. In the course of that phone call I apparently told the president that Zelensky "loves your ass." "Yes," I later said under oath. "Sounds like something I would say." On the call, the president and I also talked about Rakim

7 John Hudson, Karoun Demirjian, Rachael Bade and Paul Sonne, "Ousted ambassador Marie Yovanovitch tells Congress Trump pressured State Dept. to remove her," *The Washington Post*, October 11, 2019, https://www.washingtonpost.com/national-security/ousted-ukraine-envoy-marie-yovanovitch-expected-to-testify-in-impeachment-inquiry-today/2019/10/11/d571830e-eba0-11e9-85c0-85a098e47b37_story.html.

Mayers, better known as A$AP Rocky. Mayers was arrested in Stockholm and held for five weeks before being convicted of assault on August 14.

The press went crazy when the A$AP Rocky phone call came up. Here's why: Trump obviously had personal involvement in this high-profile, international criminal case. Trump had pressured Sweden's prime minister to release A$AP Rocky on bail (despite the fact that Sweden has no bail system) after the rapper was detained in July after a street brawl. Trump was very vocal in his support for the rapper, repeatedly calling for his freedom and even lashing out at Sweden's prime minister on Twitter after the rapper was charged. Also, that phone call's importance was blown out of proportion; apparently Daniel Goldman, majority director of investigation in the House of Representatives, implied it was a sign of my being a supposed national security risk. Later he asked why this conversation was held on an unsecure line—I replied that this type of call happened all the time. The president knew it was an open line. We weren't discussing anything classified. Others thought the conversation represented a smoking gun because I mentioned that I believed Zelensky would indeed do as Trump asked and announce that he was restarting investigations into Burisma.

As the news kept coming, October turned to November and soon enough, the moment I was dreading arrived. I was going to have to provide a public testimony in front of the House Intelligence Committee. Formally, the US House of Representative Permanent Select Committee on Intelligence is chaired by California Congressman Adam Schiff. With the Democrats in control of the House, he would be running the show when I testified and joined by twelve other Democrats. Devin Nunes was the ranking member of the minority, the Republicans, and there were eight other Republicans with him on the committee. Nancy Pelosi and

Kevin McCarthy would also be there as ex officio members of the committee. This was not going to be fun.

I fly back to Washington. I've already been prepping with attorneys Bob Luskin and Kwame Manley. Bob and Kwame and the larger team at Paul Hastings come through for me big time. The other person completely in my corner, and upon whom I rely a great deal, is my friend and counsel Jim McDermott, who I've known for twenty years. While talking to Jim later, once the whole episode was over, I realized exactly the magnitude of what he'd done for me. On my case alone, he put in over 300 billable hours of work in one month. All he did was eat, work, and run. And I don't doubt that my case preoccupied him in many of those hours too.

When I arrive in Washington, my murder board puts me through my paces. These guys ask me all the tough questions that I need to anticipate. They tell me the committee is not out to find facts impartially. No way are they prepared to announce—if the evidence reveals this conclusion to be true—"yes, this all looked really bad for the president, but in the end, we didn't find anything of substance." There is no way Adam Schiff, chairman of the Intelligence Committee and attack dog, would let that happen.

But in my opinion, Schiff made one fundamental mistake: he made the whole trial a blatant referendum on Trump. He built the house first and then drew the plans. The foregone conclusion was that Trump should be impeached; the only question was what to use to support that. What were the means to achieve the end? It's as if the committee had been clawing and clawing at Trump, looking for something to grab to use against him and impeach him, and finally snagged on something. What they got their hands on was this small scrap of a situation in Ukraine, which now they were going to use to tear into the president with all their might.

Bob Luskin advises me to remember the Hippocratic Oath during questioning: do no harm. The implication was to answer the question you are being asked with the truth as you remember it, without pandering to either side. That's it and that's all. If you have any doubt about what you recall, that's all you need to say: "I don't recall." If I had hired a hard-hitting Republican lawyer, that kind of "keeping to the middle lane" wouldn't have been possible. Everything I said would immediately be seen as biased and intended to obfuscate. Luskin has the street cred with the committee to be seen more as an impartial advisor, one who would not necessarily do anything to help make the case for impeachment but would also not help a Trump sycophant lie to protect the president. After all, I am just a third-party witness. I didn't do or say anything that implicated me in anything criminal. With that in mind, I constantly go back to the fact that my first goal is tell the truth, keep to what you know you know, and don't perjure yourself.

I heard that it was said, "If you want us [the committee] to go easy on him, he needs to say loud and clear that the president had a quid pro quo with Zelensky," the quid pro quo being "give me dirt on Hunter Biden, Burisma, and on the server connected to Hillary Clinton's 2016 campaign, and I'll give you a White House visit (and release your military aid)." The thing is Trump never said any of this, certainly not to me directly. He never said those words. But he did imply a lot of it in various forms and in various conversations. When the Ukrainians began asking, "Why is our aid tied up? Is it related to the investigations?" I said, "I have no idea. You'll have to ask around for yourself." So, how were we going to best convey this complexity to the House Intelligence Committee? Trying to figure that out kept me up at night and kept my lawyers very busy.

There are hundreds of hours of testimony you could go back and watch, hundreds of thousands of printed book pages, and millions of websites you could visit to learn almost anything you want to know about the proceedings. So what I want to share is not so much what I said in my testimony, which is part of the public record, but more about the behind the scenes leading up to and on November 20, the day I gave my public testimony, and what happened next.

Around 4 a.m. on November 20, 2019, I awake feeling groggy. I haven't slept so much as tossed around in the bed for a few hours. The swirl of thoughts in my head are picking up speed and force, and I can't let them. I am going to have to navigate myself through this day no matter the windspeed. So I get up, take a shower, and get dressed in the still-darkness. I pick out a dark blue suit—nothing flashy, but I also don't want to look like an undertaker. A benign tie, quiet shoes—of course, it isn't enough. It can never be just right. The press decide to go wild over...my watch. *GQ* writes a piece saying "lifelong civil servants wear a certain kind of watch, one that effectively symbolizes their substance-over-flash approach to governing, or that puts their love for America on their sleeve... when Sondland appeared in front of Congress flaunting a watch commensurate with his fortune, it was not unlike appearing in a jersey announcing what team he played for. And until at least a few weeks ago, we *definitely* knew which side he was on. In early October, Trump called Sondland a 'really good man' and 'great American'..."[8]

But it is just a watch. I am not on one side or the other, and this isn't a game. Or is it? I think of a book I'd just read by Simon Sinek, *The Infinite Game*.

> Finite games are played by known players. They have fixed rules. And there is an agreed-upon objective that, when reached, ends the game...

8   Cam Wolf, "Impeachment Watch: On Gordon Sondland's $55,000 Impeachment Watch," *GQ*, November 21, 2019, https://www.gq.com/story/impeachment-watch-gordon-sondland.

Everyone agrees that whichever team has scored more points by the end of the set time period will be declared the winner, the game will end and everyone will go home....

Infinite games, in contrast, are played by known and unknown players. There are no exact or agreed-upon rules. Though there may be conventions or laws that govern how the players conduct themselves, within those broad boundaries, the players can operate however they want. And if they choose to break with convention, they can.... And they can change how they play the game at any time, for any reason.

Infinite games have infinite time horizons. And because there is no finish line, no practical end to the game, there is no such thing as "winning" an infinite game. In an infinite game, the primary objective is to keep playing, to perpetuate the game.[9]

If the whole thing is a game, I don't need to win. I just need to find a way to stay aloft.

I walk out of the hotel and get a car to take me for a drive. As we pass near the White House, I see a small park, and I ask my driver to pull over and, if he would please, wait for a while. I get out and walk to a small coffee kiosk. I take my paper cup to a bench and sit for a while in the cold, letting the steam drift up into my face, contemplating the day ahead.

My entire personal and professional reputation is on the line. I have decades-long relationships at stake, my immediate career as

---

9   Simon Sinek, *The Infinite Game*, (New York: Portfolio, 2019).

an ambassador, the future of my business, and my family's well-being to worry about. Part of me feels that if I could just say everything, put it all out there, people would understand. But most of the time it's better just to shut up. Because transparency in a crisis is not a black-and-white issue. Full and absolute exposure of everything going on at any given moment can cause panic, hinder an investigation, and do irreparable damage to your reputation. Some people say I have to be transparent; I have to say whatever I know right now. No, you don't. And that doesn't make you a hack or a crony. It makes you strategic and responsible.

In business and in the ambassador job, people often say one thing in a face-to-face meeting, only to walk out and communicate something completely different to a different audience (welcome to politics—and to legal battles). And in the absence of an expert, someone will want to act like one. But on November 20, it isn't going to be me. I don't need to be an expert or a hero. I just need to get through it.

As I feel the winds building in my brain again, I tell myself, think of your parents. Think of how it was for your father, surviving WWII in work camps and eight years of separation from your mother. Think of all her hardships—making it in a foreign country as a pregnant teenager with no partner. And I also think of how far I'd come myself, from a department store janitor to an ambassador to the second largest economy in the world. I have the confidence that will carry me through this. As I start to calm, I think about my objective on that day, in that context. I am not going to be able to clear my name or to make everyone like me or understand my point of view.

One of the things that my legal team pushes me on in preparation for trial is "what are you most afraid of?" What question, what implication, what outcome would really upend you? This is not to terrify me—it is to try to de-weaponize anything the committee could come at me with. (My "murder board" sure earned their moniker.) The *Washington Post* gives us a nice crib sheet with a piece they publish a few days before my testimony where they ask:

1. Were you acting of your own volition, or at the direction of Trump?

2. What did you say to Trump—and Trump to you—on a July phone call from Kyiv?

3. You told the Ukrainians their military aid would come when their president made an "anti-corruption statement." Was that code for investigations into the Bidens/the 2016 election interference?

4. Why didn't you remember the offer you gave to the Ukrainians in your original testimony?

5. Why did you agree to testify?[10]

When facing these questions, many of which I am actually confronted with in court, my goal needs to be to tell the truth to the best of my ability. And then stop. That's it. The point is not to "win."

Eventually, I have to get my ass off that bench and get to the hearing. So off I go in the direction of the Longworth House Office Building, just south of the US Capitol. The building itself looks relatively unremarkable from the outside—a typical neoclassical-Washington behemoth. Room 1100 is the largest in the lower chamber. It looks like a small theater, which in some ways it is, especially on the day I am there. On stage is the Trump impeachment show, and I am a side player—a little bit of a Mercutio: the natural entertainer who plays to the crowd, who has friends in both enemy houses but has an allegiance to one. Oh yeah, and he's

---

10   Amber Phillips, "The 5 questions Gordon Sondland needs to answer," *The Washington Post*, November 19, 2019, https://www.washingtonpost.com/politics/2019/11/14/questions-gordon-sondland-needs-answer/.

also the guy who ends up dying in a tragic mishap during a mock battle, while uttering the curse "a plague on both your houses..." But that isn't going to be me. Not today.

The cavernous room 1100 is decorated with two sculpted eagles sitting atop giant floor-to-ceiling pillars; the original forty-bulb cast bronze chandelier hangs from the ceiling. Heavy gold curtains behind the hand-carved dais were designed by Barnet Phillips, a New York architect who also designed much of the building's furniture.[11] And I am right smack in the middle of it. Bob, Kwame, and Jim flank me, and a swarm of photographers and reporters crowd in front. The scene would have been surreal and amusing if it hadn't been my lived reality.

Before we enter the room, I review my testimony in a holding room with my legal team, scribbling corrections at the last second. Up to the minute, testimony is being leaked and things are coming out in the media that we have to react to: the other witnesses' recollections jog my memory or people made assertions about my whereabouts, statements, or actions that I have to try and remember. Then it is go time. I walk into the room and take my seat at the table. The room takes several minutes to settle. At 9:09 a.m., I take a deep breath and begin my opening statement.

My key points are first, Secretary Perry, Ambassador Volker, and I worked with Mr. Rudy Giuliani on Ukraine matters at the express direction of the president of the United States. We did not want to work with Mr. Giuliani, but if we did not, we would lose an important opportunity to cement relations between the United States and Ukraine. Second, although we disagreed with the need to involve Mr. Giuliani, we did not believe that his role was improper at the time. Third, precisely because we did not think that we were engaging in improper behavior, we made every effort to ensure

11   Jordy Yager, "Come to Order," *The Hill*, July 19, 2010, https://the-hill.com/capital-living/109679-come-to-order.

that the relevant decision makers at the National Security Council and State Department knew the important details of our efforts. Fourth, as I testified previously, Mr. Giuliani's requests were a quid pro quo for arranging a White House visit for President Zelensky, demanding Ukraine make a public statement announcing investigations of the 2016 election/DNC server and Burisma. Fifth, in July and August 2019, we learned that the White House had suspended security aid to Ukraine. I later came to believe that the resumption of security aid would not occur until there was a public statement from Ukraine committing to the investigations of the 2016 election and Burisma, as Mr. Giuliani had demanded. Finally, at all times, I was acting in good faith. As a presidential appointee, I followed the directions of the president. The others and I worked with Mr. Giuliani because the president directed us to do so. We had no desire to set any conditions on the Ukrainians. And was there a "quid pro quo?" As I testified previously, with regard to the requested White House call and White House meeting, the answer is yes. Everyone was in the loop: Pompeo, Giuliani, Pence, Mulvaney, and many others knew what was going on.

I take a deep breath as I finish my statement. We have a short break; then it is time for the fun part: questioning by House lawyers Daniel Goldman and Steve Castor, along with Adam Schiff and Devin Nunes. Schiff and Nunes take the lead in needling me. Then comes Goldman, the panel's senior adviser for the Democrats, and Castor, the House Oversight Committee's general counsel for the Republicans. This is supposed to be forty-five minutes of questioning by the chairman and majority counsel [Democrats], then forty-five minutes of questioning by the ranking member and minority counsel [Republicans]. It turns into several hours. Some of what they fire at me includes the following:

Nunes: On July 25th, you knew nothing about military aid being withheld?

Castor: Did the President ever tell you personally about any preconditions for anything?

Castor: OK. You testified that Mr. Giuliani was expressing the desires of the president, correct? But how did you know that? Who told you?

Castor: So it wasn't an order or a direction to go talk with Mr. Giuliani, correct?

Castor: You mentioned on July 25th, before you went to Ukraine, you called the President, but there was no material information on the 25th call, correct?

Castor: And why don't you tell us, what did the President say to you on September 9th that you remember?

Castor: OK. But you have—and we got into this a little bit in your deposition. You know, you said that the President gave you a special assignment with regard to Ukraine, correct?

Schiff: You've testified that [Mick] Mulvaney was aware of this quid pro quo, of this condition that the Ukrainians had to meet, that is, announcing these public investigations to get the White House meeting. Is that right?

Goldman: And you understood that there was a lot of activity within the State Department and elsewhere to try to get that [security assistance] hold lifted. Is that right?[12]

---

12   "Impeachment Inquiry: Ambassador Gordon," U.S. House of Representatives, Permanent Select Committee on Intelligence, November 20, 2019, https://www.congress.gov/116/meeting/house/110233/documents/HHRG-116-IG00-Transcript-20191120.pdf.

A lot was made of the whole idea of irregular channels of diplomacy, which is a bit disingenuous. Career diplomats are the subject matter experts—but the secretary and the ambassadors are boss. They are appointed by the president, and they are there to follow his agenda, through his designated channel—so tell me how that is irregular. Another global point is that as president, if you want to conduct domestic policy, you have to involve Congress. If you want to conduct foreign policy, sure you should consult people, but ultimately, you can do whatever you want short of signing a treaty. There is no constitutional restriction. So when I was accused of being part of an "irregular channel," I did not agree. At all. I was simply following the president's mandate.

After an initial round of questioning, Schiff calls for a brief recess. I don't know it at the time, but the Democrats have gone out to hold a press conference on the supposed bombshells I had dropped. After they finish with me a little after one p.m., we have a brief lunch break where I scarfed down a stale sandwich. Then there is an opportunity for five-minute rounds of questioning by Intelligence Committee members, which they could yield to colleagues so any House member was able to ask what they wanted. Rep. Sean Patrick Maloney (D-NY) rips into me, asking a number of leading questions. I had already said that with the benefit of hindsight, it was clear that investigations into Burisma meant investigations into Biden. Maloney harps on this point multiple times, insinuating that I was not being forthcoming in my testimony—it's clear he is pissed off that I am not being explicit in condemning the president. Castor and Rep. Jim Jordan (R-OH) question me as to why I don't mention the specifics of a call where Trump says, "I want nothing. I want no quid pro quo." Michael Turner accuses me of being circular and contradictory in his answers.

Rep. Michael Turner, R-Ohio: Nobody on this planet told you that Donald Trump was tying aid to these investigations, is that correct?

Plenty of other representatives take a whack at me too. I just stay calm, sip my water, and fly on.

In the midst of my testimony, President Trump apparently scribbled down some of what I said with a Sharpie. He recited his notes to reporters as he walked out on the White House lawn to the awaiting Marine One, its rotors noisily running in the background. As the *New York Times* reported,

> "Ready?" Mr. Trump yelled at reporters on the South Lawn, having stopped on his way to boarding Marine One. "Do you have the cameras rolling?"
>
> The president then began reading from a notepad of talking points scrawled in Sharpie paraphrasing his comments in the phone conversation, as recounted by Mr. Sondland: "I want nothing. I want nothing. I want no quid pro quo. Tell Zelensky" — referring to President Volodymyr Zelensky of Ukraine — "to do the right thing."[13]

The president looked downright gleeful as he emphasized the next part: "This is the final word from the president of the United States: I want nothing."

The hearing ends at 3:47 p.m., clocking in at over six and a half hours of testimony. I want to get the hell out of there and to the airport as fast as I can. The sooner I could put an ocean between me and Washington, DC on that day, the happier I would be.

---

13   Katie Rogers, "'I Want Nothing,' Trump Says, Quoting From Sondland's Testimony," *The New York Times,* November 20, 2019, https://www. nytimes.com/2019/11/20/us/politics/trump-sondland.html.

As I'm walking through the corridors at Dulles Airport, I'm getting high-fived, offered free drinks, and congratulated like some kind of sports hero. I was the only political appointee to testify, and people recognized that I was doing my duty as a citizen and a public official. And in the end, the Left got what they wanted—the words "quid pro quo"—and the Right thought I hadn't said anything directly damanging to the president. In fact, I came out saying that President Trump told me he wanted nothing at all from Ukraine—what more could the Republicans want from me? My legal team lauded that I'd done exactly what they wanted in toeing a very careful line by refusing to either condemn or exonerate President Trump. I had the enormous pressure of my career and reputation at stake with millions of eyes on me, and somehow I'd come through to cheers and congratulations.

Even my mishap with my luggage on the airplane made the news. After the Twitter-sphere erupted with speculation about whether I was going to make it to Dulles in time for the last flight to Brussels, I barely made it on board for the 5:50 p.m. departure. Even when I shoved my bag into the wrong overhead bin and quipped, "My whole day has been like this," apparently that was newsworthy.[14] There was also a CNN reporter who learned what flight I was on and managed to book himself a ticket just to see what I would do for the next seven hours. Sorry to disappoint you, Zach, but as you saw, I pretty much slept the whole way. Still, he made an article out of it somehow, talking about my choice of beverage (sparkling water) and how I was warmly greeted by several of our fellow passengers.[15]

---

14   "Sondland put his luggage in the wrong overhead bin, and said 'my whole day has been like this,'" *CNN*, November 20, 2019, https://www.cnn.com/politics/live-news/impeachment-hearing-11-20-19/h_809c2c9ededd78624e71553c7817ad3d?utm_term=image&utm_medium=social&utm_source=twCNNp&utm_content=2019-11-21T00%3A25%3A08.

15   Zachary Cohen, "Seven hours in the air with Sondland after he implicated Trump in his impeachment testimony," *CNN Politics*, November 23, 2019, https://www.cnn.com/2019/11/21/politics/gordon-sondland-flight-brussels/index.html.

I landed in Brussels and was ready to dive back into being a diplomat. Instead, I had to deal with another bullshit hitjob related to incidents that allegedly happened well over a decade before.

But regardless of what I did or said that proved my innocence, the damage was done. Yes, there were business repercussions, but what really bothered me was the toll on my family. To have to deal with these allegations on the heels of the media circus of the impeachment trial—it was all too much. Not to mention it felt like things were coming to a head just before Thanksgiving. Suffice it to say, it was the worst holiday I'd ever experienced and one of the lowest moments of my life. My marriage was coming apart at the seams.

There was nothing to do but keep on keeping on. I put my head down and dove back into my work. Brussels was a more friendly place than my kitchen table at that point. In fact, given my higher profile, I now had even better access to whomever I want to meet with. I was the primary channel to Washington for many European leaders. Radoslaw Sikorski, the head of the European Parliament's delegation for relations with the United States and a vocal Trump critic, even said of me: "I think he's found his feet. He has in the last year found a way of forcefully arguing for American interests and point of view without giving offense. He is well-briefed and states it like it is."[16] As the *Washington Post* put it, "Sondland, for his part, is still playing along, holding on to his post in Brussels with a cheerful tenacity, according to nine associates and diplomats who have interacted with him in recent months."

Jean-Claude Juncker's turn as president of the European Commission came to an end, and the incoming president, Ursula

---

16   Michael Birnbaum, John Hudson, Josh Dawsey and Aaron C. Davis, "Gordon Sondland plugs away in Brussels while playing a central role in Trump's impeachment trial," *The Washington Post*, January 22, 2020, https://www.washingtonpost.com/politics/gordon-sondland-plugs-away-in-brussels-while-playing-a-central-role-in-trumps-impeachment-trial/2020/01/22/13fb1902-3c85-11ea-8872-5df698785a4e_story.html.

von der Leyen, took office on December 1. This changing of the guard triggered a flood of meetings and opportunities to reengage on a whole host of issues from trade to energy to security.

I went to Strasbourg in mid-January for the European Parliament's first plenary session of 2020 where I met with dozens of members of European Parliament on a variety of issues, including Iran, trade, 5G, energy security, and China.[17] When Interim President of Venezuela Juan Guaidó was in Brussels in late January 2020, I met with him and the international community to reinforce our support in restoring democracy and supporting human rights and the rule of law in Venezuela. A few days later, I met with Colombian Ambassador to Brussels Felipe Garcia Echeverri to discuss how the US and EU could partner with Colombia to address the refugee crisis and growing FARC crime along the Colombia-Venezuela border. On January 25, I hosted US Department of Agriculture Secretary Sonny Perdue to celebrate the twenty-fifth anniversary of the US-EU spirits agreement and highlight the recently enacted flag of United States High Quality Beef Memorandum of Understanding.[18] So again, I had a lot going on.

Though I received a hero's welcome with many foreign leaders in Brussels, some of the career staff within the embassy didn't know what to do with me in the aftermath of my testimony—they were fearful that association with me might be a risky proposition. Some careerists around me went into self-protect mode and steered well clear of me.

---

17   U.S. Mission to the EU (@US2EU), ".@USAmbEU Sondland was in #Strasbourg this week for the @Europarl_EN's first plenary session of 2020. Watch his video message below for highlights," Twitter, January 16, 2020, https://twitter.com/US2EU/status/1217844702025789442?s=20.

18   Ambassador Gordon Sondland (@USAmbEU), "Last night I had the pleasure to host @SecretarySonny to celebrate the 25th anniversary of the U.S.-EU spirits agreement and highlight the recently-enacted US High Quality Beef MOU with some fantastic drinks and steaks!" Twitter, January 28, 2020, https://twitter.com/USAmbEU/status/1222153635263586304?s=20.

As for me, I hoped that by staying quiet and going about my business I could stay out of the spotlight of the impeachment drama unfolding back in Washington. The trial was moving towards its conclusion, and millions of people were following its developments minute by minute. The Democrats were still trying to get to Trump's inner circle through subpoena and pressure, but the refusal of figures like Bolton, Pompeo, and Esper, who received legal cover from their various departments in order not to appear (whereas no such protection was extended to me), meant I continued to stand out. And not in a good way.

CHAPTER NINE

YOU'RE FIRED!

On February 5, 2019, the Senate acquitted President Trump on both articles of impeachment. The votes were clearly and almost completely divided along party lines. The only surprise was Senator Mitt Romney, the lone Republican to break party rank on one of the two articles, becoming the first senator in history to vote against a president of his own party in an impeachment. However, the conclusion of the trial was decisive: Trump would be keeping his job. Little surprise that I wouldn't.

Two days after the impeachment debacle concluded, I meet with Ulrich Brechbuhl in his office at the Department of State. The meeting is my idea; I often stopped in on him while in town and at State for other meetings. As I recounted earlier, I planned to discuss the idea of leaving my post in Brussels later in the spring. I had an inkling that my days might be numbered, and I wanted to exit as gracefully as I could. I heard two Trump campaign sources said that by implicating Trump and top administration officials in a quid pro quo, I had "blindsided" aides in the White House, high-level operatives in the Trump reelection campaign, and some Republican lawmakers.

Another person I could tell was less than pleased with me was Jared Kushner. I talked to him on the phone not long after my public testimony. He was cagey and evasive. He made a comment to the effect of "people around here aren't too happy about what you did." I replied that my goal in my testimony was not to be injurious to the president; it was only to tell the truth to the best of my ability, given my recollections. In retrospect, Kushner likely already knew Pompeo was going to can me. Maybe he even told him to. Or who knows, maybe Kushner himself was the one to tell the president to get rid of me. We had several workmanlike conversations in the intervening months between my testimony and Trump's acquittal, but our relationship had cooled.

As for Pompeo, I suspected he felt I hadn't been loyal to the president and therefore couldn't be counted on to continue pursuing Trump's agenda abroad. That wasn't true at all, but good luck convincing him of that…. I knew that the second I had mentioned the secretary's name in my testimony, he would be pissed that I had dragged him in. But for me to have testified in any other way would have amounted to a series of false statements. Once I made clear Pompeo's knowledge of what was going on related to Ukraine, I surmise the secretary became upset with me and wanted me out. When I went back to Brussels at the end of November, we continued to have direct exchanges when required, but more often, we communicated through intermediaries.

On February 7, 2019 when I walk into Brechbuhl's office with the thought that I might resign, my idea is that I'd spend the next few months tying up loose ends, paving the way for my successor, and making the rounds with European leaders. Then I'd be ready to step down. It's not unusual for an ambassador to do so before his or her term is over. Aside from the reasons mentioned above, I was feeling the strain of being away on both my marriage and my business. I tell Brechbuhl my thoughts about stepping down. He agrees with that part but not with my timeline. "How about this afternoon?" he says. "We'll make it easy for you. We'll say you resigned;

we'll keep it as quiet as possible. You can go back to Brussels ASAP, pack up, leave post, and that will be that. The president wants to distance himself from 'everything that happened' during the trial." His tone makes it clear that this is all but fait accompli.

I am utterly taken aback. "That's not happening," I tell him. "If you want me out of here immediately, you're going to have to fire me." He bristles. I stand to leave, and I tell him I need to talk to my legal counsel. He says I have until three p.m. to let him know of my decision.

After leaving his office, I immediately call Bob Luskin and Jim McDermott. Both of them agree with me and with my gut instinct: don't resign. It looks like you're running off because you're guilty of something. And you've done nothing wrong. If they want you to leave post immediately, they should fire you. Otherwise, you should continue with the plan you suggested: get your things in order and prepare for a graceful exit in the spring. I'm not going to resign in ignominy. I am going to push back, to try and do things my way. There is still a sliver of hope that I might still have a chance to do that.

But then the news broke that Lt. Col. Alexander Vindman had been fired from his job at the White House, along with his brother, Lt. Col. Yevgeny Vindman, former deputy legal adviser for the National Security Council. It looked like the president wanted to clean house. I would clearly be the next one swept out the door. The Friday after he was acquitted, retribution was swift. Others like Fiona Hill, Marie Yovanovich, and Kurt Volker had been fired or left their posts much earlier. Fiona Hill, deputy assistant to the president and senior director for Europe and Russia, left the White House of her own accord in June 2019 to return to the Brookings Institution. On September 27, 2019, Volker resigned from his unpaid position as special representative for Ukraine negoti- ations (his full-time job was running the McCain Institute for

International Leadership at Arizona State University), hours after House Democrats announced they would be interviewing him. Marie Yovanovich, ambassador to Ukraine, was suddenly recalled by Washington two months earlier than planned in May 2019.

After the Vindman firing, others saw the writing on the wall for me too, and they came out forcefully in my support. Several senators made calls to the White House on my behalf: Ron Johnson, Olympia Snowe, Thom Tillis—they all relayed the same plea: Don't fire Sondland; he didn't throw you under the bus, he had to walk a fine line in the trial, and he just wants to get back to work. Tillis talked to President Trump directly. He recounted that the president said that it was Pompeo's decision to "make a change." Again, it's not like I wanted to bring up Pompeo in my testimony. But if I didn't raise his involvement, it would have perfectly supported the myth that I was acting as a "lone wolf," out there conducting "irregular diplomacy" that I made up as I went, and that simply wasn't true. So I didn't have a choice.

I appreciated all the support, but in the end, it didn't matter. I learned that the White House was going to recall me that afternoon. I put out a press release before they could say anything. They told me they weren't going to put out an announcement, but I knew better—they would have leaked the news about me with a fire hose. So I wanted to have the first word. My statement said,

> "I was advised today that the President intends to recall me effective immediately as United States Ambassador to the European Union. I am grateful to President Trump for having given me the opportunity to serve, to Secretary Pompeo for his consistent support, and to the exceptional and dedicated professionals at the US Mission to the European Union. I am proud of our accomplishments. Our work here has been the highlight of my career."

It was over. Now I needed to make plans to get back to Brussels to collect my affairs and to tie up whatever loose ends I could. But even that wouldn't be easy. That night, Brechbuhl did something vindictive: he sent a cable to the embassy in Brussels and told the staff that I was forbidden to enter the grounds, something like, "Ambassador Sondland has been terminated, he cannot come onto the property or enter the residence." I was persona non grata. I told Bob Luskin what I had learned, and he called Marik String, the legal adviser of the Department of State. Luskin said, "Come on. This just isn't right. We won't stand for it." Soon enough, the order was rescinded.

But the obvious spite really bothered me—not only did the State Department refuse to pay my legal fees, as they promised to when I was first called to testify, but now they were going to restrict me from entering the residence and the mission, making me look like a black sheep, if not a traitor. Ambassador to Belgium Gidwitz (who eventually assumed the job as acting EU ambassador in addition after my departure) got the cable in the middle of the night saying as much.

If things had gone my way, I would have had several weeks to conclude my work. I would have remained as ambassador up to the last second; I still could have been effective in my role in the meantime. But I didn't get that chance. Instead, I flew to Brussels on my own dime on February 12. When I landed that evening, I had to get my own ride from the airport; this time, there was no security detail, no motorcade, no blue lights. I spent the first night in a hotel. The next day, I went to the residence, most likely under heavy surveillance. I said goodbye to the staff, took a few personal items, made sure the rest of my belongings were ready for pack-out, and went to the embassy to clear out my desk. Again, I felt lots of eyeballs on me, but everyone present treated me with the same respect and deference as ever.

It wasn't anywhere near the proper farewell that I wanted, but I planned a small cocktail party on my second and final night at a venue adjacent to the US-EU mission called De Warande. It isn't technically on the grounds of the embassy, but you still have to go through the gates of the mission to get there, so it's not open to the general public. I didn't know what to expect that evening. I invited forty or so people. About 200 showed up. I knew that most of the embassy staff, like the State Department at large, was largely left-leaning and for that reason alone tended not to be fans of mine since I was a Trump appointee. Despite this, I got a truly heartwarming response to the news of my departure. Many, many people came up to me that night and said that it was unfair and uncalled for that I had been recalled, that they appreciated my testimony, and were disappointed to see me go. I got a lot of hugs and kind words. The marines gave me a flag, nicely framed, that had hung over the embassy during my tenure. All of this made me feel much better about my forced departure and made things a little easier when I got on the plane the next day to head back to the States.

I left for Portland on February 14th and arrived the next day. If things were awkward at the mission, I didn't feel particularly welcome at home, either. Understandably. The past few months had been sheer hell for my family. As difficult as that time was for me, I was responsible for my actions. Some of those actions, as well intentioned as they were, had been misguided. And I made my share of mistakes along the way. My family had to suffer the intense and incessant press scrutiny and ridicule, the spectacle of the trial, and the repercussions on our family business and our name. Now it was time for me to make amends—and to make some money. I planned to dive back into running my hotel business in earnest in 2020.

Well. That didn't work out either. COVID put a full stop to the hospitality industry. It used to be that when one of our hotels was down in revenue by 30 percent, that was an all-out crisis. Now every single property was down 90 percent. It was as if a massive fire, earthquake, tsunami, or tornado had struck in every city where we owned property. Simultaneously.

It's hard to imagine that 2020 was quite as bad for Zelensky as it was for me, but it wasn't a cakewalk for him either. As rabidly as millions of people followed what was going on with Ukraine previously, the country and its president were all but an afterthought for most Americans once the impeachment trials ended. That, of course, would change quite dramatically once again in a few years' time.

When Zelensky was first elected, there was an immediate wave of optimism for Ukraine's future, both internally and abroad. During the impeachment inquiry, Zelensky tried to keep out of the news, despite regularly being pestered to offer his opinion. He largely stuck to his talking points that as the leader of Ukraine, he didn't want to see his country's image dragged through the mud and become synonymous with political quagmire and corruption, etcetera. Zelensky couldn't afford to alienate Trump by sounding off, but his country was so focal in the impeachment inquiry that he couldn't escape making some kind of comment. Unfortunately, the impeachment inquiry derailed much of the early optimism Zelensky brought into the role.

Secretary Pompeo traveled to Kyiv at the end of January 2020 to reassure Ukrainian officials the US remained committed to the country. But Pompeo still did not extend a formal invitation to Zelensky to visit the White House—one can only assume that this was a massive disappointment to Zelensky personally. Ukrainians decried the snub; after all, Russian Foreign Minister

Sergey Lavrov had been invited to the White House twice during Trump's presidency.[1]

Later in the year, Zelensky's wife and then he contracted COVID (they fully recovered). He finally got his long awaited White House visit with President Biden on September 1, 2021. He quipped that "I would like Ukraine to be known, not notorious,"[2] but the meeting was uneventful, and Ukraine then again faded from view as far as being an energy and security priority, despite Russia's near-completion of the Nord Stream 2 pipeline. Zelensky's approval ratings took a dramatic downturn compared to the early days of his presidency. Then, of course, the tides again turned: Ukraine was invaded by Russia in February 2022, rightfully eliciting sympathy and outrage from most of the world. Zelensky became known as a global hero and heartthrob, staying put and bravely defending his homeland despite grave danger to his own life. Once more he was a household name, though this time for being an exemplary, inspiring leader willing to put his life on the line for the future of his country.

As for what happened with the EU ambassadorship after my departure, once I was recalled, my deputy chief of mission became the temporary chargé d'affaires. Many foreign leaders cancelled meetings I'd scheduled; the new DCM was a capable and intelligent guy with lots of subject matter expertise, but the Europeans wanted to meet with someone who had access. To borrow George Orwell's phrase from *Animal Farm*, "All animals are equal, but some animals are more equal than others." Same goes for ambassadors.

The role of the US ambassador to the EU has become more complex, in part due to the evolving nature of the EU itself. What

1 Edward Wong, "Amid Trump's Trial, Pompeo Visited Ukraine. Here's How It Went." *The New York Times*, January 31, 2020, https://www.nytimes.com/2020/01/31/world/europe/ukraine-pompeo-zelensky-trump.html.

2 Maegan Vazquez and Kevin Liptak, "Ukrainian President accomplishes years-long quest for a White House visit with Biden meeting," *CNN*, September 1, 2021, https://www.cnn.com/2021/09/01/politics/ukraine-volodymyr-zelensky-biden-white-house/index.html.

was once a loose coalition of countries plagued by war and discord has now become the largest economic bloc in the world. The politics of the EU have taken on an increasingly American tone and style in recent years, with candidates for the top EU jobs campaigning, debating, and jockeying for power. In this increasingly partisan European environment, the US needs to behave as an evenhanded and reliable ally, steadying the ship rather than adding to the turbulence.

Enhancing and elevating the role of the US ambassador to the EU can help with this. The ambassador needs to be the tip of the spear when it comes to US policy towards the EU. To act in such a fashion would require the full support of the National Security Council.

The US ambassador to the EU should have a direct counterpart at the highest level in the NSC with whom they have weekly check-ins and updates. This goes both ways—the ambassador would relay information gathered at post to the NSC, and his or her partner at the NSC would respond in kind. The same goes for trade. The US ambassador to the EU needs to be in direct contact and partnered with a senior USTR (US Trade Representative) official. The ambassador should be included in most, if not all, conversations with EU trade officials. It's obvious that the EU ambassador needs to be given greater capacity in light of their large responsibilities. Most other ambassadors are responsible for tracking one government, not twenty-seven. That alone is enough reason the role of the EU ambassador needs to be reevaluated and bolstered. If the US ambassador to the EU doesn't have access to certain levers or is unwilling to use them because they're worried about upsetting expectations, the transatlantic relationship will degrade.

Even as the role of the ambassador should be enhanced, the US Mission to the European Union needs to be made leaner and meaner to "close" this agenda—something I'd argue is the case at many of our other embassies worldwide. Our missions abroad need to be incentivized to innovate and encouraged to take risks, as well as reduce redundant roles. The culture of the State Department needs to be updated for the twenty-first century, including more flexibility in recruiting and the expansion of programs for professional development and skills to strengthen staff. China has doubled its spending on its diplomatic corps under Xi Jinping, so we need to be lean and mean to stay relevant.[3] I also continue to strongly believe in the need for political appointees in our diplomatic corps. There is no substitute for their real-world expertise in business and negotiation, their connections and access, and their ability to take risks that career diplomats can't because they are worried about maintaining their position for the next post and the one after that and the one after that.

One more thing. The IT in the State Department needs a total overhaul. Enough with the leftover equipment from the 1990s. The whole system needs a swift and complete global revamping to bring it up to present-day standards.

Reflecting on my boss and how he closed out his time in office, I hope I've made clear that President Trump had strengths and weaknesses as a commander-in-chief. Many times, his strengths got lost in the outcry over his far more obvious weaknesses. He almost always made what he wanted crystal clear but did a less exemplary job explaining why it was a worthy objective. If President Trump had expressed not through grievance but through explanation why policies he made were good for the American people, he would have gotten much further in terms of the impact he was able to make during his presidency. Too often he got sidetracked by feeling aggrieved by a problem (for instance, NATO being under-

3   Charles Clover and Sherry Fei Ju, "China's diplomacy budget doubles under Xi Jinping," *Financial Times,* March 6, 2018, https://www.ft.com/content/2c750f94-2123-11e8-a895-1ba1f72c2c11.

funded by countries like Germany) and frustrated in the fact that people wanted him to explain why he felt so. He wanted to find a solution to the underlying problem, and when that progress was stymied, he often responded not by explaining his position but by lashing out—at German Chancellor Merkel, for example.

President Trump was more than willing to let those he liked and trusted perform whatever tasks need to be performed even if those tasks weren't traditionally in their purview. On the plus side, this allowed people to excel at what they do best—but it also meant occasionally people got in over their heads. Trump liked to delegate things to people in a somewhat ad hoc fashion—this allowed for quick action and avoided the overthinking and hand-wringing that often accompanies policy making. But it occasionally meant that efforts were being duplicated or that people charged with a task initially felt their toes were being stepped on when another person entered the scene at the president's behest. President Trump was willing to give people a lot of rope to do things the way they knew best, and he also made himself accessible to people far beyond the cabinet. But this also led to people making judgment calls in situations that required more oversight or where additional information could have been helpful and led to many simultaneous conversations happening at the same time in isolation of each other. I'm sure part of the president's thinking was, "If I have a conversation with ten people about this task maybe one of them will actually get something done…"

Regarding his loss in the 2020 election to Joe Biden, if President Trump had calmly explained that he believed that the American public would be better served by examining and exposing potential anomalies in our voting system and said that he was going to litigate until those anomalies were either uncovered or proven to not exist, that would have gone a long way toward helping the country feel less divided and rancorous. Tell people what is motivating your actions and how it connects to their interests. Even better would have been to say, "If the electoral college says that Biden has won the election, I will attend the inauguration and turn over the keys." It's that simple. But we are far from the days when George H. W. left a note on his departure from the White House, in which he told Clinton, "Don't let the critics discourage you or push you off course. You will be our President when you read this note. I wish you well. I wish your family well. Your success is now our country's success. I am rooting hard for you."[4] I hope that at some point we can return to such civility between the parties.

The vast majority of Trump's political ambassadors got the boot immediately. That's to be expected. A changing of the guard in Washington triggers the same at our embassies worldwide. Whomever holds the EU post has a tough job—and a very important one, now more than ever.

4   Joel Shannon, "A 'fine letter to be remembered by': Read George H.W. Bush's gracious letter to Bill Clinton," *USA Today*, December 1, 2018, https://www.usatoday.com/story/news/politics/2018/12/01/bush-letter-clinton-read-george-h-w-bushs-letter/2173692002/.

CHAPTER TEN

THE NEXT ACT

If you wanted to read a treatise on the biggest global threats facing the United States and the European Union, obviously this is not that book. There are plenty of great books on the subject written by foreign policy experts who know a hell of a lot more about it than I do. But I do want to express my views on the matter, based on what I witnessed firsthand as ambassador and my insights into the workings of diplomacy at the highest level. In my opinion, China, Russia, and Iran present the biggest threats to global peace and prosperity, in that order. These guys are the entire ball game. I also feel that if the US and the EU act together and act quickly, we can neutralize these threats. That's a big "if." We have serious work to do, and the hurdles are daunting. We don't have time to waste, especially when it comes to China.

Plain and simple, we are hooked on their cheap goods and cheap loans. It's worked up until now. However, we are reaching a dangerous inflection point. We are not at war with China today in the military sense. But what if we were? Would China willingly oblige us with hardware, minerals, or other materials that they and only they have and we need? The answer is obvious.

During the COVID pandemic, we discovered that the materials used for testing reagents, personal protective gear, and other needed items are controlled largely by China. Why do we continue to put our eggs into this basket, allowing ourselves to become dependent on them? Because it's easy. This has to change and change immediately. Reinvesting a portion of our defense budget to make certain that our indigenous producers can be up and running in the US on short notice, or even instituting generous tax credits to induce our manufacturers to produce vital products on our shores, is money well spent. The next time you or I buy an incredibly cheap running shoe or electronic gadget made in China, we should consider what price we are *really* paying when you factor in our loss of capability.

Imagine this: It's 2040. President Ivanka Trump is beginning her second term after securing a narrow victory against Democratic challenger Cory Booker. After years of social unrest at home, the United States has been left in a position where it has to be more pragmatic and inward-facing. We are no longer seen as the leading global superpower. China has definitively assumed the role after decades of investment in its military capabilities, economic outreach efforts, and through the propping up of new international organizations that have largely made the post-World War II Western institutions obsolete.

US federal debt continued to grow exponentially in the 2020s, and any remaining confidence in Washington's ability to rein in this debt evaporated, triggering a dollar crisis in global financial markets. The US dollar is no longer the reserve currency; it's now the euro. Because of our lack of spine, the Europeans have cast their lot in with China. Faced with massive debt plus an overstretched military, public disenchantment with foreign wars, and mounting domestic challenges, especially regarding health care, education, and immigration, Americans have lost their appetite for much engagement abroad. China, meanwhile, spent much of the 2020s and 2030s supplanting the US role as the top trading partner for many countries. It has invested in infrastructure in dozens of countries, financing roads and bridges for a fraction of the cost of competitors, and setting up lucrative repayment plans that have essentially rendered half the world indebted to China. Their lauded rollout of 5G and 6G telecommunications devices and the 2042 launch of 7G towers have made China the technological hegemon of the world. Shenzhen has supplanted Silicon Valley as the go-to place for tech geniuses and entrepreneurs. The World Bank and International Monetary Fund are seen as forgotten relics, propped up by a small contingent of countries who still hope to extract something from these failing organizations. The UN has further slid into irrelevance; China has enough influence over the majority of each regional working group that it can override any vote with a few phone calls and threats to cease investment. There are still eruptions of interstate violence, but overall, the global battles are over trade and spheres of influence. China has slowly brought Southeast Asia into line, turning it into a manufacturing hub for its burgeoning middle class. China has also invested so heavily in southern Europe and the Balkans that it has enormous sway over European affairs. Countries in Latin America and Africa, too, are beholden to Chinese interests and propped up with infrastructure from Chinese companies and funding from Chinese sources.

Remember the movie *Demolition Man?* The sci-fi film set in the future where every single restaurant on earth is now a Taco Bell? I feel like we're heading for a similar scenario where all the companies in the US are run by China, even if you can't tell from the outside. In 2040, American habits and tastes have not shifted drastically, but fewer and fewer of the companies producing the food you eat and manufacturing the products you buy are American; they are owned by Chinese conglomerates, and proceeds are funneled back to China. Your personal communications are monitored by advanced Chinese Communist Party algorithms, and if you are too outspoken about China, you find yourself mysteriously unable to travel freely, muzzled on social media, and struggling to get a new job or finance a move. The movies streaming on TV feature Chinese actors, and most are dubbed in English, although more and more are subtitled in English as the number of people who speak Mandarin worldwide increases. The news comes from Chinese sources though it's not designated as such. Chinese Communist Party propaganda filters its way into households across the country. Every time you send money electronically, each transaction goes through a Chinese system and is recorded in computers accessible by the Chinese Communist Party. The world order has completely changed. The Western era is over, and the East reigns supreme.

Hopefully, this scenario is nothing more than a nightmare I had after one too many egg rolls. What's already come true is that China is a huge threat to the Western way of life, the values shared by the United States and Europe, and to the economic health of both of sides of the Atlantic.

China is really good at practicing the art of gradual incrementalism. The US right now is like the frog in a pot of water as the heat is slowly rising. Eventually, it's too late: the frog doesn't realize it's been boiled alive. In the same way, the US has stood by and watched China enter developing markets and create dependencies, buy up strategic assets globally, modernize and expand its military, and undermine our ability to manufacture the things we need ourselves. At what point are we going to realize the water is about to boil?

Russia is another country of grave concern as the US and EU look to the future.[1] [2] We've been reminded of this recently, and we need to pay attention. Here are a few of the main reasons: One, disinformation and cyberattacks—Russia has engaged in cyber-re-

---

1   "U.S. Sanctions on Russia," Congressional Research Service, updated January 18, 2022, accessed August 19, 2020, https://crsreports.congress.gov/product/pdf/R/R45415.

2   "Russia: Background and U.S. Policy," Congressional Research Service, updated August 21, 2017, accessed August 19, 2020, https://crsreports.congress.gov/product/pdf/R/R44775.

lated influence operations that, according to the US intelligence community, have targeted the 2016 US presidential election and also elections in Europe. Russia has extensive "troll farms" whose sole purpose is to lie and sow discord in the West using social media. Troll farms create posts on social media and create memes shared widely, often using incendiary messages that stoke race, religion, and political issues. A page on Facebook that shared patriotic messages about Texas that in reality was a front for Russian trolls trying to push for Texas secession gathered 250,000 followers before it was shut down in 2017.[3]

Two, coercion abroad—Russia encroaches on its neighbors and also has several active military campaigns in more far-flung parts of the world. Nearby, there's the annexation of Crimea and funding of separatist forces in addition to a war in Ukraine, while further afield is the Russian support of the ousted Assad regime in Syria and a flaring up of tensions in northern Georgia. We should also pay attention to their propensity for weapons proliferation and international treaty violations—Russia has blatantly violated numerous nonproliferation agreements and treaties. The Intermediate-Range Nuclear Forces (INF) treaty and Open Skies treaty, in particular, have not been adhered to with little consequence. The INF treaty, signed by Reagan and Mikhail Gorbachev, was the first time the US and then-USSR agreed to de-escalate nuclear tension by eliminating an entire type of weapons. Since 2014, the US has had reasonable proof that Russia is no longer abiding by this treaty and developing new ground-launched cruise missiles.[4] The Open Skies treaty allows countries to conduct a flyover of each other's military bases with little notice to collect data, creating transparency and

---

3   Davey Alba, "How Russia's Troll Farm Is Changing Tactics Before the Fall Election," *The New York Times*, March 29, 2020, https://www.nytimes.com/2020/03/29/technology/russia-troll-farm-election.html.

4   "The Intermediate-Range Nuclear Forces (INF) Treaty at a Glance," Arms Control Association, August 2019, https://www.armscontrol.org/factsheets/INFtreaty.

ensuring neither side escalates tensions. In recent years, Russia has interfered with these requests for flyovers and has not been fully transparent with other countries.[5] Russian weapons regularly turn up across Europe and the Middle East, particularly in Syria.

Three, human rights—Russia, like China and Iran, has an abysmal human rights record. Certain parts of the country, especially around Chechnya, are cut off completely from the rest of Russia, and its inhabitants are closely monitored. The people in this region have few rights and are the victims of some of the worst human rights abuses in the world. The rule of law is a sham in much of Russia. In mid-2020, the State Department blacklisted the leader of Chechnya for human rights abuses dating back more than a decade, including torture and extrajudicial killings, which had apparently only worsened amidst the COVID lockdowns.[6]

In considering the underlying nationalistic psyche of the two biggest threats to global peace and security, here are some thoughts in broad strokes. There is a sentiment among some Chinese that their civilization is the one true civilization—that they are superior to others. The Chinese state is still licking its wounds over what it perceives as past injuries, issues where China feels it's been exploited by foreign countries and excluded from global affairs— everything from the Opium Wars with the British in the late 1800s, which the Chinese still feel rancor over, to the perceived lack of Chinese voices in international organizations. A Chinese-led world would certainly mean less personal freedom, as the state would rely on technology to monitor and control the population. Propaganda would be pervasive, broadcasting the values of the

---

5   "The Open Skies Treaty at a Glance," Arms Control Association, December
      2021, https://www.armscontrol.org/factsheets/openskies.
6   Carol Morello and Paul Sonne, "U.S. blacklists strongman of Chechnya for human
      rights abuses," *The Washington Post*, July 20, 2020, https://www.washingtonpost.
      com/national-security/us-blacklists-strongman-of-chechnya-for-human-rights-
      abuses/2020/07/20/1a1b2d4a-caa6-11ea-89ce-ac7d5e4a5a38_story.html.

Chinese Communist Party, mostly Confucian values like those that emphasize the needs of society over the individual, the importance of order over privacy, and a close linkage between the CCP and the army.

Speaking again in generalities, the Russian outlook is suffused by a sense of loss and mistreatment by the world. Those who fall in this camp view the existence of the Soviet Union to have been a great achievement and feel the profound loss of the many territories (and ethnic Russians in those regions that remained) when the Soviet Union collapsed. Putin invaded Ukraine as an attempt to reclaim Soviet glory. To put it in perspective, imagine if the US government collapsed one day, and even though it eventually returned as the United Federation of States (after a decade of unrest and as a shadow of its former self) these states didn't rejoin: Montana, Wyoming, Washington, Idaho, Oregon, and Utah (about 24 percent of the Soviet Union's territory was lost in its break-up). The Russian people see this as a great blight on history; they imagine the kind of power they could be today without the turmoil of the 1990s, and they feel an intense desire to reunite Russian people "trapped" in other countries when the Soviet Union collapsed. Crimea played into this sentiment—the Russian people see the capture of Crimea as righting a historical wrong and that these were ethnic Russians who were rejoining their country after being cut off by arbitrary political boundaries.

So, what can we, the US and EU, do together to counter the threats posed by these states?

On Iran, the Joint Comprehensive Plan of Action (JCPOA) deal failed to address Tehran's missile program, the regime's support for terrorism, and its gross human rights violations. The economic stranglehold on the country *was* working, so either we return to that to extract further concessions or take additional steps to ensure buy-in from the Iranian regime. The quarrel is with the government of Iran, not the people. A new agreement needs to be worked on that successfully blocks Iran's nuclear program forever and scraps its missile programs. For now, President Biden seems intent to rejoin the JCPOA as a starting point and then to broaden and expand the agreement. He's trying to use the momentum of the JCPOA, which tackles a lot of thorny issues and made significant headway, and take it a few steps further, and I hope he succeeds. A good next step would be a deal that limits nuclear development for energy purposes only and allows Iran to keep its missile program—temporarily. There needs to be coordinated pressure from the US and Europe for Iran to be willing to go this far, and many will argue that this still isn't far enough, as Iran could be developing a nuclear weapon by researching nuclear energy.

On Russia, a starting place in terms of limiting their reach and influence would be to renew several key international treaties. Already, the Biden administration has sought to extend for another five years the Strategic Arms Reduction Treaty (START) treaty, a key nuclear disarmament deal between the US and Russia that has already been renewed twice; this would limit the number of nuclear weapons in the arsenals of the United States and Russia.[7] This could then be expanded to include a de-escalation of nuclear stockpiles. Economic sanctions have negatively impacted the Russian economy but have not produced any policy changes. A new, more robust approach is needed, including a coordinated approach with European allies.

Resolving the conflict in Ukraine should be the top priority of the US-EU security dynamic. As long as this conflict festers, the EU and US are doing ill by a critical ally in the region. I'd suggest we undertake a massive overhaul of the Minsk agreements but

---

7   Matthew Lee and Robert Burns, "Biden proposes 5-year extension of nuke
      treaty with Russia," *AP News*, January 21, 2021, https://apnews.com/article/
      russia-nuclear-weapons-da58ab8ba29ff6ebd1d93bdbd0d6db38.

work to instate them—this time with more buy-in from the EU and United States. (The Minsk agreements, drawn up in 2014 and 2015, were attempts at resolving the conflict in Ukraine through a ceasefire that almost immediately collapsed. It was a bad deal. In theory, if it had worked, it would have stopped the fighting but at a cost: Russia would've walked away having gained significant leverage over Ukraine. In any event, the agreements fell apart almost immediately.) Let's help establish a true ceasefire and put an international peacekeeping force in place to maintain this fragile area (similar to the one enacted along the India/Pakistan border).

Regarding China, there are both political and economic approaches we can take to counter this rising power. Economically, more needs to be done to prevent China from gaining access to new markets. The US and some European countries already screen for Chinese investment, making sure there isn't a national security concern for a Chinese company to take control of say, a US microchip factory. If Chinese companies start buying up too much of a particular sector, such as chip manufacturing, this would be against our national interests, as suddenly, we wouldn't have any US-controlled chip companies and would be vulnerable to price fluctuations controlled by China. But currently, there's no mechanism to intervene. More than just screening Chinese investment and denying them access to US and EU markets, there needs to be a joint US-EU fund that can be tapped into to outbid China when it comes to infrastructure projects and other ventures.

For instance, consider the case of the Port of Piraeus in Greece. With Greece in tough financial straits, it put this port up for sale in 2016, and China now owns a majority stake in it. China now wants to turn the port, which sits in a key location between Europe and Asia, into the biggest transit hub between the two continents and the largest port in Europe. And you know what? China bought the port with no competition. Now they have a toehold in the EU.

Politically, China has many governments in its pocket due to the heavy amount of investment it has undertaken in other countries worldwide. Acting together, the US and the EU should be running interference, inserting ourselves as a far more accountable and benign, if not benevolent, alternative partner. We should be the entity that other countries turn to when they are looking for investment or help with development. Another warning sign is what's happening in Serbia. China has invested heavily in the country, which is now ostensibly in the pocket of China as trade ties between the two increase and joint projects multiply. In a telltale sign of China's level of interest in Serbia, the largest Chinese cultural center in Europe isn't being opened in Paris or Berlin, but Belgrade.[8]

We need to wean ourselves off of Chinese goods and Chinese loans. I would gladly, over time, pay more for the price of independence and national security. This is the critical area where our relationship with the EU and the Five Eyes (a security alliance the US has with New Zealand, the UK, Canada, and Australia) could pay off big time. For example, consider the PPG that we all find we desperately needed at the start of the COVID pandemic. Instead of relying on China for supply, the alliance could pick, say, France to be the provider of last resort for PPG for the entire group. I would rather call Paris than Beijing when things get tight.

If the US and the EU worked together as a cohesive unit, China's hegemonic ambitions would be significantly contained and our combined Western global footprint (the US and EU, and also factoring in Canada, Australia, New Zealand, and the UK) would have a dramatic positive impact on the security and prosperity of the US and its allies.

---

8   Sebastian Shukla and Oren Liebermann, "China's clout is growing on the edge of the EU, and the US is worried," *CNN*, September 14, 2019, https://www.cnn.com/2019/09/14/europe/serbia-china-investment-intl/index.html.

C'mon folks. Why are we arguing over GMO tomatoes and seatbelt regulations when China gears up to eat our lunch and make our car industries obsolete entirely? Above all else, it's in the interests of the US and EU to work together, as the West, to combat the rise of China. The US already views China's rise as an existential threat, representing the end of American hegemony and an American era. The EU instead refers to China as a "systemic rival"—not as an enemy, but this is noticeably sharper language than in the past.[9] Policies towards China within Europe are fragmented, with each EU country taking a slightly different approach. Harmonizing the EU position on China, as the European Commission has attempted in recent years, is step one. Step two would entail harmonizing the EU policy and US policy to present a united front as the West. As long as there's daylight between the two, there will be room for China to continue to grow in it, unchecked.

The EU, together with the US, should be promoting a human rights-based approach towards China. This is an area the EU claims it has prioritized—and it's true. With a strong human rights record and its focus on the values such a record represents, it could push China towards a middle ground, making it less of an authoritarian nightmare.[10] The EU is a powerful force for good, but the US is the motor that brings about change. That's worked OK for a long time. But now we need more horsepower if we want to stay ahead in this race for global control. The EU needs to power up its own motor and use it in combination with ours to power a real move forward.

The time for talk is done. Up until now, working together has been optional for the US and EU. Soon it won't be. We'll have no

9   Andrew Small, "The meaning of systemic rivalry: Europe and China beyond the pandemic," European Council on Foreign Relations, May 13, 2020, https://ecfr.eu/publication/the_meaning_of_systemic_rivalry_europe_and_china_beyond_the_pandemic/.

10   Tim Rühlig, "Towards a More Principled European China Policy?" *IFRI*, November 30, 2020, https://www.ifri.org/en/publications/etudes-de-lifri/towards-more-principled-european-china-policy.

choice; the water will be boiling. China will have edged us out economically, militarily, and in intellectual property. We'll be scrambling to play catch up and will be forced to act together. So let's get going now. Let's set short-term, realistic goals and metrics that will allow us to measure whether we've achieved them.

Consider the problem of 5G networking, which I also discussed in previous chapters. Currently, there is no US alternative to China's Huawei that can provide telecommunications equipment for 5G. In Europe, there are two companies that can provide this equipment, but neither can produce the equipment at the same price point as Huawei, owing to government intervention and heavy subsidies from the CCP. The US and EU should similarly subsidize or organize companies to produce 5G equipment from a Western company. Otherwise, the CCP will build these proprietary 5G networks the world over and have access to key infrastructure in Western countries. On a whim, China could shut off our power grids or collect data on individuals for extortion.

Imagine what 2040 could look like if we get our act together. First, here at home, the toxic political climate of the 2010s is abandoned in favor of a renewed sense of bipartisanship. After the 2022-2024 economic downturn following COVID-19, the US economy picks up dramatically and experiences record growth, bolstered by developments in AI and autonomous vehicles. US auto manufacturers are the first to market, and our self-driving cars quickly become the standard worldwide. Rust belt towns across America are reinvigorated and now provide millions with jobs as automobile factories spring up across the country. There's a renewed investment in infrastructure, and the first bullet train opens on the West Coast, connecting Seattle to Portland to San Francisco to Los Angeles in a matter of hours. The East Coast's bullet train system is in the works and is set to open in 2043. An AI breakthrough in 2027 brings the US into the lead with other countries around the world scrambling to develop their own AI technology. The US remains the world's superpower, but there have been no large wars or skirmishes since 2034.

Europe by 2040 is also a stronger actor on the world stage. After a wave of conservative federalists sweep into power in national elections across the bloc in the late 2020s, more power is ceded to the EU, and ultimately, a common external border is created. Finally, Europe is fully realized as George H. W. Bush imagined: whole, free, and at peace. The US and EU have a robust exchange of government personnel, fostering a stronger sense of communication. Nontariff barriers to trade have been eliminated, and trade is seamless across the Atlantic. Europe establishes itself as a player in the tech world and works with the US on its 2027 AI breakthrough. Europe looks poised to be next in line after the US to unlock the secrets of AI. Europe is stronger economically and militarily than it ever has been, although it still draws on soft-power tools when dealing with other countries. Although it no longer *needs* to work with the US on global challenges, Europe often chooses to do so. The EU has expanded further to include the Balkan countries, Moldova, Norway, and Iceland. The bloc is further uplifted by optimism surrounding the planned vote for the UK to rejoin the European Union scheduled for 2041, with many pundits anticipating a positive vote and a return of the errant island nation.

The Middle East is now a bustling economic bloc. Iran, keen to join the growing economies of the region, had set aside the resentment it harbored towards neighbors and brokered a shaky peace agreement with Israel in 2035. The Iranian government slowly loosened up its tight control in the 2030s to allow more freedom to its people and finally decided to separate church and state in 2037. The United States is now indirectly an ally with Iran, with the two cooperating strongly on scientific exchanges and through a renewed emphasis on academic programs allowing Iranians to study in the United States. Later this year, the first female president of Iran will take power after winning a close election.

Ukraine has restructured itself to be less susceptible to corruption, and so Western investment in the country has steadily increased. It now has achieved an admirable bond rating, energy independence, and a reliable stream of income from its position as a key energy transit hub. This predictable and uninterrupted income creates liquidity for infrastructure and defense, and the country is poised for even greater success, even EU membership.

Russia is a shell of itself in 2040 after its botched invasion of Ukraine. Russia struggles to maintain its vast territorial integrity, let alone project power into neighboring countries. Chairman Putin, now eighty-eight years old, has grown feeble and frequently disappears from the public eye for long stretches, prompting unsolicited rumors of his demise. After an attempt by one of his cronies to overthrow him in 2036, he purged most of the senior leadership and installed himself as a true military dictator. Now he is surrounded by young bureaucratic sycophants and servants. In 2030, it was revealed that Putin had siphoned billions from the Russian people and had dozens of properties around the world. After these revelations, the ensuing riots, and the aftereffects of his failure in Ukraine, his popularity never truly bounced back. However, he is so deeply entrenched in the political fabric of Russia that he continues to win rigged elections every few years. Between a stalled economy, a growing independence movement in Chechnya, a bored and financially burdened military, and St. Petersburg declaring itself an independent city-state in 2037, Russia finds itself largely neutered. No one refers to Russia as a great power anymore, except perhaps Chairman Putin in his long, rambling annual addresses to the nation.

China is a more responsible player in global affairs in 2040. When the Chinese economy tumbled below 5 percent annual growth in 2025, this triggered a global loss of confidence in China as a lender. As pressures mounted, China's Belt and Road Initiative fell apart, and its investments were sold off piecemeal to raise capital quickly. A series of domestic crises turned the CCP's attention further inward, as climate change activists and pro-democracy Hong Kong residents and supporters raged on against the CCP. With the world's attention on these protests, the CCP could do nothing but wait for the movements to fizzle out. China continues to be a major regional power, with Chinese investment and influence in Southeast Asia second to none. Although it considers itself a rival of the United States, many do not consider China an equal of the United States, especially after the disastrous East China Sea incident. In 2031, China attempted to unilaterally claim a series of islands off the coast of Taiwan, including the Senkaku Islands. Global backlash was swift and resulted in an immediate blockade of the Chinese navy. When the joint US-EU calls on China to retreat were effective, the UK, Japan, South Korea, Israel, and (surprisingly) Iran all united against this act of Chinese aggression. In the end, it was clear that China could not employ twentieth-century land grab tactics. After this rebuke, China's navy returned home with its tail between its legs, its expansionist dreams stymied for the time being. Overall, it's clear to everyone that the West will remain ascendant for the foreseeable future.

When I was in Brussels, we obviously didn't solve all of the major issues between the US and EU, but we made a lot of progress. And we scored some legislative and trade victories. We had a more frank and honest exchange of ideas than we've had in years. The Europeans may have chafed at President Trump's straightforward, transactional style, but many of his policies were sound, and I hope that they won't be undone by President Biden simply to be contrarian. We have to put aside the small change because this is a time unlike any other; the stakes are higher, and the demands are greater. The US and the EU now must confront aggressive regimes and autocratic leaders that threaten to undermine democracy, rule of law, justice, and many other principles that we call inalienable rights. The presidential transition in the United States cannot be like those in the past, when undoing what one's predecessor had set in place was de rigueur and expected.

We don't have the luxury of bringing progress to a halt while we reset our entire policy approach. In the meantime, Russia plows ahead with its expansionist aspirations, the Chinese Communist Party appears intent on buying up key infrastructure and defense technologies around the globe from Kazakhstan to Cameroon, and Iran ramps up its nuclear aspirations, fomented by populist outrage.

Throwing out the previous administration's playbook has been the norm since at least the Clinton era, but it's now not only a huge waste of time, it's also detrimental to US national security interests. The next administration needs to build on the frank, open conversations we've had with our allies and to reassess the long-entrenched norms that were rightly challenged under the Trump administration. Consider that when Trump took office, only three of our European allies met the 2 percent of GDP minimum spending on defense required by NATO. In 2019, nine allies met the 2 percent minimum. Sixteen allies have submitted plans to meet the 2 percent and 20 percent goals by 2024. This is real progress, due to Trump's relentless pressure on NATO members to contribute their fair share to defense. I hope the Biden administration continues to undertake similar missions in their interactions with our European allies.

As we reevaluate our country's stature in the world, we would do well to remember that the United States is exceptional but not perfect. We are the go-to country for most of the world when they want disaster relief, military protection, or an enormous and wealthy market to sell goods. And regardless of who is in power at home, it is in our DNA to step up when the world needs us. We lead, we help, we protect.

How we are then treated, particularly by those who benefit from our largesse and compassion, is something to consider. It's something I've discussed in these pages regarding Europe, but it also applies elsewhere. Many, many countries who call us an ally let us pick up the check on many things for which they can and should pay. They then turn around and make it hard for us to do business with them or pass freely in and out of their country.

Our relationships to any government should involve a real-time, sober assessment of our bilateral situation. While historical dealings carry some weight, they are often accorded too much emphasis in negotiations. I'd instead encourage this evaluation: What did we do for you in the past five years and what have you done for us? Are US workers indirectly funding a huge social safety net for, say, the Europeans by allowing those countries to contribute less than their fair share of defense costs? If so, how do US workers feel about the French enjoying a thirty-hour work week and ample vacation time while Americans bust their asses in part to facilitate this?

OK, fine. It's in our national interest to make certain that Europe is protected from Western adversaries. But what do we receive in return? How about a wide open market for our goods and services without the nonsensical excuse that some of our products just aren't safe or healthy? In many cases, we should demand separate and substantially upgraded treatment from those who have "third country" rules. We are not just *any* trading partner, protector, or source of safe investments and the world's highest quality education.

Enough crocodile tears and protestations of hurt feelings when we ask for reciprocity or VIP treatment. Does this mean that our long-standing relationships are nothing more than transactional?

Yes! Because those relationships are generally treated similarly by some of our closest friends and allies.

Bill Clinton was a lot closer to Trump in the way he conducted himself in dealing with the Europeans than he was compared to Obama or even George W. Bush. Clinton was on a first-name basis with many leaders and was a "cut the bullshit" kind of guy, but Trump, of course, took it to another level. Trump was the first president who really took Europe to task in terms of what its countries owe us. But then he faltered because he didn't focus on what he really wanted. His instincts were great. His execution was terrible. He got caught up in browbeating them but then didn't immediately pivot to make demands as to what he wanted for the US in concrete language. For instance, I want your markets open tomorrow. I want our farmers to be able to ship goods directly to Europe. We'll label everything. And if your people don't want to buy it, they don't have to buy it. I want you to quit trying to regulate global data privacy. You follow our rules; we'll follow yours. Don't impose your decisions on us or try to restrict what we do. And that's that.

There are a whole host of things that we should get in return for the safety shield we're providing Europe that we don't get. It's in our best interest that Europe is kept safe, but what we want is for Europe to give us some payback for what we've done for them over the last eighty years following the end of WWII. The reason we deserve to be treated differently than any other trading partner in the world is that we do more for Europe than anyone else does. And we want them to treat China the way China should be treated, which is that it's an adversary to both the US and the EU. Quit trying to play both sides with China.

When the United States and Europe work as partners in dealing with any adversary, we are much stronger for it. When we push back together against authoritarian rule in Russia and the single-party system in China, our cooperation legitimizes and strengthens our resolve.

Our relationship is much, much more than just a trade or security arrangement. Our partnership is based on a commitment to democracy, rule of law, open markets, human rights, and promoting peace and security. But for far too long, the bickering over small change has gotten in the way of a shared US and EU vision of a post-Cold War world. While we have been busy dithering in places like Afghanistan or arguing about the safety of a vaccine we've both approved, we've lost sight of the threats to energy security posed by Russia, to capitalism and our global financial system posed by China, and to global security posed by an almost nuclear Iran. Now we face an existential threat to our collective Western existence. With the size and heft of the US and the EU, we can easily undermine each other and stall progress. In the absence of needed agreements and strong alliances between the two of us, we will only accelerate the economic and political chaos in the West. But when we decide to stand side by side and use the might of our combined economies, defense capabilities, and intelligence, we can do anything. Independently, we are formidable. Together, we are unstoppable.

FINAL THOUGHTS

Once upon a time, in a world before COVID and before the Russian invasion of Ukraine, I hosted a party for Volodymyr Zelensky. As I described earlier, he was the "new guy" on the scene, a recently elected young president still finding his footing while his country of Ukraine was attempting to do the same. I was the US Ambassador to the EU, looking for an opportunity to bring him into the mix and introduce him to other leaders who could help Ukraine in its mission to become a fully European nation.

As I shared with you, in June of 2019, I gathered a crowd that included presidents and prime ministers and a host of other important EU officials—and Jay Leno. As a fellow comedian, I knew Zelensky would appreciate the gesture. Indeed, he went up to him and called Leno his "hero." The party was a great success and marked the start of a friendship between me and Z that continues today. It also marked what I hoped was the beginning of closer cooperation between the US and Ukraine. We of course had security working the doors to make sure only invited and vetted guests were allowed in.

How times have changed. I got fired for testifying truthfully at Trump's impeachment hearing. As a result of that botched referendum, Ukraine's reputation was tarnished and opportunity for potential partnership dimmed. Zelensky's presidency seemed likely to fizzle if not fail completely.

Nope, scratch that. New script. A few months later, all of our lives stopped. The world sputtered along for two years, rocked by a pandemic that has now reoriented us away from our imagined globalist path. Most recently, Russia invaded Ukraine, American interest in and sympathy for that country has skyrocketed, and Zelensky has proven himself to be the hero. He's now the one knocking at the doors, pleading with the EU to allow Ukraine entry—which the EU should allow immediately.

But we should have never been in this situation. How did we get to a place where Russia feels emboldened enough to invade an ally of ours, one that was making great strides toward becoming more fully European? I believe the lack of cohesion and commitment from Brussels along with US inaction enabled the Russian invasion of Ukraine. I also believe the practical, no-nonsense approach pursued by Trump, which I also pursued while Ambassador in Europe, could have kept Putin in check. Instead, President Biden's approach has essentially been a reversion to a "lead from behind" strategy, with results that embolden tyrants and bring devastation to countries like Ukraine that desperately want to pursue a more Western orientation.

Consider this (fictional) conversation between Trump and Putin:

> "Vladimir, great place you have over there, that palace. Lots of gold. Reminds me of my 50,000 square foot penthouse at my Tower in New York. You know it's the biggest in the city, right? Anyway, I like the way you run things. People do what you tell them, and everyone is respectful. No opposition. Great job! Listen, we're going to get along great and do some deals together. But don't touch Ukraine, because if you do, I'm gonna have to bomb the shit out of Moscow. So stay in your lane, and we'll be fine. Now about that blonde protocol lady of yours, is she a great piece or what..."

Contrast with the Biden/Blinken/Nuland crowd:

> "The United States strongly condemns your actions and should said actions continue we shall be forced to take stronger measures through the United Nations Security Council. Furthermore, any incursion into Ukraine, except a slight incursion which shall be permissible under certain circumstances and subject to the review and approval of attorney General Merrick Garland, who was the latest winner in the US Supreme Court consolation prize contest, will require consideration of action on our part. Now about that blonde etagere in your anteroom. Is that a period piece?"

You get the drift. Every time Putin—or any other despot, for that matter—hears an equivocation from the US or Europe, regardless of what that equivocation might be, it is a signal to him to press on. This is where our current team is failing. They are so caught up in the *process* and in a linear tit-for-tat that they don't know how to deal with Putin's exponential escalation.

The answer is simple and somewhat risky: go early and go hard. When the rumblings begin, shut them down then and there. Move in the materiel. Impose the sanctions. Make the Putins of the world understand that if they get this type of response while they are just musing, imagine what the response to action will be. Be ready for and take the criticism that you acted too hastily, too disproportionately. It is a small price to pay considering the potential alternatives.

The US must be viewed by the world, particularly our adversaries, as a supertanker that has charted a course from which it will not deviate. The course is freedom and rule of law. We are an imperfect country, but we strive for perfection—a goal we will never achieve. Instead, we should keep on course and stay focused on the ideals our country represents and the things that will further our long-term best interests. When we try to act like a speedboat, dodging and weaving, speeding up and slowing down, constantly changing course or worse yet coming to a dead stop while we wait to see what other boats are going to do, it sets the world on edge. They count on us to always be underway and on course. Our adversaries should not question whether we will deviate. They must credibly believe we will decimate them if they move to overturn freedom and the rule of law outside of their own parochial sphere. When the rumblings begin, before any action is taken by our adversaries, we need to decisively remind them where we are headed. And we need to use our considerable tools, financial, cyber, (and yes, even kinetic) early. This is not warmongering. It is keeping the tanker on course.

The same supertanker mentality should apply in our dealings with the EU. Our treatment of the EU has always been conducted with "kid gloves," and they need to come off. The EU is our most valuable business and strategic partner, not the post-World War II welfare project it used to be. We must use our alliance to strengthen our competitive position against Russia and China instead of continuing all of the public and private interactions steeped in formality and ceremony.

Trump did not wrap his queries and demands in niceties. That's just not who he is. But the most important reason was time. He wanted to "close" as many deals as possible before the clock ran out on his presidency. As a result, he cut through the small talk bullshit and got right to the point. Tariffs, market closures, the threat of a US NATO withdrawal, calling out the EU for its support of the Nord Stream 2 pipeline, pulling out of the JCPOA agreement with Iran, and turning away from the Paris climate accords were all done in order to finally get the bloc's attention and have them realize that the free ride was over. I was the primary messenger of these actions, and it pissed off my counter-parties to no end. But the message had to be delivered. The sad irony of the events now transpiring in Ukraine, China, and Iran are indicative of how right Trump was. The Europeans are finally realizing the need for increased defense spending, the reason it is necessary to keep Nord Stream 2 offline to try to end a dependence on Russian gas, and the folly that was the Iran nuclear deal, as Arab states now rally together to prevent Iran's nuclear ambitions.

Whatever happens next, the US and Europe need to act together. The future of the free world depends on it.

When I think about my own evolution over the past few years, with the benefit of some temporal distance from my firsthand experience in dealing with him, I have considered what I feel is my "red line" when it comes to Trump's behavior. I took the tweets, the narcissism, and his many personality quirks with a grain of salt. I liked most of the policy he espoused, and it was refreshing to see rapid forward movement in a whole host of areas.

But January 6, 2021 changed all of that. The incidents that day permanently altered my views on Trump as a leader. Do I believe the election was "stolen" from him? I do not. Were there attempts to falsify or toss votes, to his detriment, here and there? Probably. Could he have stopped the Capitol intrusion and violence? At the very least, he should have tried much harder.

The election had overwhelmingly been concluded in Biden's favor by January 2021. We knew that he was duly elected and would be president. Now that I am getting a taste of how dysfunctional his administration is, I wish he were not president, but he is. Case closed.

What really disappoints me is that President Trump did massive damage to the United States' "brand." I am no stranger to how important brand is—how much work it takes to establish and build one and how hard it is to refurbish one once it's been tarnished. One of the hallmarks of the United States' brand, along with our system of democracy, our individualism, and our reputation for being innovative and adventurous, is that we pride ourselves on holding the planet's most peaceful elections and elegant transfers of power. No one else does it like we do. I am talking not just about our legal norms in how we hand over the office from one president to another but also the symbols surrounding this amicable handing over of the keys and the codes.

The United States is admired around the world by those living in both autocracies and in democracies for the way we pass the baton to the elected successor. Two people, presidents past and future, who at that moment likely loathe one another, stand there and make nice not just for the domestic audience but for the world. The greetings and hugs, the limo ride together, and sitting on the inaugural platform watching the next person take the oath of office while preparing to rip your previous leadership apparatus apart—all of it is part of the show. And Trump really damaged this important and aspirational tradition. I wished he had not, and I believe that his presidency would have been more highly regarded by history if he had bowed out, shaken Joe's hand, and wished him well—and then beat him in the next election.

Looking back at the Ukraine situation, with the benefit of hindsight, Trump would have been right to investigate Burisma and the Hunter Biden connection, within certain limits. Burisma hired Hunter Biden to be a board member for a company in an industry he knew nothing about. He had no experience, they were paying him close to a million dollars a year, and no one, including Hunter Biden himself, could identify what his qualifications were other than his last name. So I don't think the investigation that triggered the impeachment avalanche, while it wasn't necessarily the Lord's work, was as bad as the Democratic members of the House made it out to be because there truly was something corrupt and perhaps illegal going on there.

The real lesson here is one of overreaction. The minute the whistleblower complaint came out, there was an overreaction by the House in thinking that they had a campaign fraud issue at stake. The impeachment debacle did a huge disservice to the country because it completely distracted from and unraveled all kinds of really good stuff policy-wise that was going on in the Trump administration.

As we move on, the related problems or allegations of election fraud are not difficult or expensive to solve once and for all. States should run their own elections using their own systems and policies. I have no problem with absentee ballots, drop boxes, early and late voting, or anything that enfranchises as many *legal* voters as possible.

One caveat is that the federal government should have a national biometric voter ID system that ensures two important things: first, that the person entitled to vote in a federal election has a legal right to do so and second, that such a person can only vote once and is thereafter locked out of voting anywhere else in that particular election. I would suggest we spend whatever federal funds are necessary so that even the hardest-to-reach voter is assisted in this endeavor at taxpayer expense. It can be done. Anyone claiming it's too hard is being disingenuous.

After this system is in place, say over a two four-year-phase-in period, any contested election would likely be limited to recounting ballots in close races. All of the other claims of "illegals voting" or the ballot box being "stuffed" would become moot. One person, one legal vote. Confidence restored, even if we have to wait for those straggling states to report their results.

I do think a lot about what the future holds for the country and for myself. The next election will be a doozy. For my part, I have been through an excruciating public trial. I usually love the lime-light, but once I found myself in the press globally and relentlessly, I realized I previously had no idea of the pressure it brings. I don't wish the experience on anyone. And yes, I brought it upon myself. Like Icarus flying too close to the sun, I soon found the wax around my wings was dripping wet. I could have flown lower—stayed out of the press, given small cocktail parties, and lived a life of relative anonymity in Brussels. Instead, I chose a different path, creating as much exposure as I could for the US-EU Mission and maximizing my time in my role as ambassador. I won't deny that it had some-thing to do with the desire to be noticed—but it's more complex than that. My desire to be seen was also motivated by my need to make a difference. If you stand in the shadows, you won't inspire much action.

Instead, I am a lightning rod, thanks to traits both innate and learned. I'm a touch arrogant, a bit showy, and yes, I like attention. My push to get the ambassador's job, combined with what it takes to get into the lottery that is the selection process in the first place, gave the press plenty of fodder to cover me in a less-than-positive light. Once it got to the impeachment trial, they were well prepared for a field day at my expense. I can bitch about the press coverage, but all in all, there was some truth to what they said about me.

Yes, I made some serious mistakes in the past two years, and I regret the pain that it caused those closest to me. But I also managed to do some good. I was fortunate enough to hold one of the most interesting and fulfilling jobs in the world. From that unique status and vantage point, I was able to accomplish positive things for our country in a relatively short period of time. I continue to speak up about the importance of the alliance between the US and the EU. It is my hope that my limited notoriety will help to secure an audi-ence for this vital topic. This relationship is not a "nice to have." It's a "gotta have" as we move into a new era. Unfortunately, I see the

EU slipping back towards its old ways. We cannot do the same. We are going to need to quickly develop a fulsome relationship, devoid of quibbling, that can be leveraged against China, Russia, Iran, and other adversaries. I will help wherever I can.

Even my role in the impeachment inquiry ended as a net positive. I told the truth. Period. In the end, that was the only thing that appeased both sides of the aisle—and somehow, both camps ended up finding me tolerable. Folks have been incredibly gracious to me since my recall on February 7, 2020. It's nice to get an occasional high five or the best table at a restaurant. Speaking of which, I recently ran into Ulrich again, whom I hadn't seen since the day he fired me in his office. I was at dinner with a friend at the Ivy in Los Angeles when I saw him across the way at a table with three other people. What are the odds? He noticed me and got visibly nervous as I stood and walked his way. I ambled up and said, "Hey, Ulrich. Nice to see you. No hard feelings. Tell Mike I said the same; I just want my money back." I had recently filed a lawsuit against Pompeo because he had not delivered on the promise he made me to pay back the legal fees I incurred for testifying at the impeachment trial. Bob Luskin is one of the best lawyers in the country, and the best ain't cheap. $1.8 million is not pocket change. The secretary had promised in front of many witnesses to pay my legal fees. I didn't mention any of this to Ulrich, but I didn't need to. He knew it all already. I cordially took my leave. And then I picked up his tab.

I've come through the storm and done my best to make amends to those I hurt. The lessons I have learned will hopefully serve me for the rest of my life.

ACKNOWLEDGMENTS

Thanks to my family for their steadfast support, particularly Katy who stood by through thick and thin. My YPO forum, Jamsheed, Craig, Jeff, Brett, Joe, Scott, Nick and Fred who have been a nearly twenty-five year source of strength, support, and wise counsel. To my friends President George W. Bush and Gov. Ted Kulongski, from both ends of the political spectrum who always exhibited wisdom, civility, and humility. Lastly to Shannon O'Neill, my great collaborator and sounding board on this book.